THE LIFE AND TIMES OF SIR KAI HO KAI
(Second Edition)

The Life and Times of Sir Kai Ho Kai

A Prominent Figure in Nineteenth-Century Hong Kong

(Second Edition)

G. H. Choa

The Chinese University Press

ISBN 962–201–873–4

First Edition 1981
Second Edition 2000

THE CHINESE UNIVERSITY PRESS
The Chinese University of Hong Kong
SHA TIN, N.T., HONG KONG
Fax: +852 2603 6692
+852 2603 7355
E-mail: cup@cuhk.edu.hk
Web-site: http://www.cuhk.edu.hk/cupress/w1.htm

Printed in Hong Kong

⟋ Contents ⟍

ᚼ List of Illustrations ᚼ

─◦ List of Appendices ◦─

—⁕ Acknowledgments ⁕—
(First Edition)

Ever since I started to write this book, I had been trying to locate some descendants of Sir Kai Ho Kai with the hope that I could gather more information and see some personal papers and documents which might have been kept in the family. In spite of the fact that Sir Kai raised a large family of ten sons and seven daughters, my initial inquiries were not successful. On 20 October 1979, a report appeared in the *South China Morning Post* under the caption "Old Hong Kong Family Honours Newly-Weds". From it, I learnt with delight that the father of the bridegroom, Mr. Arnold Hall of H. W. Turning & Co., was a grandson of Sir Kai. After I established contact with him, Mr. Hall very kindly granted me an interview. Besides telling me what he knew about the family, he showed me a bundle of papers, among which were Lady Ho Kai's application for probate, a number of debit notes and title deeds belonging to his great-grandfather the Rev. Ho Fuk-tong, and Mrs. Ho Fuk-tong's power of attorney in which she nominated her two sons Wyson Ho and Ho Kai. Later, he sent me a reprint of the chapter on the Rev. Ho in a biographic work on famous pastors (名牧遺徽). I am most grateful to Mr. Hall for all the help he gave me.

I wish to thank the staff of the University Library, the Chung Chi College Library, the New Asia College Library and the United College Library of The Chinese University of Hong Kong, the Hong Kong University Library, the Medical and Health Department's Library, the Government Secretariat's Library and the Public Record Office for their co-operation and also Dr. W. D. Wylie, F.R.C.P., F.R.C.S., F.F.A.R.C.S., Dean of St.

Thomas's Hospital Medical School, and Mr. Colin A. McLaren, Archivist and Keeper of Manuscripts, Aberdeen University, for the information they sent me.

It gives me great pleasure to acknowledge the help and advice I received from Dr. Chingho A. Chen, Ph.D., Dr. T. C. Cheng, O.B.E., D. Litt., Dr. L. Y. Chiu, Ph.D., Dr. Y. T. Chung, Ph.D., Mr. Richard Lai, O.B.E., Dr. E. H. Paterson, O.B.E., F.R.C.S., the Rev. Carl T. Smith, the Hon. Dr. P. C. Woo, C.B.E., Ph.D., L.L.D. who gave me much valuable data on his grandfather Mr. Hu Liyuan, and the Hon. Mr. Justice T. L. Yang. I am especially grateful to Dr. Jung-fang Tsai, Ph.D. who made many suggestions and corrections after reading the manuscript.

My thanks are due to Mr. A. E. Starling, M.B.E. and Mr. Rupert Chan, B.A., for correcting the manuscript and the proofs, Mr. Simon Tam, B.A. and Mr. A. R. Cayford, for their help with the research, Mr. Chow Kai Wing, B.A. for translating a Japanese reference, Mrs. Annie Tam and Miss Hilary Tam, who, between them, did all the typing.

⟋⟋ Preface and Acknowledgments ⟍⟍
(Second Edition)

There are several reasons for revising this book on the life and times of Sir Kai Ho Kai: firstly to correct some errors and mistakes; secondly, to re-arrange the contents of Chapters V, VI and VII in line with the sequence of events, thus, Health Problems, the Sanitary Board and the Public Health Ordinance are now put together in Chapter VI, the Bubonic Plague Epidemic and the Discovery of the Plague Bacillus in Chapter VII, and the Tung Wah Hospital and the Introduction of Western Medicine in Chapter VIII; and thirdly, to add in materials gathered since the publication of the First Edition.

Several books on various aspects of the history of Hong Kong have since been published, notably Dr. Elizabeth Sinn on the Tung Wah Hospital, Dr. E. H. Paterson on the Nethersole Hospital, Professor D. E. Evans on the Faculty of Medicine of the University of Hong Kong and Ms. J. C. Stewart on Sir James Cantlie. From them I learnt more about some events in Ho Kai's life-time in which he played a significant part.

Of great interest and value was an unpublished diary kept by Dr. J. C. Lowson, a government medical officer who was in charge of the Bubonic Plague Epidemic in the first few months of 1894. For access to this, I am indebted to Dr. Francis Ashburner, a descendent of Dr. Lowson, and Professor Faith Ho. After she read in the *South China Morning Post* in February 1993 about the founding of the Hong Kong Museum of Medical Sciences, Dr. Ashburner sent a photostat copy of the diary to Professor Ho. Professor Ho then kindly made it available to me. In uncompromising terms, Dr.

Lowson described the chaotic conditions seen by him in the early phase of the Epidemic.

At the XX International Congress of the International Academy of Pathology and the 11th Congress of Academic and Environmental Pathology held jointly in Hong Kong in October 1994, I presented a paper on the discovery of the Plague Bacillus during the Epidemic of 1894 in Hong Kong to commemorate the centenary of the event. The controversy concerning which of the two claims was the real discovery was recalled as a matter of historical interest.

A search of the literature revealed two papers on Ho Kai which were published in 1981 and 1992 respectively, after the appearance of the First Edition.

The most important acquisitions however were copies of two letters sent to me by a correspondent who must remain anonymous. One was written by Sir Boshan Wei Yuk to the then Governor of Hong Kong, Sir Francis May, and the other by one of Ho Kai's sons to Sir James Stewart-Lockhart, then Commissioner in Weihaiwei. These two documents contained much information on the last years of Ho Kai's life and what happened to his large family after his death, hitherto unknown to me.

I wish to thank my former secretary Ms. Annie Tam for again typing the manuscript for me. I understand that she took the opportunity to teach her two young sons how to use a word processor so I have to thank Ryan and Vernon Tam as well. Ms. Susan Au-Young also helped with the word processing. For the help they gave me, I am grateful to my friends Dr. Stanislaus Hu, Mr. Arthur Starling and Mr. Raymond Tang Jr. Lastly I thank Dr. Steven Luk, the Director of The Chinese University Press for agreeing to publish a Second Edition.

1. Sir Kai Ho Kai, Kt., C.M.G., M.B., C.M.,
M.R.C.S., Barrister-at-law
(By kind permission of Mr. Arnold Hall)

2. Sir Kai Ho Kai, Kt., C.M.G., M.B., C.M.,
M.R.C.S., Barrister-at-law
(From *Alice Ho Miu Ling Nethersole Hospital, 1887–1967*)

3. Sir Kai Ho Kai in academic robe

(From Norton-Kyshe, *The History of the Laws and Courts of Hong Kong*)

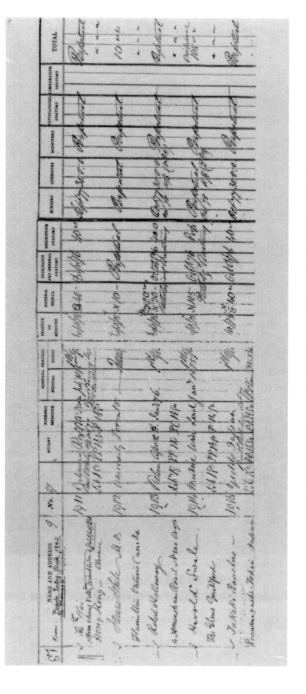

4. Sir Kai Ho Kai's record in St. Thomas Hospital's Pupil Entry Book

(By kind permission of the Dean, St. Thomas Hospital Medical School)

5. Sir Kai Ho Kai at the Opening of the Po Leung Kuk, 1896

(Hong Kong Museum of History)

6. Sir Kai Ho Kai and other members of the Legislative Council with Sir William Robinson, c. 1897

(From Cameron, *Hong Kong: The Cultured Pearl*)

7. Sir Kai Ho Kai with Qing Officials and Sir Frederick Lugard in 1907
(Hong Kong Museum of History)

8. Sir Kai Ho Kai with the students of the Hong Kong College of Medicine, c. 1908

(From Arnold Wright, ed., *Twentieth Century Impressions of Hong Kong, Shanghai, and Other Treaty Ports of China*)

9. Sir Kai Ho Kai at a meeting at Sir Paul Chater's residence, 1909
(From Harrison, *University of Hong Kong: The First Fifty Year, 1911–1961*)

10. Sir Kai Ho Kai at the Laying of the Foundation Stone Ceremony of the University of Hong Kong, 16 March 1910

(From Harrison, *University of Hong Kong: The First fifty Years, 1911–1961*)

11. Sir Kai Ho Kai at the Opening of the Kwong Wah Hospital, 1911
(From *One Hundred Years of the Tung Wah Group of Hospitals 1870–1970*)

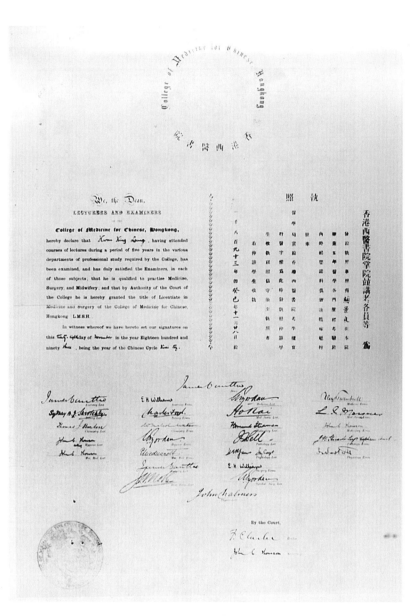

12. Sir Kai Ho Kai's signature on Dr. Kwan Sum-yin's diploma, which is kept in the Hong Kong Museum of Medical Sciences, bequeathed by the late Dr. Kwan Siu-sek.

13. Sir Kai Ho Kai's tomb at the Colonial Cemetery, Hong Kong
(From the *South China Morning Post*, 10 October 1976)

14. Alice Ho Kai
(From *Alice Ho Miu Ling Nethersole Hospital, 1887–1967*)

15. Alice Memorial Hospital on Hollywood Road, c. 1887
(From *Alice Ho Miu Ling Nethersole Hospital, 1887–1967*)

16. Nethersole Hospital on Bonham Road, c. 1893
(From *Alice Ho Miu Ling Nethersole Hospital, 1887–1957*)

17. The Four Bandits: from left to right: Yang Heling, Sun Yat-sen,
Chan Siu-pak, You Lie, standing behind: Dr. Kwan Sum-yin
(Hong Kong Museum of Medical Sciences)

18. Sir Patrick Manson
(Hong Kong Museum of Medical Sciences)

19. Sir James Cantlie
(Hong Kong Museum of Medical Sciences)

NG CHOY.

20. Ng Choy, also known as Wu Tingfang
(From G. B. Endacott's *History of Hong Kong*)

21. Mr. Hu Liyuan
(By kind permission of Dr. the Hon. P. C. Woo, C.B.E., LL.D., Ph.D.)

22. Tai Ping Shan District, c. 1880
(From Warner, *Fragrant Harbour*)

23. Victims of Bubonic Plague
(Hong Kong Public Records Office)

24. Dr. Alexandre Yersin
(Hong Kong Museum of Medical Sciences)

25. Dr. Shibasaburo Kitasato (北里粟三郎)
(Hong Kong Museum of Medical Sciences)

─◌ Prologue ◌─

"There is a history in all men's lives,
Figuring the nature of the times deceas'd."

—— *Henry IV, Part I* ——

There is also a history in the places where their lives are born and
spent. Situated on the South China coast, the territory of Hong Kong
consists of Hong Kong Island itself, a small part of the Chinese mainland,
and a number of off-shore islands. Hong Kong Island and the adjacent
islands, with a total area of 29 square miles, were ceded to Great Britain in
1841. The coastal strip on the mainland, the Kowloon Peninsula, 4 square
miles in area, was ceded later in 1860. Between Hong Kong and Kowloon is
a natural harbour, the width of which varies from one to six miles. In 1898,
another area of 370 square miles on the mainland, the New Territories, was
leased to Great Britain for ninety-nine years. The entire territory with a
total area of some 400 square miles, was returned to China on 1 July 1997
and is now a Special Administrative Region in China.

As early as the sixteenth century, European traders, attracted by the
prospect of tapping the rich resources in China, began to appear on the
China coast. The Portuguese were the first to have gained a foothold in
China, after they established themselves in Macao in 1557. Not having a
base of their own, other nationals, the Spaniards, the Dutch, the French
and the British, had to be content with using the facilities there, offered
to them by the Portuguese. In the struggle for supremacy among the
European sea-powers, the Dutch, who had by then taken Malacca from
the Portuguese, attacked Macao in 1622, but were repulsed. Eventually, in
1685, permission was given to foreign traders by the Chinese government
to trade in Guangzhou, with certain conditions and restrictions imposed.

By 1715 the British-owned East India Company, which held the monopoly on Eastern trade, was firmly established in Guangzhou as the principal European agency trading with China. At that time, the British were only interested in buying tea, as they had become a nation of tea-drinkers. Their clippers would leave India with nothing on board except the silver with which to exchange for the tea. In a restricted area on the bank of the Pearl River, the traders rented "factories" from Chinese merchants to live in and conduct their business during the trading season, which lasted from October to May. For the rest of the year, they had to withdraw to Macao. However anxious the foreign merchants were, there was little hope of China opening up more of the country for trade. With the ending of the East India Company's monopoly of the China trade, the British government sent Lord Napier out as Chief Superintendent of Trade in 1834. He found that the Chinese government had no wish to establish diplomatic or any other kind of contact with foreign powers, even after he forced his way through the Bogue, the channel leading from the Pearl River delta to Guangzhou, with his warships. The discontented British merchants clamoured for more aggressive action, and at the same time they began to think of securing an island or some islands off the Chinese coast to replace Guangzhou as their base. They had found something they could sell to the Chinese, opium. Chests* of this obnoxious stuff now filled the holds of the clippers on the outward-bound voyage. There was a demand for it even though it was listed as contraband by the authorities, but without customs charges or "squeeze", the profit could be very substantial. At first, the British government took the correct attitude of not extending its protection over this illicit trafficking. However a chain reaction was started when the British merchants were ordered to give up their stock of opium by the Imperial Commissioner in Guangzhou, Lin Zexu 林則徐, in 1839. The Chinese thought that trade relations would resume after the confiscation of the offending commodity

---

* A chest weighed between 130 to 150 pounds.

but the British merchants reacted differently. Captain Charles Elliot, R. N., who had taken over as Superintendent of Trade, refused to surrender all the opium in British hands and withdrew all British to Macao. As the Macao government did not wish to get involved, Elliot further withdrew the British community to merchant ships and proceeded to anchor in Hong Kong harbour. After what is known in history as the Opium War, the British forces occupied Hong Kong.

As the man on the spot, Captain Charles Elliot concluded a preliminary treaty with Guangzhou officials on 30 January 1841, after a naval action near the Bogue. He then reported to the home government that he had acquired Hong Kong for the British Crown. On receiving the despatch, Lord Palmerston, the Foreign Secretary, was far from pleased. He pointed out that Captain Elliot failed to secure full compensation for the opium delivered and additional openings for trade farther north, and only obtained the cession of "a barren island with hardly a house on it". A few months after the event, instead of getting suitably rewarded, Captain Elliot was recalled and dismissed for disobeying orders and instructions. He was right in acquiring a permanent base on the China coast so that the British could trade directly with China without having to use the facilities in Portuguese Macao or suffer the restrictions in Guangzhou. But even in his wildest dreams he could not have foreseen that Hong Kong would one day become an international trade and financial centre, rated as the eighth largest in the world. As for Lord Palmerston, he was certainly no man of vision as he thought that "Hong Kong will not be the mart of trade any more than Macao is so".

At the time it was ceded Hong Kong Island was populated by some three thousand fishermen living in matshed huts which they built on the beaches. In the hilly terrain, steep and rugged slopes rose from sea-level to two and three thousand feet, featuring rocky crags, woody ravines and open grassy terraces. The main attraction, however, was the natural harbour where the waters were calm and deep, offering excellent anchorage for ships. After the military occupation, European merchants came to settle in this new colony, transferring their factories over from Guangzhou and Macao. They chose the eastern part of the island to build their warehouses and homes, while the military camps were situated on the western side. The central district, which was named after the Queen as the City of Victoria, was to be developed as a business centre. Boat people soon appeared on the scene, helping to transport merchandise from the ships in the harbour to the warehouses on shore. Chinese merchants followed, coming over from Macao and Guangzhou in junks to trade, buying opium, cotton cloth, spice and other commodities, and selling tea and silk. Labour for building roads and houses was provided by men from the mainland. When the first ever census was taken in May 1841, there were 7,450 Chinese residents, consisting of 4,350 villagers and fishermen, scattered over twenty hamlets, 800 in the bazaar, 2,000 living in boats and 300 labourers from Kowloon.

From the medical and health point of view, Hong Kong was virtually a "white man's grave". The high morbidity and mortality among the early settlers and the troops in the garrison must have been most discouraging to the colonial and military surgeons who were responsible for looking after them. They were soon confronted with a killer disease which they called "Hong Kong Fever". They also had to deal with other more familiar diseases such as cholera, dysentery, smallpox and typhoid fever. The unhealthy environment was held responsible for the prevalence of diseases. The air was filled with a putrid odour arising from the decomposition of exposed refuse and excrement. The swampy soil was thick with undergrowth in which mosquitos, insects and snakes thrived. The weather was especially unpleasant in the hot humid summer months when typhoons could strike in full gale force causing extensive devastation. The houses that were built could not even withstand the heavy rains and strong winds let alone provide comfortable and clean living. Then there were the Chinese who could live under the most primitive conditions, without any regard for comfort and hygiene. They insisted on having the right to follow their traditional customs and beliefs, which no one could persuade them to change and modify. Aloof and hostile, they were a law unto themselves.

Gradually, a small town emerged, at first a rival to neighbouring Macao but soon to overshadow it as the volume of trade passing through the magnificent harbour steadily increased. In due course a second generation who would be called Hong Kong Chinese was born on this British territory. Having received a Western education, they became a new breed. They began to take up positions in the big firms, join the civil service and enter into the various professions. They were also made members of various committees, boards and councils to assist the administration. The Chinese members who sat on the Legislative Council, an advisory body in the typical government structure of a British colony or possession, were regarded as representatives of their community, though they were nominated and appointed by the governor and not elected by their compatriots. Acting as spokesmen and intermediaries, they were essential bridges between the government and the people. Among the élite who were the first to conquer new frontiers were some very distinguished personalities who left their marks in the history of Hong Kong. Perhaps the most distinguished and certainly the most versatile of them all was Sir Kai Ho Kai 何啟, barrister, physician, reformist, revolutionary and essayist.

During Ho Kai's life time Hong Kong went through a particularly interesting and difficult phase. In the Chinese quarters sanitary services were practically non-existent and environmental hygiene almost entirely neglected. To improve the living conditions of the Chinese, the government proposed to enact new public health and building legislation. They would be required to build houses with adequate light, ventilation and living space for the occupants, separate latrines and kitchens and drains and sewers for the disposal of excrement and refuse. Incredibly, the move met with strong opposition from the Chinese community as a whole. Ignoring the desirability of better accommodation for all, the landlords argued that the standards laid down would cut deeply into their profits unless they could recover their loss from the tenants, who protested that they could not afford to pay higher rents. On the other hand the Chinese were not provided with proper medical care although they only had faith in traditional medicine. A bubonic plague epidemic then broke out, ravaging the place for nearly thirty years, and causing tens of thousands of deaths, mostly among the Chinese. The measures taken by the authorities to deal with the situation were strongly resented by the Chinese. However, it was the epidemic that provided the opportunity to introduce Western medicine to them by young graduates of the Hong Kong College of Medicine. Ho Kai was in the midst of all this; indeed, as adviser to the government and representative of community for twenty-four years, he was responsible for the passage of many bills concerning the welfare, education and other aspects of life of the Chinese during his tenure. He was also either a witness or a participant in all the major events that took place in Hong Kong, spread over six governorships.

Whilst the young colony continued to grow in Ho Kai's time, far more momentous and dramatic events were happening across its border on the Chinese mainland. The Opium Wars were fought during the reign of Emperor Daoguang 道光 from 1821 to 1851, whose court was unable to resist the relentless military and diplomatic pressure applied by foreign powers for further territorial and economic gains. By the time Emperor Tongzhi 同治 reigned from 1862 to 1875, reform of the government was openly discussed and advocated by a group of intellectuals. What is known in history as the Hundred Days Reform (百日維新) failed when the movement was crushed by the Dowager Empress Cixi (慈禧太后, 1835–1908) in the Wuxu Year Coup (戊戌政變). Situated conveniently at the doorstep of China, Hong Kong became a sanctuary and a base for political refugees who fled the country. Under the protection of the British flag, they could carry on their activities and propaganda work free from persecution and harassment by Qing officials. They were joined by a new breed of local intellectuals who, having gained an insight into modern political philosophy through their Western education, became sympathizers of the Reform Movement and supporters of the Revolutionary Cause later. At heart, they were Chinese who were deeply interested in and committed to the affairs of the mother country. Among them was none other than Dr. Sun Yat-sen

孫逸仙, who succeeded in toppling the Qing dynasty to become the founder of the Republic of China. Although he was born near Macao in a village in Guangdong province, he went to school in Hong Kong and graduated from the Hong Kong College of Medicine. He was certainly qualified to be a Hong Kong belonger.

Ho Kai, born and brought up in Hong Kong and educated in Great Britain, was a supporter of the Reform Movement originally. After its failure he went over to Sun his former student at the College of Medicine as an adviser behind the scene though not important enough to be an eminence gris. He used a pen as his weapon, not a sword. His essays on political reform received some attention by the activists but had little impact on their plans and actions. Nevertheless, no student of the modern history of China could ignore his contributions to the political literature of the period. Had his background been different he might have been given a fairer appraisal and perhaps a higher rating among such prominent intellectuals of the day as Kang Youwei 康有為 (1856–1928) and Liang Qichao 梁啟超 (1873–1929) who dominated the political scene of the last days of the Qing dynasty. Ho Kai's relatively short life was certainly a full and eventful one.

Family History

After China was opened up in the nineteenth century, Chinese from the coastal provinces, particularly Guangdong and Fujian, began to migrate to Southeast Asian countries, the United States and Australia. During the Taiping Rebellion (1850–64) (see Chapter XI) many people left their homes in the south for Hong Kong. However, Hong Kong itself experienced recession during the Arrow War of 1856–57 (see Chapter XI), because the Guangzhou authorities stopped trading and supplying food to the territory. The hardship suffered by the local Chinese made them turn against the foreigners. Their feelings became so strong that there was an attempt to poison the entire foreign population by putting arsenic in their bread. This incident which happened in January 1857, was said to have been instigated by the mandarins in Guangzhou, but no great harm was done as the poison was detected early and the bread was produced by one single bakery. The number of Chinese emigrants reached a new high level at this time, their destination being either the old or the new Golden Mountain as San Francisco and Australia were called respectively. Their dream was to seek better prospects abroad, amass a fortune, and return home to enjoy their last years. Literally treated as human cargo, they were herded together like cattle and confined in small airless holds of junks and ships on their outward-bound voyage. After they landed, as most of them did not possess a skill, they were used as cheap labour in warehouses, factories and mines. They could survive only if they were strong enough to endure the untold physical hardship, for instance, building the transcontinental railway and digging gold in the States or working in the tin mines and rubber plantations in Malaysia, and those who succeeded in the end would have been fitter, more resourceful or luckier than the others. Having sur- vived, instead of returning home, some would settle down in wherever they were, and with a little saving, send for a bride or marry a local woman to raise a family. Their descendants would fare differently in their adopted countries. Having received an education, they found many careers and opportunities open to them. They emerged from this process of social tran- sition as members of a new community, ready to take their rightful places in the society in which they lived. Ho Kai himself was a typical product of the era as his family history followed this pattern closely. However, his fore- fathers were of a different caste, being Christians who worked for the Church. His grandfather migrated from Guangdong to Malaysia where he settled in Malacca. He was probably a semi-skilled or skilled artisan, employed as a cutter in a printing press operated by a Protestant Missionary Society, and he became a Christian. Some early Christian converts were called "rice Christians" contemptuously because they converted for the sake of getting more congenial work, better pay and more comfortable living conditions. Whether grandfather Ho was one such or not we do not know, but, Ho Kai's father who returned to Hong Kong, was a pastor.

In 1807, Dr. Robert Morrison, D. D. (1782–1834) arrived in Macao, the first Protestant missionary sent to evangelize China by the London Mis- sionary Society. On his mission to acquire the Chinese language in order to translate the Bible into Chinese, he was immediately warned of the diffi- culties. He would not be able to obtain permission to enter China from the Chinese government officials to whom all foreigners, whether traders or missionaries, were *persona non grata* to be treated with open hostility. Indeed, the mandarins were so violently xenophobic that the common Chinese were prohibited under the penalty of death from teaching the language to foreigners. And even if he could gain entry by some means or other he would have nowhere to live because according to the regulations of the British-owned East India Company only their employees and traders could stay in their factories in Guangzhou. Then, should he remain in Macao, his presence would not be welcomed because of the jealousy of the local Catholic bishop and priests. Undeterred by these seemingly insurmountable obstacles, and with providence no doubt on his side, Morrison eventually proceeded to Guangzhou with the help of some American friends. Such was the beginning of a life and career of devotion and scholarship that made him a legend in his own time and won him lasting fame as a great missionary and sinologist. The Morrison story is relevant to ours because this many-sided man of remarkable foresight founded the Anglo-Chinese College in Malacca with which the Ho family was associated. Realizing that conditions in China would continue to be difficult for missionary work, Morrison began searching for some other field in which to extend his activities. He turned his eyes towards Malaysia. Malacca was then the chief port of Malaysia, strategically situated at that crossroad between the east and the west, the Strait of Malacca. The city was founded in 1400 by the Malays but in 1511 it was conquered by the Portuguese. After a siege and heavy fighting it was wrested from the Portuguese by the Dutch in 1641. The Dutch rule in turn was interrupted by the British in 1795, and eventually Malacca was ceded to Great Britain by Holland in 1824 when the Treaty of London was concluded. The fact that Malacca changed hands three times in its history provided proof of its importance as a trading centre in those days before it was overtaken by the development of Singapore. On a visit to Malacca, Morrison found that under European rule there was freedom of religion while the Malays, like the Chinese, had yet to be enlightened. He was satisfied that it was the right place to establish another base. Thus, in 1818 the foundation stone of the Anglo-Chinese College in Malacca was laid. It was put in charge of the Rev. William Milne by Morrison whose idea was to set it up for the purpose of training missionaries to work in the field beyond the Ganges, and as a central point for organizing and controlling the British Asiatic missions. It included a language school and a press for the training of both Europeans and Asiatics.

In the press section Milne had with him a Mr. Leung Fat 梁發 who helped him to produce the *Chinese Monthly Magazine* (察世俗每月統記傳), a pamphlet containing mostly religious articles but also some news items and modern science reports. In fact Leung did most of the work, writing some of the articles, cutting the wood-blocks and printing the paper. In this respect he could be regarded as the first Chinese newspaper publisher, editor and reporter. The magazine lasted for only six years from 1815 to 1821. After the death of Milne in 1822, Leung Fat returned to China and, helped Morrison with his work. Having been baptized in 1816, he later became the first Chinese evangelist to preach the Gospel.

There was another cutter in the press section by the name of Ho, who left his family in his native village Xiqiao 西樵 in the county of Nanhai 南海 in Guangdong province. His son later joined him in Malacca, and while father worked in the press, the boy attended the school. This was Ho Fuk-tong 何福堂, otherwise known as Ho Tsun-shin 何進善, or Ho Yun-yeung 何潤養 who in time was received into the Church. In 1843, it was decided to move the Anglo-Chinese College from Malacca to Hong Kong, which had by then been established as a British colony. Dr. James Legge (1815–97), who was in charge of the College, and Ho Fuk-tong were both transferred to Hong Kong. Dr. Legge was the other great missionary and Chinese scholar of his day, in every respect the worthy successor to Morrison who had died in 1834 before the curtains rose on Hong Kong. Translator of many Chinese Classics, he was appointed the first Professor of Chinese at Oxford University after he returned to Great Britain from the East. To complete the story of the Anglo-Chinese College after its transfer to Hong Kong, it was closed down in 1856, but in 1914 was re-opened as the Ying Wah School (英華書院).

The circumstances in the young colony were at once favourable and encouraging for the pioneer missionaries. In the newly formed administration, the Rev. V. J. Stanton was appointed as the Colonial Chaplain. After setting up the Anglo-Chinese College, members of the London Missionary Society became active, using the premises as a church where baptisms were performed. Other missions soon arrived, some having been transferred from Macao and other parts of China. By 1850, the first bishop of the diocese of Hong Kong was appointed. He was Bishop George Smith who consecrated the new St. John Cathedral shortly after his arrival. A period of increased missionary and educational activities now set in. Ho Fuk-tong became the first Chinese to be ordained a priest, and in 1846 was appointed as a minister in the Hop Yat Church (合一堂).

The Rev. Ho Fuk-tong was born in 1818. At the age of 21, he was baptized. Apparently, it was in deference to the wishes of his father and the missionaries that he took the step as his faith was not particularly strong at that time. However, after studying the Bible, he was greatly enlightened and became a truly devout Christian. Besides attending the Anglo-Chinese College in Malacca, he also studied in a missionary school in Calcutta at one time. After completing his studies, he became proficient in English and other subjects such as scripture, theology, Church history and world history. He even learnt some Hebrew and Greek from Dr. Legge so that he could read the Old and New Testaments in the original. At this stage he was already able to preach a sermon with remarkable eloquence. After he returned to Hong Kong, with his knowledge and education, he could have obtained a good position in any commercial firm or the civil service, but he chose to dedicate his life to work for the Church. When it was arranged that he should get married, he made it clear to his relatives and friends that the wedding ceremony must be conducted according to Church rites. However, when he arrived at his village home, he found out that it was to follow native customs. To everybody's surprise and horror, he was not to be found on the appointed day, having absconded to Hong Kong. Eventually, his wish was granted and the ceremony took place in Hong Kong in church. Mrs. Ho Fuk-tong was taught how to read and write by her husband. She too became a Christian.

Having been ordained in 1845, the Rev. Ho Fuk-tong soon established a reputation as a preacher. One day he chose as his subject "The Patience of Job". When he described how Job had to relieve the itchiness of the sores

on his body by scratching them with a slate, his oratory was so effective
that the entire congregation felt an intense itch which they proceeded to
scratch. On another occasion, when he spoke on the fourteenth verse of
Psalm No. 139, (I will praise thee; for I am fearfully and wonderfully made;
marvellous are thy works; and that my soul knoweth well.) he kept the
congregation enthralled by describing the intricate structure of the human
body, and comparing the functions of the hands of man and animals. In
preparing his sermons he only made some notes on a piece of paper but
when he started to speak, thoughts readily flowed in his mind and words
also came to him easily. Dr. Legge, who greatly admired his preaching, said
that he was better than some of the famous preachers of the day in the
United Kingdom. The Rev. Ho was once asked why the Chinese would
only listen but were not keen to seek salvation. He pleaded that it would
require a great deal of patience to convert the Chinese but with divine
guidance, success would come in the end. His fame soon spread from Hong
Kong to the neighbouring districts in Guangdong province. Inspired by
him, a follower started an evangelical mission in Boluo 博羅 but unfortunately he was regarded as a fanatic and became a martyr to his cause. The
mission however survived and grew steadily. Encouraged by Dr. Legge, the
Rev. Ho took up writing, and published a monthly exhortation which was
widely read. He also wrote explanatory notes on the gospels of St. Matthew
and St. Mark, but he did not complete the cycle because he was too busy
carrying out his pastoral duties. In 1870, he had a stroke. A year later he
became critically ill. Asked by Dr. Legge if his mind was at peace, he said
that since he had long established contact with Christ, he was neither in
fear nor doubt. He died on 2 April 1871, aged 53.

The Rev. Ho Fuk-tong was not only a good preacher but a remarkably
good man of business. Having bought a lot of property at the right time
with his savings, he became a rich man. When he died, his estate was sworn
at over $100,000 which would make him a billionaire today. This fortune
was evidently used to send two sons to go to England to study, and also his
son-in-law through the dowry which his daughter received. It was said that

because he did not think the head of the mission would like him to have too great an interest in money, he used several aliases in his transactions. However, in a letter to the *South China Morning Post*, Professor Dafydd Evans expressed his opinion that the Rev. Ho made no secret of his land dealings and certainly did not endeavour to conceal his business activities from the London Missionary Society. The use of aliases was certainly common practice at that time in Chinese society. In 1862, the Rev. Ho purchased a portion of the Society's original property for $26,325, not a small sum in those days so it could be assumed that the Society must know that the preacher was a man of means. Professor Evans also wrote that Ho's first incursion into real estate had come in 1846 when he bought a lot in the Lower Bazaar for $150 and two years later he was in the moneylending business, charging five per cent per month on $400 on a security of a Lower Bazaar lot. Among the papers kept by his great-grandson Mr. Arnold Hall, there were six title deeds and two debit notes from which it was evident that the Rev. Ho was also active in dealing with the people in his native village in moneylending and land sales. The six title deeds showed that he bought land, houses and rice-fields for a total of about 200 taels, between 1857 and 1871, the year he died. In one of the debit notes, dated 1866, on a security of several acres of rice-fields, he lent out 17 taels, charging an interest rate of 20 per cent per month, to be paid four times a year, for two years on the condition that he could take over the property if the principal sum was not repaid at the end of the period. The other, dated 1869, was taken over by him from another moneylender, the sum involved being 20 taels, with an annual interest of two taels. The interest rates charged by moneylender in those days were indeed high.

The currency used in China and Hong Kong should be described. In the Qing dynasty, except for copper cash for everyday use, the Chinese had no coin currency. Their medium of exchange was silver as a metal, and the unit used was the tael, or Chinese ounce. Silver ingots of various weights and shapes were in circulation. Trade was carried on by weighing out silver and testing its fineness. Foreign silver currency such as the Spanish dollar, was acceptable to the Chinese not as a coin but as so much silver. The English had to pay Chinese merchants in Spanish dollar or silver ingots for the tea and silk they bought, later, back in England, the prices would be converted to sterling according to the relation of silver to gold. Before 1873, a tael was worth six shillings. The value of the Hong Kong dollar in the early years was pegged to the East India Company rupee at $1 to 2.5 rupees in 1845, thus it was worth 4s. 7d. in sterling as 1 rupee was equivalent to 1s. 10d.

The Rev. Ho had five sons and six daughters. The names of the sons were Shan-chee 神賜, Shan-tim 神添, Shan-po 神保, Shan-kai 神啟, and Shan-yau 神佑. Of the characters in a Chinese name, the first is the surname, and each has a meaning. Ho literally means "why" or "which" though it does not seem plausible that originally someone should choose it for a surname. Shan means god, thus Shan-chee is god's gift, Shan-tim god's addition, Shan-po god's protection, Shan-kai god's enlightenment and Shan-yau god's blessing.

Little is known about Shan-chee except that he died in his native village of Xiqiao in 1890. Shan-tim started life as interpreter in the government civil service in 1873 but left in 1875 to become a real estate broker. He was a large speculator in the 1881 land boom but when it collapsed, he became bankrupt and moved to Guangzhou. Eventually he came back to Hong Kong where he died about 1907–8. Shan-po otherwise known as Wyson Ho (何衛臣), had the distinction of being the first Chinese solicitor to practise in Hong Kong. He served his articles in England, and on his return in 1887 was admitted to the roll of attorneys. He was apparently not a very forceful personality, and though respected he did not take advantage of the opportunities open to him. He died in Hong Kong in 1898. Shan-yau was at first an articled clerk to his brother Wyson Ho the solicitor. In 1897 he accompanied his brother-in-law Wu Tingfang 伍廷芳 (1842–1922) to the United States. Wu was then the Chinese Minister to the United States and Ho was eventually appointed as Chinese Consul-General in San Francisco in 1900.

Of the Rev. Ho's six daughters only one, Ho Miu-ling 何妙齡 (1847–1937) need be mentioned. In a short account of her life, she was described as a devout Christian, very intelligent and well-educated. Having finished school early she married Wu Tingfang at the age of seventeen. To enable her husband to study law in London, it was said that she supported him with her dowry and savings. Later, when Wu became a Chinese diplomat, she travelled and lived abroad with him. After Wu's death in Guangzhou, she came back to live in Hong Kong in 1922. She donated generously to many charities in Hong Kong such as the Hop Yat Church building fund, established scholarships at the Ying Wah School, and paid for the building cost of a hospital which was named after her. It was estimated that in all she probably gave away as much as $200,000, a large fortune in those days. She lived on to the ripe old age of 91 before she died in 1937.

Wu Tingfang was known as Ng Choy 伍才 in Hong Kong. The surname was in fact same, pronounced Wu in Mandarin and Ng in the Cantonese dialect. He was born in Singapore in 1842 and educated in Guangzhou and Hong Kong where he studied in the St. Paul's College which was established by the London Missionary Society. He started his illustrious career as an interpreter in the Supreme Court of Hong Kong in 1862, a year before he married Miss Ho. In 1874, he went to London and was admitted into Lincoln's Inn, three years later he was called to the bar. He returned to Hong Kong in 1877 to become the first Chinese to be admitted as a barrister in the Supreme Court. He achieved another first when in 1880 he was appointed to the Legislative Council by Sir John Pope Hennessy who at the time was Governor. He could even have been the first Chinese to act as Attorney-General when the substantive holder of the post went on leave in 1879. However, there was so much opposition that the appointment was never made. In 1882 Ng Choy left Hong Kong and as Wu Tingfang, he began a second career in China that was to earn him a place in the history of the Republic. He first went to Tianjin to join the secretariat of Li Hongzhang 李鴻章 (1832–1901) who was then perhaps the most influential man in the Qing court. He assisted Li mostly on foreign affairs, for instance, the treaty negotiations at the end of the Sino-Japanese War in 1895. In 1896, he was appointed Minister to the United States, Spain and Peru. On his recall in 1902, he served on the Board of Commerce and the Board of Finance as Vice-President. In 1907, he was again posted to the United States as Minister for two years. From 1911 to 1922, the year he died, Wu served as Minister for Foreign Affairs, Minister of Finance and Minister of Justice in several governments set up by different factions at various places during a period of severe teething trouble which tormented the young republic.

Unfortunately, when Ho Fuk-tong died in 1871, members of the large family he raised had not made their marks yet. At that time the most outstanding of his sons, Shan-kai, who was the fourth, was still studying at school.

Personal History

〜〜〜

Ho Kai was born on 21 March 1859 in Hong Kong. Though he was given the name Shan-kai he chose to drop the middle character Shan which was common to all the brothers. In any case, within the family, he would be called by the last character Kai. After he was knighted, he should have been addressed as Sir Shan-kai Ho or Sir Kai Ho but instead he used the designation Sir Kai Ho Kai. Following the common practice among Chinese scholars of giving themselves courtesy names by which they are called by their friends, Ho Kai was known to have another name Yuk-sang 沃生 meaning literally fertile growth, or fertile scholar. Ho Kai is also known in Chinese history as He Qi, the way his name is pronounced in Putonghua.

After studying privately he entered the Government Central School in 1870. This school was established in 1862, and was the forerunner of the present Queen's College, the name having been changed in 1894. The government's education policy then was to teach local boys English so that they could become clerks and interpreters, there being a demand for both by government departments and commercial firms. For instance, as mentioned in Chapter I, Ho Kai's brother-in-law, Ng Choy, and his brothers Shan-tim and Shan-yau started life as interpreters in the government civil service. To receive a bilingual education, local Chinese boys would have to study some Chinese first and then English in either the Government Central School or a missionary school such as the St. Paul College (established in 1851), the Diocesan Boys' School (established in 1869), and the St. Joseph College (established in 1876). In 1871, the year

after Ho Kai entered, there were 144 boys in the Government Central
School. The headmaster was Dr. Frederick Stewart (see Chapter X). Some
idea of how the school was run could be obtained from the following
description:

> No fees were charged and text-books, including dictionaries, when available,
> were provided free of cost. There was a lower vernacular section and upper
> English study section. The school was divided into upper school, classes 1, 2 and
> 3; lower school, classes 4, 5 and 6; and preparatory school, consisting of classes 7
> and 8. The study of English was not compulsory. After passing an entrance
> examination in Chinese, pupils were admitted to the preparatory school where
> they study vernacular. Thereafter, on leaving the preparatory school, they did
> four hours of Chinese in the morning and, if they wished, four of English in the
> afternoon. It was a long day, 6 a.m. to 4 p.m. with breaks for breakfast and lunch,
> for those who elected to join the English classes, and most did. In 1865, fees were
> charged to all pupils, $1 monthly in the English classes and 50 cents in the
> Chinese section.

Ho Kai was admitted to class 4 in 1870 at the age of eleven. This indicated
that he must have already learnt some English otherwise he would have to
start from the lowest form class 8. He spent only two years in the Government Central School, as apparently he was so clever that he completed
four years of study in half the time. It was recorded that "his promotion was
rapid, for on September 1st 1871 he was in class 1, then the top form".

In 1872 when he was thirteen he was sent to England where he entered
the Palmer House School in Margate, Kent. After leaving school he
started studying medicine. He registered in the Aberdeen University in
September 1875, from the address 3, Elgin Street, Hong Kong. Four years
later, in 1879, at the age of only twenty, he received the M.B.C.M. degree
(Bachelor of Medicine, Master of Surgery). His clinical study, however,
was done at St. Thomas's Hospital in London. In the Pupils Entry Book
of this medical school, his address was recorded as "Bom Chum" Villa,
Griffith Road, Wimbledon. He paid 110 guineas and some laboratory fees

to register as a "perpetual pupil" which probably meant that he was a long-term full-time student as there could be others who paid smaller fees to attend courses on a part-time basis. His academic record was very good for he obtained a certificate of honour in his first and second years and a college prize in the second year. He also passed the examination for the membership of the Royal College of Surgeons of London in 1879. It was common practice for medical students in Great Britain to do their clinical studies in one of the London teaching hospitals although they had enrolled at some other university than London University itself. At the end of their training the students could take the qualifying examinations of the Royal Colleges, and became a L.R.C.P. (Licentiate of the Royal College of Physicians) and M.R.C.S. (Member of the Royal College of Surgeons), besides sitting for the degree examination at their own university. The degree of Bachelor of Medicine and Master of Surgery in Aberdeen was replaced by that of Bachelor of Medicine and Bachelor of Surgery in 1889. The fact that Ho Kai was a Master of Surgery and a Member of the Royal College of Surgeons did not necessarily imply that he had specialized in surgery as both were basic qualifications.

In the year 1879, after he qualified in medicine, he was admitted into Lincoln's Inn. It is not clear whether his original intention was to practise both professions simultaneously. Nowadays doctors who have also read for the bar usually embark on a career as medical administrators, forensic pathologists or coroners. Such openings were not available in Hong Kong in Ho Kai's time. From various sources, it would appear that his future wife was responsible for persuading him to study law as well. He had by then met a Miss Alice Walkden of Blackheath, a south-east suburb of London, near Greenwich. She was born on 3 February 1852, seven years before Ho Kai. Miss Walkden's father Mr. John Walkden was reputedly a member of Parliament, but nothing else is known about the family. One could assume that it was while Ho Kai was studying at St. Thomas's Hospital and living in Wimbledon that he did his courting. They became engaged, got married in 1881 and returned to Hong Kong early in 1882. They made their home in a house named "Craigengower" on Bonham Road. This was probably the first Anglo-Chinese marriage ever and even more unusual, it took place in racist Victorian society, the Walkden family must be very liberal-minded.

Ho Kai did just as well in law as in medicine. In the three years at Lincoln's Inn he was Senior Equity Scholar and Senior Scholar in Real and Personal Property. He was called to the bar in 1881. When the news reached Hong Kong, the then Governor, Sir John Pope Hennessy, made the following remarks at a Legislative Council meeting held on 7 February 1882:

> Mr. Ho Kai, in opposition to members of various Universities had passed his examinations at Lincoln's Inn with credit. This young gentleman who was expected to arrive in the Colony had taken the highest honours at Lincoln's Inn. It was something that a gentleman belonging to the Colony should have gained such honours.

Ho Kai was indeed fortunate to have had such an excellent education. The institutions which he had chosen, or had been chosen for him, were all of the highest standing. With his intelligence and brilliance, and no doubt through hard work as well, he had acquitted himself so well that he had earned an illustrious place in the annals of all of them. The Government Central School or Queen's College was the most prestigious school in Hong Kong, though not the oldest. St. Thomas's Hospital which was opened in 1213 and refounded in 1551, is the second oldest of London's several voluntary hospitals, the oldest being St. Bartholomew's Hospital which preceded St. Thomas's by some ninety years. The date of foundation of the Medical School at St. Thomas's Hospital was 1723. Aberdeen University was founded in 1494, being the third one in Scotland after St. Andrew's and Glasgow but before Edinburgh. The Aberdeen Royal Infirmary with which the medical school was associated was opened in 1742. Lincoln's Inn is one of the four Inns of Court in London, the others being Gray's, Inner Temple and Middle Temple, where barristers read for the bar. Situated in Chancery Lane, the Inn was named after the landlord who sold the estate to the Church. The early history of the Inns of Court is very obscure, and the date of their respective foundation cannot be precisely determined. What is certain is that by the beginning of the fifteenth century, all four Inns of Court were well established with traditions behind them.

Ho Kai was not the first Chinese from Hong Kong but the second to study in a school in England. The first was Wei Yuk 韋玉 who became Sir Boshan Wei Yuk 韋寶珊 (1849–1922). He went to Leicester Stonygate School in 1867 at the age of eighteen after he attended the Government Central School. In 1868 he proceeded to the Dollar Academy in Edinburgh. After he returned to Hong Kong, he succeeded his father as compradore* in the Mercantile Bank of India. Although Wei Yuk was older than Ho Kai he entered public life later. He was appointed to the Legislative Council in 1896 and received his Knighthood in 1919, respectively six and seven years after Ho Kai.

Nor was Ho Kai the first Chinese to study Western medicine. This was Wong Foon 黃寬 (c. 1827–79), who, together with two other students, was taken to the United States in 1847 by the headmaster of their school, Dr. A. S. Brown. He attended the Monson Academy in Massachusetts, but studied medicine at the Edinburgh University from which he graduated in 1853. After a few more years of post-graduate studies, he returned to Hong Kong in 1857. He practised for only a short time in Hong Kong and moved to Guangzhou where he worked for a while at the Missionary Hospital 博愛 醫院 which Dr. Sun Yat-sen first entered as a medical student. However he was back in Hong Kong in 1860 when he was posted to the Government Civil Hospital. He then left again to become medical adviser to Li Hongzhang. Eventually he took up private practice in Guangzhou, helping out at the same time at the Missionary Hospital. He died in 1879, the year Ho Kai got his medical degree from Aberdeen University.

---

* A compradore (買辦) was a Chinese manager of a foreign firm, serving as middle man in the company's dealings with the Chinese customers, a lucrative job giving the occupant prestige and standing in society besides a good income from commissions.

After his return to Hong Kong Ho Kai first went into private medical practice but not for long. To quote from his obituary in the *China Mail*, "he found, unfortunately, that his compatriots were unwilling to receive Western medical treatment unless it were given gratis." Having been admitted as a barrister in the Supreme Court on 29 March 1882, the second Chinese to join the roll, he practised law instead.

Soon after he settled down Ho Kai became active in public life. He was appointed a Justice of the Peace in 1882, and a member of the Sanitary Board in 1886. He was offered the position of acting police magistrate in 1887 but declined it. In 1890 while Sir William Des Voeux was Governor he became the third Chinese to sit on the Legislative Council, the first being his brother-in-law Ng Choy whose appointment in 1880 was mentioned in Chapter I, and the second Wong Shing 黃勝 who was appointed in 1884.

Wong Shing (1825–1902) also known as Wong Ping-po 黃平甫 was one of the other two students who went to the States with Wong Foon, the third member of the trio being Yung Wing 容閎 (see Chapter XI). The three were students at the Morrison Education Society's school which was moved to Hong Kong from Macao in 1842. Wong Shing, like the other two, entered the Monson Academy in 1847, but because of illness he left the States in less than two years without entering a University. After returning to Hong Kong in 1848 he first worked in the printing department of the *China Mail* and in 1853 he was put in charge of the printing press of the London Missionary Society under Dr. James Legge. He became the first Chinese to serve as a member of the Jury in the Supreme Court in 1858. For a brief period between 1862 and 1863 he was in Shanghai serving under Li Hongzhang. Back in Hong Kong, he became associated with Dr. Legge's collaborator, the famous scholar and translator Wang Tao 王韜 (see Chapter XI), with whom he founded a Chinese newspaper the *Hsün Huan Jih Pao* 循環日報 in 1873. About this time, he gave up his local printing business to serve the Chinese government again. He set up a printing office in the Tsungli Yamen in Beijing and took a group of young Chinese students to study in the States under a scheme administered by Yung Wing. After three years in the States, he returned to Hong Kong. Having established himself in the business community, he entered public life. Wong Shing was one of the founding directors of the Tung Wah Hospital which was opened in 1870. He sat on the Legislative Council from 1884 to 1890 when he was succeeded by Ho Kai. Sir Boshan Wei Yuk, who was mentioned in a previous paragraph, was Wong Shing's son-in-law.

Besides the Sanitary Board and the Legislative Council, on which he sat for a record of twenty-four years, Ho Kai served on a large number of boards and committees, including the Public Works Committee, the Standing Law Committee, the Examination Board, the Medical Board, the Po Leung Kuk Committee, the District Watchmen Committee, the Tung Wah Hospital Advisory Committee, the Governing Body of the Queen's College and as a founding member of the Hong Kong College of Medicine and the University of Hong Kong. The functions of these boards and committees and the contribution made by Ho Kai will be discussed in the following chapters. In short, it may be said that he had the distinction of sitting on every board and committee and his time had been given ungrudgingly in the public service no matter what sacrifice to his own interests and as a professional man. Hence, he was looked to by the Chinese for advice in their dealings with the government, and consulted by the government in transactions with the Chinese community. These were the comments written by the contributor to the *20th Century Impressions of Hong Kong*. His interest in education was not confined to his old school, the Queen's College; he was also a founder of the St. Stephen's Boys' College in 1902. It was originally situated on Bonham Road under the management of the Church Mission Society. His many services to the community were recognized by the award of the C.M.G. (Commander of the Order of St. Michael and St. George) in 1902 and a knighthood in 1912. He was the first Chinese to receive both these honours. But another first eluded him. During the governorship of Sir William Robinson in 1895, there was talk of appointing a Chinese to the Executive Council and his name was on the mind of the governor. However he never received the appointment, which went to Sir Shouson Chow 周壽臣 (1861–1959) in 1926, twelve years after the death of Ho Kai. Sir Shouson Chow was one of the students sent to the United States by the Chinese Education Mission by Yung Wing. He served in the Customs and Consular service in Korea, which was then under Chinese rule, and held posts in the Chinese railway and customs service under the Qing dynasty. He came to Hong Kong after China became a Republic.

From photographs of Ho Kai which appeared in a number of publications, one could get some impression of his physical appearance. A half portrait which has been kept in the family and another which appeared in the commemorative pamphlet *Alice Ho Miu Ling Nethersole Hospital 1887–1967* are reproduced as Figures 1 and 2 respectively. Also reproduced as Figure 3 is a rather rarely seen full-size portrait showing him standing, dressed in the cap and gown of presumably a bachelor of medicine of the Aberdeen University, in Norton-Kyshe's *A History of the Laws and Courts of Hong Kong*. It is evident that he was a big, heavy-set man, perhaps somewhat taller than the average Chinese. In the two half-portraits, he was dressed in the conventional European style of the day, wearing a wing-collar and a bow-tie. A Chinese would still be wearing a queue in those days, for instance, in the class photograph of the first batch of students of the Hong Kong College of Medicine, all of them could be seen with their queues. Ho Kai must have had his cut early, presumably before he went to the United Kingdom. In fact, his well-brushed hair was already showing signs of thinning and recession. He wore a big moustache, with well-waxed tapering ends. One could say that he had a distinguished and intelligent look whether from observation or hindsight, and it must be admitted that he had rather handsome features set on a broad face. These photographs must have been taken in or after 1902, the year Ho Kai was awarded the C.M.G. for he was wearing its insignia on his left lapel. In appearance, at any rate, he was certainly not typically Chinese but thoroughly westernized.

Another indication that Ho Kai was very much westernized was that he was a freemason.* In his book on the history of freemasonry in the Far East, *The Craft of the East*, Christopher Haffner explained that freemasonry "is the product of an evolutionary process whereby the operative stonemasons who built the great Gothic churches of Europe developed into a society of 'speculative' masons, at the same time taking simple medieval legends in the art of building, the Bible, and folklore, and developing them into complex rituals capable of universal appeal." He added that this process was formalized by the creation of Grand Lodges and spread throughout Europe and North America and in just over forty years reached the Far East. He did not say forty years from when. The Chinese jokingly call it the "foreign devil's triad society". Indeed, the freemasons adopt certain practices and rituals not dissimilar to those of the Chinese triad societies, for instance, members are bound by the spirit of a brotherhood to help one another. It is not necessary to elaborate further. When the University of Hong Kong was opened in 1912, it was proposed to found a university lodge. Dr. Francis Clarke, the dean of the Faculty of Medicine, was a deputy district grand master, and the application, forwarded to the Grand Master in Scotland, was approved. Ho Kai, together with Wei Yuk, his colleague on the Legislative Council were already initiated in the Lodge St. John No. 618 SC. They both took an active part in forming the University Lodge of Hong Kong No. 3666. They must have been the first Chinese to be admitted into the Society, so was Hu Liyuan 胡禮垣 (see Chapter XI) according to Dr. P. C. Woo, himself an active member*. Unlike other societies, the freemasons certainly did not have any racial discrimination in admitting members. It was perhaps of this bond of brotherhood that Wei Yuk undertook to help the family of Ho Kai after he died as we shall see later.

However, Ho Kai was very much a Chinese at heart. With reference to the Chinese calendar, he was born in the ninth year of the reign of Emperor Xianfeng 咸豐 which lasted from 1850 to 1860. He lived throughout

---

* This information was kindly provided by Dr. P. C. Woo, who is Hu Liyuan's grandson.

the reigns of Emperor Tongzhi (see Prologue), Emperor Guangxu 光緒 from 1875 to 1908 and Emperor Xuantong 宣統 from 1909 to 1911. The most active years of Ho Kai's public life therefore coincided with Emperor Guangxu's reign, a most turbulent period in the history of the Qing dynasty. From outside the country, though near enough, he got himself involved in the politics of China by advocating a change in the constitution. As we shall see, he was a monarchist, loyal to the throne at first but circumstances made him change his stand later. He saw the birth of the Republic but lived for only four years afterwards.

When Ho Kai died on 21 July 1914, aged only 55, he left a widow and a large family of ten sons and seven daughters. He was twice married. The first marriage ended tragically when Alice Walkden died on 8 June 1884. They had been married for only about three years. Mrs. Ho Kai apparently died of typhoid fever shortly after given birth to a daughter, who was taken back to England to be brought up by her mother's relatives and died young without having been married. Ho Kai subsequently re-married Miss Lai Yuk-hing 黎玉卿 whose father was reputedly an American. Lady Ho Kai died in 1945, having survived her husband for thirty-five years.

Incredible as it might seem but Ho Kai, a barrister-at-law, with a large family, who had to retire early because of ill-health, died intestate, without a will. The evidence was provided by a document in Arnold Hall's possession.

SUPREME COURT OF HONG KONG

PROBATE JURISDICTION

LETTERS OF ADMINISTRATION

Be it known that on the Sixth day of March, One thousand nine hundred and sixteen, Letters of Administration of all and singular the personal estate and effects of Sir Kai Ho Kai, C.M.G. late of No. 45B Robinson Road Victoria in the Colony of Hong Kong, Barrister-at-law deceased who died on the 21st day of July, One thousand nine hundred and fourteen, at No. 45B Robinson Road Victoria aforesaid intestate, were granted to Lily Ho Kai of No. 31 Queen's Road

Central Victoria aforesaid, the lawful widow and relict of the said deceased she
having been first sworn well and faithfully to administer the same by paying the
just debts of the said intestate and distributing the residue of his estate and effects
according to law and exhibit a true and perfect Inventory of all and singular the
said estate and effects and to render a just and true account thereof whenever
required by law so to do.

(Signed) Hugh A. Nisbet

Registrar

In actual fact, Ho Kai died penniless, leaving nothing but the furniture
in his house and some law books in his office, altogether probably worth
less than a couple of thousand dollars. He was in debt to Au Tak 區德 (see
later) for at least seven thousand dollars. His financial affairs were described
in detail by Wei Yuk in a letter dated 20 August 1914 addressed to the
Governor, Sir Francis May, appealing to him for help to educate Ho Kai's
children. Wei Yuk, as a fellow Legislative Councillor, told the governor
that he had to make the appeal on compassionate grounds because Lady
Ho Kai found herself in dire straits, unable to feed the large family. In
pleading his case, he reminded the governor of the unpaid services Ho Kai
had rendered to the people of Hong Kong and the great sacrifice he had
made in so doing.

According to Wei Yuk, Ho Kai, on his return from England, after
straightening out his elder brother Ho Tim's affairs (see Chapter I), in-
herited $20,000 and he began to earn from his legal practice, so he was
quite comfortably off. After the death of his first wife in 1884, he sent the
daughter back to England and settled on her everything left by her mother.
Ho Kai then spent his savings to pay for the cost of construction of the
Alice Memorial Hospital (see Chapter V). His troubles began in 1895 with
the bankruptcy of Ho Tim. In the early days of Hong Kong, there was a lot
of speculation on land and real estate as development progressed on the
Island, then the Kowloon Peninsula and eventually the New Territories.
There had been several booms one of which burst during the governorship

of Sir John Pope Hennessy in 1882, affecting none other than Ng Choy, who probably left Hong Kong that year to evade his creditors. When the New Territories were leased in 1898, a land syndicate spread the rumour that the British would soon confiscate all privately owned land. The local inhabitants duly panicked and sold off their family land cheaply, which was swept up by the syndicate, thus making a large fortune. Ho Kai was alleged to have been associated with the syndicate but there was no evidence to substantiate the allegation. As we shall see later, he had never been a wealthy man.

To settle his brother's affairs, which included the rebuilding of a dilapidated theatre, Ho Kai had to borrow $50,000. When the mortgage was due the next year, 1896, he was so pressed that on the advice of Wu Tingfang, as Ng Choy had now become, he went to Shanghai to serve as adviser to Sheng Xuanhuai 盛宣懷 (1844–1916) for a salary of 1,500 taels a month. Sheng was the prototype of the Shanghai tycoon. He was general manager of the China Merchant's Steam Navigation Company but he also controlled several other companies, including the Shanghai Cotton Mill, a company started by Li Hongzhang. The time was when, under the enlightened administration of Li, technology was being introduced to modernize China's industries. By using government loans and transferring funds to and from other companies without consulting the shareholders, Sheng tripled the capital base of the Mill between 1887 and 1893. He died a multi-millionaire, and it was said that his funeral expenses amounted to 300,000 taels. Ho Kai was not happy with his job and stayed for only two months. On his return to Hong Kong, with the help of a friend, Fung Wah-chuen 馮華川, he succeeded in selling the theatre. Having got back about $20,000, he bought himself a home, No. 7, West Terrace, where he lived from then on until 1912. The house next door, No. 8, was originally bought by his sister, Madame Wu Tingfang, but later she wanted Ho Kai to take it over and Ho Kai had to borrow $12,000 to complete the transaction. Between 1897 and 1908, his annual income from his legal practice was between $4,000 and $5,000. In the meantime the family was growing and he had to provide schooling for his children. Madame Wu advanced money to him from time to time to meet family expenses but Ho Kai was again in debt because he had to pay for repairs of the roofs of the two houses. It was then that his friend Au Tak, whose daughter was married to Ho Kai's eldest son, came to his rescue, becoming his creditor, lending him money to keep up his position and his family. Now follows the story of Kai Tak Bund (啟德 濱) and the Kai Tak International Airport.

Au Tak (1840–1920) was the proprietor of a furniture shop named Chiu Loong Tai 昭隆泰, situated on Chiu Loong Street (昭隆街) in the Central District. The street still exists but not the shop. Besides furniture, imported sundry goods and photographic equipment were also sold at the shop. Au was one of Hong Kong's earliest developers, the owner of houses on such prime sites in the Central District as Chiu Loong Street and On Lan Street (安瀾街) . In 1912, Ho Kai went into partnership with Au Tak to form a company to develop a piece of land formed by reclamation. It was planned to build something like a garden estate there with houses, recreation grounds etc. for private tenancy. For this venture, Ho Kai sold his two town houses on West Terrace, for which he received $12,000 and took up residence at 45B Robinson Road. This house valued at $22,500 was bought for him by Madame Wu Tingfang and Au Tak who paid $10,000 and $12,500 respectively. The development company was formed with a capital of $1 million, divided into 50 shares of $20,000 each. It was hoped that Ho Kai would have been made managing director with a competent salary and be entitled to one share of the company free. But the venture was a failure, it had not taken off in the two remaining years of Ho Kai's life and eventually went into liquidation in 1924, ten years after Ho Kai died.

The land, which was named Kai Tak Bund, after the two principal partners, was taken back by government. In 1925, an American pilot, Harry Abbot, leased the land to start a flying school there. Abbot was said to have fought on the side of Sun Yat-sen as a mercenary during the civil strives among the warlords in the early years of the Republic. At the opening of the school, everything went wrong. The merchanic who demonstrated a parachute jump was drowned after he dropped into the harbour instead of landing on the airfield. For the next few years, the airfield was used by the Hong Kong Flying Club for the purpose of teaching people to fly an aeroplane, with facilities for members to enjoy weekend flying. The Royal Air Force and the Royal Navy also used it as a base for their planes. The first commercial flight to arrive in Hong Kong touched down on 24 March 1936 from Penang. In the same year, Pan American Airlines' Philippine Clipper arrived after its inaugural flight from the United States, taking ten days to complete the journey. Then came the War in 1941. On 8 December, Japanese bombers appeared early in the morning, and destroyed the few obsolete planes on the ground which was also heavily damaged. The Japanese later extended the airfield for the use of the Ocupation Force by demolishing the houses around it. After the War, further extension work was carried out from time to time. Between 1958 and 1974, two runways were built on reclaimed land to bring it up to international standards. Known as the Hong Kong Kai Tak International Airport, one of the busiest in the world, it has now been replaced by a new one at Chek Lap Kok which was inaugurated in July 1998. For all that Ho Kai had done for Hong Kong, no street or building had been named after him. He is remembered only as the Kai of the old airport, which was built originally on his business venture, Kai Tak Bund. After its demolition, Ho Kai and his friend Au Tak will be forgotten, unless the housing estates to be developed on the site will still be named Kai Tak.

In the same year 1912 when Ho Kai went into business with Au Tak, he was earning only between $2,000 and $3,000, while his family expenses increased to $9,000 to $10,000. At the same time his health was deteriorating and he was prevented from taking up much more work, besides, he had to spend money on his illness. His income in 1913 was about $2,000 but for the first half of 1914, it dwindled down to only $395. Besides Au, another friend, S. W. (Seen Wan) Tso 曹善允, a solicitor, had been kind to Ho Kai, paying his office rent since 1912 and giving him the service of a clerk. Tso (1868–1953), nine years Ho Kai's junior, was the senior partner of the law firm Tso and Hodgson. He was born in Macao where his father was a prominent figure, having been knighted by the Portuguese government for services rendered. He was educated in England, where he went to Cheltenham College in 1886 and later qualified as a solicitor in 1896. Tso took up most of Ho Kai's public offices after the latter's death, including appointment to the Legislative Council from 1929 to 1937. Au Tak, Tso and two other friends contributed $750 each to meet Ho Kai's funeral expenses and the immediate needs of the family.

Ho Kai's ten sons, in order of seniority, were named: Wing-ching 永貞, Wing-hang 永亨, Wing-kin 永乾, Wing-yuen 永元, Wing-lee 永利, Wing-on 永安, Wing-hong 永康, Wing-kam 永錦, Wing-tak 永德, and Wing-tse 永謝. The seven daughters were: Sui-kam 瑞金, Sui-ngan 瑞銀, Sui-tung 瑞銅, Sui-tit 瑞鐵, Sui-sek 瑞錫, Sui-wah 瑞華, and Sui-mee 瑞美. At the time of Wei Yuk's letter, dated 20 August 1914, one month after Ho Kai died, sons Wing-ching and Wing-hang, daughters Sui-kam, Sui-tit and Sui-tung were married and required no assistance. According to Professor Lo Hsiang-lin 羅香林, Wing-ching and Wing-hang enrolled at the Hong Kong College of Medicine in 1909 but did not complete their studies. Others still studying for whom tuition fees had to be paid were Wing-kin (aged 22) and Wing-yuen (aged 20) who were studying engineering at the University of Hong Kong, Wing-lee (aged 19) who had just matriculated and waiting to enter University, Wing-on (aged 14) and Wing-hong (aged 11) who were studying at St. Paul's College and Wing-kam (aged 5) who was attending a preparatory school. The other two sons were only 4 years and 20 months old respectively. Of the daughters, Sui-sek (aged 16) and Sui-wah (aged 13) were studying in a preparatory school. In the end, on Sir Henry May's recommendation, the Secretary of State for the Colonies gave approval to provide tuition fees for the five sons Wing-kin, Wing-yuen, Wing-lee, Wing-on and Wing-hong, respectively the third, fourth, fifth, sixth and seventh. The amount granted was $1,440 per annum. It is not known for how long was this assistance made available, but four years later, the entire family was relocated in Shanghai.

Further news of the family was given in a letter written by Wing-lee dated 8 October 1918 from Tianjin to Sir James Stewart-Lockhart (see Chapter X) who made inquiries as an old friend of Ho Kai's. Wing-ching was Commissioner of the Shanghai-Nanjing Railway, Wing-hung was with the Bank of China, Wing-kin and Wing-yuen had graduated from the University of Hong Kong, Wing-lee was working at the Shanghai-Putong Railway, Wing-on had left college the year before and was working in the Shanghai-Nanjing Railway. The four younger ones, were studying in Shanghai.

All Ho Kai's male descendents had therefore left Hong Kong for Shanghai. It was Arnold Hall's impression that they were influenced by their uncle by marriage, Wu Tingfang, to go to him and put themselves under his patronage. Wing-kin, Arnold's father, and his brother Wing-yuen, graduated in engineering, went into partnership as Hall and Hall Associates to practise as architects. Arnold himself was born in Shanghai, but he went to school at King's College in Hong Kong, then went back to Shanghai to enter St. John's University. Eventually he again came back to Hong Kong to start his business, but he has since left for the States. Some of Ho Kai's daughters married well. The eldest, Sui-kam, married her cousin, Dr. Wu Chaoshu 伍朝樞 (1887–1934), the son of Wu Tingfang. Dr. Wu followed his father's steps closely. After studying at Lincoln's Inn, he was called to the bar in 1911. He then joined the Chinese diplomatic service and rose to become Minister at the League of Nations and Ambassador to the United States in 1929. Sui-tit, married Dr. Herbert To, a dentist in Hong Kong. Sui-sek was the wife of Dr. Foo Ping-sheung 傅秉常 (1895–1965), a graduate of the University of Hong Kong who became a diplomat, first serving as Wu Tingfang's private secretary. Subsequently he was appointed Ambassador to Russia during 1943–1949, in which year he returned to China as foreign minister, the last in the Nationalist government.

The Legal Profession:
Barristers versus Solicitors

For legal advice on problems concerning their properties or business, the Chinese had to turn to legal practitioners admitted into the rolls of the Supreme Court. In the rapidly growing city, Crown land was being offered for sale by auction to people who were interested in acquiring and developing properties. In all land and real estate transactions, title deeds had to be carefully drawn up and duly registered. Any departure from the usual procedure and faulty documentation could give rise to rather complicated consequences. For example, it was said that because the Rev. Ho Fuk-tong used aliases, several law suits were instituted in the course of administering his will and estate after his death. Dealing with European firms the Chinese had to follow their normal commercial practices. Legal action would be taken if any party failed to be responsible for securities, guarantees, promissory notes and contracts as illustrated by a case actually handled by Ho Kai which will be described later in this chapter. There were undoubtedly sufficient cases and problems to keep the legal profession busy. Until members of the illustrious Ho Family were admitted into the profession, Ng Choy and Ho Kai as barristers and Wyson Ho as a solicitor, all legal practitioners were expatriates. Because they knew neither the law nor the language, the Chinese, when they had to consult a lawyer, had to rely on English-speaking Chinese clerks employed by solicitors firms for help. However, some few bad elements among the clerks might demand a commission for their services. Thus a client sometimes had to pay both the solicitor and his clerk. To add to his difficulties, after consulting a solicitor, he might be told that counsel's opinion would have to be sought. The ordinary Chinese must have found it not only frustrating but expensive to obtain legal advice. It would seem that some of the expatriate lawyers were undesirable characters of the beachcomber type. Having lost their credit-ability and licence to practise at home, they now hoped to make some money out of ignorant people in the young colony, where the natives were mostly ignorant and perhaps easily intimidated. The entry of their own people into the legal profession must have been greatly welcomed by the Chinese community. It can therefore be readily understood that Ho Kai easily succeeded in the legal profession although he failed in his medical practice. Before he was admitted into the local bar, there was a long battle between the barristers and the lawyers which went on for years. It will be necessary to describe this battle briefly in order to give the reader some idea of the kind of work done by a barrister in early Hong Kong.

The removal of the Criminal and Admiralty Courts in Guangzhou to Hong Kong by order of the Privy Council in 1843 was the first step in establishing an administration of justice in the Colony. Crime was a particularly serious problem, created by the common occurrence of burglary and armed robbery ashore and piracy in adjacent waters. On 1 October 1844, the Supreme Court was formally opened, presided by the first Chief Justice, J. W. Hulme, who then admitted the first Attorney-General, P. I. Sterling, to practise as a barrister of the Court. Two rolls were in fact established: a roll of barristers admitted to practise before the Supreme Court of Hong Kong, and a roll of proctors, attorneys and solici-tors admitted to practise before the Supreme Court of Hong Kong. Two barristers were admitted in 1844, one in 1846, one in 1851, one in 1854, three in 1855, and none until 1859. Only one solicitor was admitted in 1844, followed by three in 1845, three in 1846, one in 1849, two in 1850, one in 1851, one in 1853, one in 1854, two in 1855 and one in 1858. The record thus showed that by 1858, there were eight barristers practising in Hong Kong and sixteen solicitors. The significance of this date will be appreciated later. At the beginning both barristers and solicitors practised separately according to the code governing the two branches of the legal profession.

On 15 April 1851, the Chief Justice, Mr. Hulme, admitted Mr. William Thomas Bridges into the roll of barristers. Almost immediately afterwards, while appearing for a case before the Chief Justice, Mr. Bridges called the attention of the Court to the inadvisability of solicitors being allowed to continue to appear as counsel for prisoners. His argument was that it was not part of the function of a solicitor to appear either in civil or criminal cases if a barrister could be retained, and he said that there was now more than one barrister practising at the local bar. By these remarks, he therefore disclosed that the legal profession had in a way amalgamated, or at least solicitors were in some cases acting as barristers. The Chief Justice replied that solicitors had been allowed to plead from absolute necessity and as such necessity no longer existed, the ordinary practice of the English courts would be observed. Mr. Bridges subsequently had an interesting career in Hong Kong. He acted as Attorney-General and Colonial Secretary when these officers went on leave. While acting as Colonial Secretary in 1857, he was involved in a big scandal of the time. He was alleged to have ordered the destruction of evidence which could incriminate a government official, D. R. Caldwell, who held the office of "Protector of the Chinese" (撫華道), for taking bribes to protect pirates, opium smugglers and brothel-keepers.

In January 1858, a date mentioned above, the Attorney-General, T. C. Anstey, was approached by the barristers on the subject of amalgamation of the legal profession. In a letter addressed to him, three barristers, W. T. Bridges, H. Kingsmill and J. Day, said that practical experience had convinced them that there did not exist in Hong Kong as at home a necessity for the division of the two branches of the profession. They were willing to give up their peculiar privileges and consent to an amalgamation. Bridges would appear to have changed his stand but he gave his reasons as we shall see later. It has already been recorded that by that time, there were eight barristers and sixteen solicitors in Hong Kong. The barristers included the

Attorney-General himself, and one who had by then ceased to practise. Bridges, Kingsmill and Day were respectively the fourth, seventh and the eighth barrister admitted into the roll.

In his reply the Attorney-General proposed a meeting of the profession to discuss the following subjects: (1) the propriety of the suggested change, (2) the practical method of effecting it, (3) the future status of the two branches, (4) the mode of securing the expected advantage to the community and (5) the precautions to be taken for its protection against the wrong. He communicated his views to the Law Society, whose secretary denied the allegation that dissatisfaction was felt by the general public at the rules which imposed separate duties on barristers and solicitors. The solicitors felt that as much and perhaps a greater necessity existed in Hong Kong for the division of the two branches as at home and were against amalgamation.

When the meeting was held on 12 January besides the Attorney-General, who took the chair, Messrs. Bridges, Kingsmill and Day were present. Bridges was apparently acting Colonial Secretary at that time. Another barrister, F. W. Green sent his apologies saying that he was unable to attend because of illness, and that while he admitted the necessity for a change of some kind, he dissented from the proposal of his learned brethren. There were five solicitors, Messrs. W. Gaskell, A. Parsons, E. K. Stace, G. Turner-Cooper and W. Moresby. Bridges said that the question should not be put to vote as the barristers would surely be outvoted, three against five. Gaskell then moved the following resolution: "That there does exist here as at home a necessity for the division of the two branches of the profession." The barristers argued that the business of attorney and barrister had been carried on most satisfactorily by one gentleman. They did not wish to injure the attorneys, but the general public was not prepared to pay two lawyers instead of one. They had heard no more of their briefs after they turned down the direct approaches by clients. The solicitors said that the functions of the two branches were essentially different and should be kept distinct. Their time being fully occupied in the details of a general practice, they could not acquire the knowledge requisite for the discharge of the duties of a barrister. Towards the end, there was an exchange concerning barrister's fees. Bridges commented that he did not care what the ordinance said about a fixed retainer. He meant to draw a larger amount as the ordinance merely said that more should not be allowed on taxation. Gaskell observed that if Bridges were to have his way, the difference disallowed on taxation of his retaining fee would have to come out of the attorney's pocket. The meeting ended with the resolution being carried, the barristers not voting against it while the solicitors were all in favour.

In spite of the outcome of the above meeting, in May 1858, a number of bankers and merchants memorialized the Attorney-General on the subject of the amalgamation of the two branches of the legal profession. In the petition, it was said that the change was not desired on account of the expenses attending legal proceedings but no compelling reason could be seen to employ two advisers when it would be more convenient to confide in one. It ended with a statement that in a young and small community like Hong Kong, there should be but one class of practitioners, and that unrestricted competition between all the properly admitted members of the Supreme Court would be a great improvement on the existing state of affairs. The Attorney-General submitted the memorial in the Legislative Council which ordered it to be read and printed. The Law Society then presented its memorial to the Chief Justice, pointing out that amalgamation would be very prejudicial and unfair to the attorneys and of no advantage to the community, who, not regarding expense, might have all they could desire under the present system. The Society also presented another memorial to the Governor and the Legislative Council. The attorneys said that the people who signed the original petition were ignorant of the subject and had done so only because two legislative councillors headed the list of signatories. They maintained that no complaint had been made against their profession, and that the change would only benefit members of the bar. They even doubted the competence of the colonial government to deal with the matter and asked for an independent Committee or Commission.

This petition was presented to the Legislative Council by the Chief Justice, who was an official member. Following its submission, the Council considered an Ordinance for Practitioners in Law. At the second reading on 24 June, the views of the Law Society were heard, with Mr. Parsons as its spokesman. He argued against the case for amalgamation. The request for amalgamation was however supported by the community and the press. When the Legislative Council reassembled on 6 July, events took an unexpected and farcical turn. The Law Society disowned Mr. Parsons as its representative and spokesman. As no other person was now present to support the petition, it was, by resolution, declared a fraud, and the order to lay it upon the table was rescinded. On 12 July, the Council resumed the second reading of the ordinance. The Governor remarked upon the necessity for checking the practice of enormous charges being imposed on the Chinese. The Ordinance for Practitioners in Law was then passed as No. 12 of 1858. "This enactment was neither more nor less an ordinance to empower barristers to act as attorneys" noted Norton-Kyshe.

The successors to Hulme and Anstey as Chief Justice and Attorney-General, respectively W. H. Adams and J. J. Smale, were both against amalgamation of the two branches of the legal profession. The government had acted on the advice of the profession while the general public appeared to be satisfied with the system. In 1862 a surprise move was made by the Attorney-General who introduced a motion in Legislative Council to repeal the Amalgamation Ordinance No. 12 of 1858. Two unofficial members were against the motion. They said that no complaints of extortionate charges had been heard, and they deprecated the re-opening of the door to undesirable characters in the legal profession. The Chief Justice did not agree with the inference that attorneys would sooner or later become drunkards or scamps. He was also against the appointment of a Commission of Inquiry. In the end, it was agreed that a reasonable delay should be given for these professionals who had been practising as barristers and attorneys to adjust themselves. The Amalgamation Ordinance of No. 12 of 1858 was allowed to continue in force until 31 December 1864, while the Ordinance repealing it was passed on 3 July as No. 13 of 1862. The principal provisions of this new ordinance were: "(1) Every barrister who is now by faculty privileged to act as a notary in Hong Kong shall be entitled to continue so to act after this Ordinance shall have come into operation, and (2) on the first day of January 1865, every barrister who is now practising as a legal practitioner in this Colony shall elect whether he will act from that time as a barrister, or an attorney and solicitor, and shall sign the court roll accordingly, declaring the way in which he has exercised the option hereby granted."

In 1873, the question of amalgamation of the two branches of the legal profession was again raised. At a meeting of the Legislative Council on 9 July, a new bill was introduced. An unofficial member, Richard Rowett of Holiday, Wise and Co. suggested that some steps should be taken to enable people to take the opinion of counsel without the intervention of attorneys in respect to matters which were not before court. The Attorney-General, J. Pauncefote, said he should object to any proposal to amalgamate the two branches if that was what Rowett had in mind. Rowett said that he was not advocating amalgamation but he was only trying to save unnecessary expense. In support, W. H. Alexander who was Registrar of the Supreme Court but sitting as an unofficial, agreed that people should be permitted to take the advice of counsel direct, as it would save them trouble and expense if told they had no case. The Governor then proposed that the Bill be referred to a special Committee, consisting of the Chief Justice (J. J. Smale), the Attorney-General and the Registrar of the Supreme Court. It will be recalled that Smale, when he was Attorney-General, was largely responsible for repealing the amalgamation ordinance of 1858.

Rowett's resolution gained the support of the community at large who addressed the Governor on the subject. This letter was laid before the Legislative Council at a meeting on 19 August. Rowett then introduced his motion, that "for the convenience, and in the interest of the public, it is desirable that all barristers-at-law admitted to practise as advocates of the Supreme Court in this Colony, shall be permitted to take business from clients personally, without the intervention of attorneys, in all cases except those in which litigation has been actually commenced in the Supreme Court, and that at the earliest convenient opportunity the government of this Colony shall adopt such means as may be necessary to that end." The Attorney-General however proposed an amendment: "The Council, having regard to the expression of opinion contained in a letter recently addressed to the government by a large proportion of the mercantile community, are of the opinion that it is expedient to modify to a certain extent the rules of the legal profession which restrict barristers from giving consultations and transacting other business, in certain cases, without the intervention of an attorney, but that such modifications should be expressly defined and limited, in such a way as may be deemed advisable, so as to meet the reasonable requirements of the public without effecting an amalgamation of the two branches of the legal profession." The amendment was carried by a clear majority when put to vote. An ordinance meeting the amendment proposed by the Attorney-General was accordingly drafted by him and submitted to the Council. It was passed on 30 September, entitled "An Ordinance to regulate and define the practice of barristers and attorneys admitted and enrolled by the Supreme Court and to amend the law in relation thereto", No. 15 of 1873. The following were the principal provisions: "(1) A barrister may, without the intervention of an attorney, hold consultations with clients and give opinions in all matters whatever, (2) a barrister may, without the intervention of an attorney, appear for a client in all criminal proceedings before the Supreme Court, and in all proceedings in the Court of Summary Jurisdiction, and in all proceedings whatever before any Court of Inferior Jurisdiction, (3) a barrister may receive any fee directly from a client, for any professional business which he may transact without the intervention of an attorney."

The question of remuneration for counsel was raised by the Chief Justice, now Sir John Smale, who stressed that no defence could be perfect without counsel having the assistance of a solicitor, when he dealt with a case before him in 1877. In September that year, he wrote to the Colonial Secretary, saying that in murder trials, the government should provide counsel for the defence, and besides the nominal retainer, a refresher should be paid if the case lasted for more than a day. He also pointed out the difficulties facing counsel without the assistance of a solicitor. The Governor thus gave instructions that the advice and opinion of the Chief Justice be followed. Henceforth, a solicitor would be instructed and counsel retained in capital cases notwithstanding the relevant section in Ordinance No. 15 of 1873. When the Secretary of State for the Colonies was consulted, the opinion given was that it was not the duty of the State to furnish prisoners with counsel and solicitors for the sake of elucidating the truth, but that at the same time it was right and reasonable, especially in colonies where the prisoners might be ignorant of the laws and the language, that the judges should be authorized to assign counsel with powers, if necessary, to employ a solicitor at the expense of the State. In 1879 fees were fixed for the remuneration of counsel and solicitors employed by the government. The fee to counsel before the Supreme Court was fixed at fifty dollars for each case, and that to the solicitor for a first attendance before a magistrate at fifteen dollars and for each subsequent attendance at ten dollars and for defending each case in the Supreme Court at twenty-five dollars.

Such then was the state of affairs regarding the practice of law in Hong Kong when Ho Kai returned in 1882. His name was the thirty-third on the roll of barristers. Having gone through the essential details of the battle for or against the amalgamation of the two professions up to 1879, one could assume that as a barrister in 1882, Ho Kai could deal with clients directly and collect his fee without the intervention of a solicitor, and in certain cases at least, he could appear in court without the assistance of a solicitor. Very little is known about Ho Kai's career as a barrister. In the section on his life in *Biographies of Famous Chinese in Hong Kong*, there was a reference to his legal practice:

> He insisted on being fair, strict and clean. He often said that the rich could not
> be benevolent, and vice versa. Whenever he was consulted on cases of brothers
> fighting over estates, he would first lecture them on principles before settling the

dispute for them. Because of these qualities, although he practised law for many years, he remained a poor man.

To search for records of cases handled by Ho Kai as a barrister, two works were consulted, Norton-Kyshe's *A History of the Laws and Courts of Hong Kong, from the Earliest Period to 1898*, and *Hong Kong Law Reports*, from the earliest edition of 1905 to that of 1914, the year Ho Kai died. The results were not gratifying. It could be that he did most of his work in chamber rather than in court. Also, during the period 1905–14, he was probably too busy in his public life to appear in court frequently. However, a few references to him were found.

In Norton-Kyshe's book, it was recorded that on 21 January 1885, W. Keswick, an unofficial member, presented a petition to the Legislative Council by the solicitors in Hong Kong praying for legislation to improve the land laws in force in Hong Kong. It called for the extension of two Acts of Parliament, the Real Property Limitation Act 1874 and the Vendor and Purchaser Act 1874, to Hong Kong, and the simplification of the procedure of deposition of title deeds with the lands office. This petition was signed by a number of residents and landowners. Acting as her attorney Ho Kai signed on behalf of Ho Lai Shi 何黎氏 who was in fact his mother. Among Arnold Hall's papers was an unsigned document dated 1888 in which Ho Lai Shi nominated and appointed Wyson Ho and Ho Kai as her attorneys and agents.

There was also mention of a criminal case in which Ho Kai appeared for the defence. On 18 September 1897, Wan Hung murdered his wife Chan Sze-kui. He then absconded but returned to Hong Kong early in June 1898 when he was arrested. At the Criminal sessions held on 19 July 1898, he was convicted and sentenced to death. "The last penalty of the law was carried out at the usual place and in the form now used on the morning of August 3rd."

In *Hong Kong Law Reports*, Ho Kai's name was mentioned in two cases. The first case of *Lai Chi-chin versus Leung Shun-hing and Wing Tsoi*, was heard on 28 August 1907. Ho Kai apparently appeared for the defendants. Leave to appeal was granted by the full court on the motion of Ho Kai which was based on the desire to introduce fresh evidence. At the re-hearing on 15 January Mr. Slade for the appellant applied for leave to introduce fresh evidence. Mr. K. C. Pollock for the respondent objected that no notice of motion had been served and no affidavits filed. Slade then made his motion indicating the nature of the new evidence which he desired to produce. The principal ground was fraud, the books on which the appellent had been found in the summary jurisdiction action to be a partner being alleged to have been fabricated. Pollock for the respondent contended that the grounds now alleged could have been taken at trial. Eventually, the court granted the appeal and decided to hear the case *de novo*.

The other case was that of *Wai Lee Firm versus Ku Chung Ming*, Summary Jurisdiction No. 235 of 1911, with Ho Kai appearing for the plaintiffs, Mr. F. B. L. Bowley, a solicitor for the defendants. The nature of the case was described by the following summary:

> Where there is a lump sum contract for the performance of certain building work, payment is not to begin until a certain stage in construction is reached, if owing to circumstances over which neither party has any control (in the instance, a collapse or the intervention of the building ordinance requiring a complete change of plans) the completion of the work becomes impossible before the time for any payment under the contract has arrived, the contract is at an end, and the builder cannot recover on a quantum merit for work already performed. Nor can he recover for materials worked up into the building, but he may remove, or sue for the value of, materials brought on the land but not yet used, the property in which has not passed to the building owner.

The judgment given was that the plaintiff was entitled to his own materials and could either remove them or recover their value.

In an article published recently but not in his thesis, Jung-fang Tsai wrote that Ho Kai once defended none other than his great friend and literary collaborator, Hu Liyuan (see Chapter XI) in a law suit over an unpaid debt. The case was heard from 22 to 24 April 1896, and the judgment delivered on 30 April, by the acting Chief Justice, Mr. W. N. Goodman. A report of the summing up and judgment appeared in the 30 April edition of the *China Mail*. The plaintiff was Tso Tsz-ki and the defendant U Lai-woon, which was Hu Liyuan pronounced in Cantonese, but the names of counsel were not given. Tso was suing Hu for the recovery of $16,600, of which $10,000 was the principal sum lent to Wong Tsik-hing on 17 December 1889, guaranteed by Hu, and $6,600 interest accrued over the years. The story centred on Wong Tsik-hing who was the comprador of the shipping firm, Douglas Lapraik & Co. It was the established practice of all European firms to require their comprador to deposit a sum of money with the company as security. If the security was provided by other people, then the comprador would have to give them a share of his profit. It served as a guarantee for the comprador and his staff who were responsible for handling all cash transactions. Wong's security was originally $40,000, provided by three persons, Hu Liyuan, Lo King-chee and Leung Man-shik. Hu himself put up $16,000. Unfortunately, Wong became indebted to Douglas Lapraik & Co. as a result of heavy losses in speculating on stocks and shares, in the amount of $30,000, in December 1889. He was required to have his security increased by $20,000. When Tso Tsz-ki was approached to provide it, he said he would take over the entire amount of $60,000. The three original guarantors agreed to retire in his favour. However, because of defects in the title deeds which he produced, Tso was unable to satisfy the Company and did not provide the security at once. He was asked to lend Wong $10,000 first, so that the latter could pay off some of his debts. Hu acted as a guarantor for this loan. A promissory note was issued, with the following statement:

> Now borrowed from Mr. Tso Tsz Ki $10,000 in current bank notes. It is agreed
> that interest at the rate of $10 per $1,000 per month shall be charged. The use of
> the money is limited to two months, after which the principal and interest to be

repaid in full. This is proof. Securities for the repayment, U Lai Woon and Lo King Chee. Witness: Lo Moi Sang, 17th December, 1889. This note is made by Wong Tsik Hing true handwriting.

It was further agreed that the two guarantors would be employed, Hu as a shipping clerk and Lo as an accountant. There was also an understanding that the promissory note would be replaced by a new one after two months. A year later, in December 1890, Wong declared bankruptcy. Six years later, in December 1896, Tso decided to recover his debt with interest by taking Hu to court. Ho Kai was successful in defending Hu Liyuan.

The following remarks were made by the Acting Chief Justice when he delivered his judgment.

Unfortunately in this case there is considerable conflict in testimony and, as the parties did not wish for a jury, I must decide upon the facts as well as upon the legal effect of these facts. Wong being largely indebted, and having no money to pay that if he lost, continued largely to speculate in shares. Such conduct is so dishonourable that I discount the value of his evidence when it conflicts with that of a man against whom nothing is known, but I see no reason why the defendant is now as worthy of credit as the plaintiff, and Wong's evidence collaborates the defendant's version. The defendant and Lo King Chee were already sureties for a large sum for the comprador. They only agreed to be surety for the extra $10,000 on certain conditions. There was a time limit. It was agreed the plaintiff was to become surety for the comprador in the first moon, that is, within a month after 21st January 1890, and that a new promissory note (in which, in my opinion, the defendant's name was not to appear) was to be given and the old one cancelled in that first moon, and as a further consideration for becoming surety for the two months the defendant was to be employed as a shipping clerk. The plaintiff failed to carry out his agreement to become surety, and in my opinion, because he did not use and did not wish to use due diligence to put his title deeds right. He changed his mind, I believe, about becoming surety and did not carry out the arrangements which induced the defendant to become guarantor. The defendant never got the post of shipping clerk, and yet in July 1895, has a writ issued against him and he is asked to pay $10,000 and $6,600 for interest. After carefully considering the whole evidence I find as a fact that the plaintiff in 1890 by his words and conduct did wilfully cause the defendant to believe and act upon the belief that the plaintiff no longer looked to him for payment of the $10,000, and that his liability as surety was considered by the plaintiff to be at an end. I find that in so doing he altered the position of the defendant, who, under the belief that the plaintiff no longer looked to him, might well take no further steps to insist on payment of the note by the principal debtor or upon the new promissory note being given and his own suretyship being cancelled. In the witness box, the defendant said "I took no proceedings against the plaintiff to get back my guarantee as the note was of no use." Accordingly I find for the defendant and give judgment for the defendant.

Having practised as a barrister for so long and with his standing in both the profession and society, Ho Kai never "took silk" to become a Queen's Counsel. The English bar from time immemorial is divided into a senior and a junior section. After ten years of practice a barrister can apply to be appointed as a Queen's Counsel or "take silk" as it is known, and thus become a member of the senior bar. The term "take silk" originates from the silk gown which a Queen's Counsel wears as against that of common material worn by junior counsel. A Queen's Counsel charges higher fees than a junior, and when he appears in court, he leads, or is assisted by, a junior. Ho Kai could certainly benefit in every way by taking silk but for unknown reasons he never took the step. It could be that in the early years of colonial rule in Hong Kong such an appointment would not be given to a Chinese barrister.

The Medical Profession: Western Doctors versus Traditional Practitioners

Ho Kai set up medical practice after he came back to Hong Kong in 1882. The first local Chinese to qualify in medicine, he was also the only private practitioner in town. He soon found that he could not earn a living as a doctor because patients who would consult him expected him not to charge them. He then turned to his other profession. The Chinese had great faith in traditional medicine which was a distinctive aspect of their culture, one of the oldest in civilization. Being intensely xenophobic, their first contacts with foreigners resulted in cultural shock, hence they regarded Western medicine with not only disbelief but also suspicion. For thousands of years they had been treated by traditional medicine with no other alternative and with good results, so they could see no reason why they should now abandon it for Western medicine. To understand their initial reaction to Western medicine, it is necessary to discuss briefly how the principle and practice of traditional medicine differed from Western medicine but first, the laws governing the practice of traditional medicine in Hong Kong should be explained.

After the cessation of hostilities with China, by a circular dated 20 January 1841 written from Macao, Captain Charles Elliot announced the cession of the island and harbour of Hong Kong to the British Crown. On 2 February 1841 Captain Elliot, now on board H.M.S. *Wellesley* at anchor in Hong Kong Bay, issued a proclamation in which he declared that "the island of Hong Kong, having been ceded to the British Crown under the seal of the Imperial Minister and High Commissioner Keshen [Qishan] 琦

善, it has become necessary to provide for the government thereof, pending Her Majesty's further pleasure". Continuing, he said:

> And I do hereby declare and proclaim that, pending Her Majesty's further pleasure, the government of the said island shall devolve upon, and exercised by, the person filling the office of Chief Superintendent of Trade of British Subjects in China for the time being. And I do hereby declare and proclaim that, pending Her Majesty's further pleasure, the natives of the island of Hong Kong, and all natives of China thereto resorting, shall be governed according to the laws and customs of China, every description of torture excepted.

The Chinese inhabitants of Hong Kong were addressed the day before, on 1 February, in a manifesto written in Chinese, issued over the joint names of Captain Charles Elliot, Plenipotentiary, and Commodore Sir James Bremer, Commander-in-chief. It contained the following passage:

> The inhabitants are hereby promised protection, in Her Majesty's gracious name, against all enemies whatever; and they are further secured in the free exercise of their religious rites, ceremonies, and social customs, and in the employment of their lawful private property and interests. They will be governed, pending Her Majesty's further pleasure, according to the laws, customs and usages of the Chinese (every description of torture exempted) by the elders of the village, subject to the control of a British magistrate …

In simplified terms the Chinese were given assurance that they could continue to live according to their own ways, and do anything they liked except using tortures. Of the many "customs and usages" the Chinese certainly considered the practice of traditional medicine as included among them. Indeed, at the beginning, the authorities had no intention of interfering. Later on whenever attempts were made to impose some measure of control in order to safeguard public health, the Chinese would put up strong opposition and resistance. The relevant passages in the proclamations would invariably be cited as evidence that in effect the practice of traditional medicine had been given official approval and recognition. For this historic reason traditional practitioners were not required by the laws of Hong Kong to be registered, nor were they subject to professional examinations and disciplinary procedures.

In later years legislation was enacted to define and control the practice of traditional medicine. Section 31(1) of the Medical Registration Ordinance, revised edition 1975, stated that "subject to the provisions of Section 32 nothing in this Ordinance shall be deemed to affect the right of any person of Chinese race, not being a person taking or using any name, title, addition or description, calculated to induce anyone to believe that he is qualified to practise medicine or surgery according to modern scientific methods, to practise medicine or surgery according to purely Chinese methods and to demand and recover reasonable charges of such practice." The treatment of eye diseases was however not allowed. Section 32(1) stated that "Notwithstanding the provisions of Section 31, no person unless he is a registered medical practitioner or is provisionally registered shall hold himself out as being qualified, competent or willing to undertake the treatment of diseases of the human eye or the prescriptions of remedies therefor, or the giving of advice in connection with the treatment thereof." In the case of the prescription and sale of Chinese herbs, no restriction was imposed. However, if any patent medicine, whether pills, mixtures, ointments or lotions, was found to contain any poisons, dangerous drugs or antibiotics, the proprietor would be prosecuted. Similarly, if any practitioner of traditional medicine was found to use Western methods for treatment, for example, giving an injection, or having in his possession poisons, dangerous drugs or antibiotics, he would be charged for offence against the provisions of the Medical Registration Ordinance, the Pharmacy & Poisons Ordinance or the Antibiotics Ordinance.

Chinese traditional medicine was based on the concept that a continuous interaction of the dual forces of Yin 陰 and Yang 陽 was behind all natural phenomena, including the constitution and function of the human body. In the medical classic *Nei jing* 內經 attributed to the Yellow Emperor (黃帝), it was explained that the maintenance of the proper balance of

Yin and Yang within the body was essential for good health. As diseases were due to imbalance of the two forces, so treatment should therefore be aimed at restoring the equilibrium, whether by medication, dieting, acupuncture or just proper conduct and mental hygiene. It should be noted that the idea of balance or equilibrium was also basic to the classical theories of Greek and Hindu medicine. In addition to the concept of Yin and Yang, there were other naturalistic ideas about the composition and working of the universe, the most important being the theory of the five elements, gold, wood, water, fire and earth. The organs of the body were classified according to the five elements: gold for the lung, wood for the liver, water for the kidney, fire for the heart and earth for the stomach and the spleen. Consequently, the organs could react with one another in the same way as the elements, for example, the lung with the heart as gold with fire. Diseases were therefore accounted for by abnormal reaction between the elements manifested as one organ being stronger or weaker than the other. Treatment should thus be directed at re-establishing the normal reaction, by the strengthening of the weaker or suppression of the stronger organ, mainly by the use of the herbs of which there were thousands of varieties. The active principles of some of them had been assayed, the best example being ephedrine from Ma Huang 馬璜, hence its effectiveness in treating asthma. Acupuncture, the insertion of needles into specific points on the body and moxibustion, the burning of small cones of dried herbs on these points, were occasionally used for the relief of pain and other complaints. Surgical operations had been performed by only a few legendary figures in the long history of traditional medicine. The most famous was Hua Tuo 華佗, 141–201 A.D. who reputedly was able to perform all kinds of operations, including a craniotomy, after giving his patients an anaesthetic herb flos daturae (洋金花) to take by mouth. Bone-setters were not regarded as members of the profession, as some of them were no more than boxers or in any case they practised in close association with exponents of the martial art. They treated sprains with massage, trauma with external applications, dislocations and fractures with splints, and internal injuries by medication but practically never performed debridement, suturing or amputation.

Ho Kai's counterpart would be a scholarly looking individual, usually of middle age, wearing the conventional long gown covered by a short jacket and a skull cap, practising in a herbalist shop by agreement with the proprietor on mutually beneficial terms. He would have learnt his medicine from an older member of the profession, often his own father, by studying under him for a number of years. He would have read a number of standard textbooks such as the two on internal disorders, *Essay on Typhoid* (傷寒論) and *Synopsis of the Golden Chamber* (金匱要略), both by Zhang Zhongjing 張仲景 (*c.* 200 B.C.) often referred to as the Hippocrates of China. For the changes in the characteristics of the pulse in various disease conditions, he would have to learn from the writings of Wang Shuhe 王叔和 (*c.* 200 A.D.). He must study the pharmacopoeia *Chinese Materia Medica* (本草綱目) compiled by Li Shizhen 李時珍 (1519–1593), an indispensable guide to the knowledge of herbs and their actions without which he would not know how to treat and prescribe for his patients. For the consultation, he sat opposite his patient across a table on which were put paper, brushes, an ink-slab and a pad for the patient to put his wrists upwards one after the other for his pulse to be felt. The clinical examination was conducted according to the four standard procedures: observation (望), listening (聞), history taking (問) and feeling the pulse (切). The last was the most important. After observing the patient's appearance, listening to his speaking voice and asking what his complaints were, by determining the rate, rhythm, amplitude and quality of the pulse, the physician could diagnose all disease conditions from say typhoid fever to pregnancy. He seldom had to touch any part of the patients' body, sometimes he could not even touch a female patient's wrist if she would not give consent. That would mean physical contact between the two sexes, regarded as taboo according to the very strict rules governing social behaviour of the day. To overcome this awkward situation, it was said that a piece of string would be tied to the lady's wrist so that the physician could then feel the pulse waves transmitted as

movements on the string, a rather tall story one would have thought. However, it was true that a lady would use a porcelain model of a female body to
point out where she felt uncomfortable or pain instead of touching her own
body to maintain decorum.

After the consultation was over, the physician would write a prescription of various ingredients and the quantity of each in *qian* 錢 or *fen* 分 for
the patient to hand over to a shop-assistant who in fact was a dispenser.
The herbalist shop was of a standard design. Behind the counter were drawers
lining the walls from top to bottom and large porcelain jars standing between niches, in both of which herbs and other materials were stored. To
prepare them for dispensing, herbs were cut by a specially designed chop-
per, mineral substances were ground up by a mortar and nuts and kernels
were crushed by a testle. All these instruments were on display in the shop
and the works carried out in full view of everybody. Having been given the
prescription, the dispenser would collect the ingredients, weigh them up
with a steelyard or Chinese hand-held balance, wrap them up in paper and
give the packet to the patient. He then instructed the patient to make a
concoction by boiling the contents with so many bowls of water to start
with and then let it simmer down to one bowl before drinking it. Usually
the medicine was to be taken once a day only and unless a repeat was
advised, the patient was expected to see the physician again the next day.

The Western doctor could not have been more different. The age of
scientific medicine was about to dawn in Ho Kai's time. Medical students
had to learn chemistry, anatomy, physiology and pathology at university
level before taking up clinical studies in a teaching hospital, graduating
with a degree. Western doctors also used four standard procedures in
examining patients: inspection, palpation, percussion and auscultation. For
diagnosis, they used a stethoscope and for treatment, they used leeches and
enemas and various kinds of instruments to perform operations although
anaesthesia and asepsis were still to come. One could picture Ho Kai in his
frock coat and wing-collar, waiting in his consulting room otherwise known
as surgery, waiting for patients to turn up but often in vain.

From what they had observed through their limited contact with the Europeans, the Chinese found certain European customs and practices difficult to understand, in fact, they would even consider some of them as uncivilized. In the field of medicine particularly, apart from the difference in philosophy, the Chinese could raise a number of objections to the methods used for diagnosis and treatment by Western doctors. For instance, no female could ever subject herself to the kind of physical examination that would be carried out on her by a Western doctor because she would have to take off her clothes. Accustomed to drinking long draughts of herbal concoctions, they could not see how only a tea- or tablespoonful of some fluid often with a peculiar odour or taste could be as effective as a bowl of herb medicine. Procedures such as blood-letting, blistering by leeches and purgation by enemas were regarded as illogical and harmful as they would further weaken the patient's already debilitated state. The use of instruments by Western doctors to perform surgical operations absolutely horrified them, so did the very high incidence of sepsis and mortality which strengthened their argument that surgery was only a painful, mutilating and dangerous procedure, unable to save life or restore function. Furthermore, they somehow suspected that Western doctors would cut out certain parts of the anatomy of their patients in order to use them for preparing their medicine. Tales of eyes and livers of abandoned babies being removed for this purpose were widely spread, probably because doctors had performed autopsies on them.

There had been Western doctors in Hong Kong before Ho Kai came on the scene but they were no more successful. Dr. Benjamin Hobson of the London Missionary Society (see Chapter V) moved a general hospital from Macao to Hong Kong in 1842. He set it up on Morrison Hill to treat Chinese patients free of charge. Initially, attendance was quite satisfactory, for instance, for the first three months, from 1 June to 31 August, he saw 1,311 out-patients and admitted 106 in-patients but then the figures gradually decreased. This hospital was closed ten years later when no more doctors were available (see Chapter V).

Also in 1843, the government started a medical service with the appointment of a colonial surgeon, Dr. Alexander Anderson. In addition to other duties, he was put in charge of a public dispensary, which was mainly for the sake of European residents and other nationals. It was not until 1850 that a Government Civil Hospital was opened. From the reports of the colonial surgeons it was evident that their contacts with Chinese patients were confined to those admitted into the prison hospital, the lunatic asylum, the lock hospital for the treatment of venereal diseases and the Government Civil Hospital. In the 1881 annual report, the Superintendent of the Government Civil Hospital (which post was also held by the Colonial Surgeon) wrote that "very few Chinese patients sought admission. This may be that they do not appreciate Western scientific medical treatment but it is probably that the fee charged of $1 a day has more to do with it". He went on to recommend that "it would be well if the Government considered the advisability of reducing the fee and at the same time make arrangements for free out-door attendance to those who might apply at fixed hours on certain days of the week."

The Chinese had a hospital of their own named the Tung Wah Hospital (東華醫院) which was opened in 1872, the year Ho Kai went to England. In spite of its name, traditional medicine was used for treating patients not Western medicine. The existence of this Hospital was an obstacle to the introduction of Western medicine to the Chinese as we shall see in Chapter VIII.

Two events which took place later made the Chinese finally change their attitude towards Western medicine. The first was the establishment of both the Alice Memorial Hospital and the Hong Kong College of Medicine to train young Chinese as Western doctors in 1887 (Chapter V) and the second, the Bubonic Plague Epidemic which broke out in 1894 and its effect on the Tung Wah Hospital (Chapters VII and VIII). Ho Kai played a prominent role in both.

The Alice Memorial Hospital and the Hong Kong College of Medicine

Although he did not practise medicine, Ho Kai made two major contributions in the medical field. In order to make Western medicine acceptable to the local Chinese, there were two obvious considerations. Firstly, more hospitals should be built so as to offer Western medical treatment to the Chinese on a larger scale. Hitherto, there was only the Government Civil Hospital which the Chinese did not like for various reasons, including the rather high daily maintenance charge of $1 and the restrictions imposed by the European medical and nursing staff regarding diet, visiting hours, etc. There was no other hospital for them except the Tung Wah Hospital where, as already explained, the patients were treated entirely by traditional practitioners. Secondly, a medical school should be established locally to teach Western medicine to the Chinese. It was a logical step to take because Western-trained Chinese doctors could do much more to convince the Chinese to accept Western medical treatment than the Europeans. Putting the two together medical care for the Chinese should in future be in the hands of Western-trained Chinese doctors.

It was mentioned in Chapter IV that in 1843 the London Missionary Society opened a hospital on Morrison Hill with Dr. Benjamin Hobson in charge. He was transferred to Guangzhou in 1848, and his replacement Dr. H. J. Hirshberg stayed for five years before he was sent to Xiamen in 1853. The work then ceased altogether. In 1881 a new beginning was made. A small committee was formed with Mr. H. W. Davis of the accountant firm of Linstead and Davis as Chairman. The members included Dr. William

Young, a medical practitioner, and two members of the London Missionary
Society. It was decided to start a medical mission dispensary in the Tai Ping
Shan district to be named the Nethersole Dispensary after the mother of
Mr. Davis. Attendance at the Dispensary was so encouraging that the
Committee soon began to consider the possibility of erecting a new hospital. The Committee was then enlarged by the addition of more members
representative of all sections of both the Chinese and non-Chinese communities. Among the Chinese members was Ho Kai. At this point in time,
Ho Kai's wife had died. As a memorial to her, he offered to provide the
cost of the proposed hospital building. The amount involved has not been
recorded in the literature, for instance, Dr. E. H. Paterson's A Hospital
for Hong Kong, a history of the Alice Ho Miu Ling Nethersole Hospital.
Other financial details are known. A site was purchased on Hollywood
Road for $22,000. The London Missionary Society contributed $14,000
and the balance was raised by public subscription. Besides Ho Kai's
donation towards the building cost, Mr. E. R. Belilios (1837–1905) made a
further gift of $5,000, the interest of which was to be used for the purchase
of drugs. Mr. Belilios was a local philanthropist of Portuguese-Indian stock,
after whom the Belilios Girls' School was named as he provided the money
for the original building. A successful stock and bullion broker, he distinguished himself as the Chairman of the Board of Directors of the Hong
Kong & Shanghai Bank who solved the difficulties which beset that institution in 1876–77. In 1881 he was first appointed to the Legislative
Council where he sat as an unofficial member until 1900. For the many
public services he rendered, he was made a commander of the Order of
St. Michael and St. George (C.M.G.) in 1893. It was the first time a dec-
oration was given by the British government to an unofficial resident
in Hong Kong. The hospital, named the Alice Memorial Hospital, was
opened on 16 February 1887. On the instructions of Ho Kai the management and control of the Hospital were placed in the hands of the London
Missionary Society, which would also send out a missionary doctor to take
charge of the medical work, while a Finance Committee, consisting of

supporters of the Hospital with Ho Kai as Chairman, helped with raising funds.

The Hospital met with immediate success. Some six months after it was opened, Dr. Patrick Manson, in an address at a ceremony to mark the inauguration of the Hong Kong College of Medicine, said:

Although Hong Kong has been a Crown Colony since 1841, and its population and prosperity have steadily and rapidly increased and although hospitals for the treatment of the Chinese have been for years established and are flourishing in nearly all of the Treaty Ports and in many other towns of the Empire, yet in Hong Kong, which ought to be a centre of light and guidance to Chinese in all matters pertaining to civilisation, it was not until this year that a hospital devoted to the treatment of Chinese on European principles was opened. It is true that before this there were hospitals of a sort. But the Tung Wah Hospital, according to European notions of what a hospital ought to be, is not up to the proper standard, and is by its constitution and the spirit of many of its directors and supporters, closed to European methods of cure and administration, and the Government Civil Hospital, besides having association of a kind not pleasing or attractive to the native mind, is too rigidly foreign in its ways and discipline to suit the great majority of the sick Chinese. Attempts have been made from time to time to supply what was felt to be a public want but it was not until February this year that they were consummated. As soon as the Alice Memorial Hospital was opened, its erection received its justification: the beds were at once filled and crowds of out-patients came for treatment. Its success was established within a month of its being opened.

There were originally five wards for the accommodation of eighty patients in the Alice Memorial Hospital. Soon the number of beds was increased to ninety. But further extension was still necessary. As there was no land adjacent to the Hospital on Hollywood Road, another site on Bonham Road was made available by the London Missionary Society. Mr. Davis, who kept up his interest in the Alice Memorial Hospital, now offered to meet the cost of the new hospital. In 1893, the Nethersole

Hospital with accommodation for thirty-five in-patients was opened. The work of the two hospitals was coordinated, both being under the management of the London Missionary Society. The Nethersole Hospital was used for women and children. Before the death of Ho Kai there were further developments. In 1903, a separate block was added to the Nethersole Hospital for maternity cases. It became the Alice Memorial Maternity Hospital. In 1906, another hospital was built behind the Nethersole on Breezy Path. This was known as the Ho Miu Ling Hospital. Ho Miu Ling, it will be remembered, was Ho Kai's sister and the wife of Ng Choy or Wu Tingfang. As the hospital was donated by her, it was named after her. The Alice Memorial on Hollywood Road was closed in 1921 and a new one built on Bonham Road, which was opened in 1929. The Nethersole was also closed in 1933 and reopened in 1938. Eventually, the four hospitals were merged into one, with the unusually long name of Alice Ho Miu Ling Nethersole Hospital, but it is commonly called just the Nethersole Hospital.

With the opening of the Alice Memorial Hospital, the Hong Kong College of Medicine for the Chinese was also founded, in 1887. In the inaugural address already quoted Dr. Patrick Manson explained why it was necessary to establish a medical school.

> In this hospital the care of the sick devolves on four of the civil practitioners of the town, on a native house-surgeon, and on a staff of dressers or students. To qualify the latter properly to discharge their duties, they require a certain amount of teaching. If we have to teach a few we may as well teach a large number. The same staff and time will do for sixty as is required for six. Hence has arisen the idea of forming a school of medicine within this Hospital, with these medical men and these students or dressers for a nucleus.... The object of it, of course, is the spread of medical science in China, the relief of suffering, the prolongation of life, and, as far as hygiene can effect this, the increase of comfort during life. We think that the present is the opportunity for Hong Kong to take up a manifest and long-neglected duty to become a centre and distributor, not for merchandise only, but also for science. I do not doubt our ultimate success, and

when we succeed we shall not only confer a boon on China but at the same time add to the material prosperity of this Colony.

It was not the first time medical education was initiated for the Chinese. After he settled down in Macao, Robert Morrison (see Chapter I) saw so much illness and misery among the Chinese that he started a medical clinic for them. Not being a medical doctor, he asked the ship surgeons of the East India Company to take charge of it as charity work. The surgeons were so appalled by what they had to deal with that they wrote to missionary societies at home asking for volunteers to come out to help. In response, a new breed of missionaries who were both doctors and ordained ministers, belonging to various Protestant denominations, began to arrive in China. Known as medical missionaries, their mission was to heal the sick, which was their motto, by introducing Western medicine into China and through their contacts with patients to spread the Gospel among them. They had another objective which was to take on pupil-assistants to train them as Western doctors so that these young Chinese could serve their own people. The first of these medical missionaries, Dr. Peter Parker (1804–88), an American, arrived in Macao in 1834. He opened a hospital and there he trained a pupil-assistant named Kwan Ato. Kwan must be regarded as the first Chinese to practise Western medicine as Dr. Wong Foon, the first qualified Western doctor, did not graduate until 1853 (Chapter II).

In later years at the Tong Wen Guan (同文館) in Beijing which was founded in 1864 to train young Chinese in languages, mathematics and science, a course in Western medicine was started by Dr. John Dudgeon of the London Mission but apparently it was not well-organized and did not achieve its purpose of turning out well-trained doctors. A medical college in Tianjin was established in 1881 which later in 1893 became the Bei Yang Medical College (北洋醫學校) whose founder was none other than Li Hongzhang who had faith in Western medicine after witnessing how the wounded was treated after battles and also having been cured of an illness by Western medicine. This College should thus be regarded as the first medical school in China.

Neither was Manson the first to think of training young Chinese in Hong Kong as Western doctors. Earlier on, it was already mentioned that Dr. Benjamin Hobson moved over to Hong Kong in 1843. An Englishman, he was a graduate of the University of London from University College. In the Medical Missionary Hospital on Morrison Hill (named after Robert Morrison who died in Macao in 1834) Hobson took on Chinese students and trained a pupil assistant named Lam Atsung. Proficient in Chinese, he wrote and translated textbooks for them. At the first meeting in May, 1845 of the China Medico-Chirurgical Society which was formed by doctors practising in Hong Kong to exchange ideas and discuss problems, the President, a Dr. Tucker, a Naval Surgeon, expressed the hope of seeing a medical school in Victoria city. Following him, Hobson, who was briefly the Society's secretary, wrote to the Committee in which he made the following remarks:

> If we are to effect any change in the low empirical state of medical science in China, it must be in my opinion by educating the Chinese in the principles and theory of the medical art, according to the more modern practice of the West. And in Victoria, there are facilities and advantages to secure this interesting object of our hope, which no other place possesses.

He went on to propose that the premises of the Medico-Chirurgical Society and the medical school should be in the same building. The Society held a special meeting in July to discuss Hobson's proposal but as the problem of obtaining suitable premises proved to be insurmountable, nothing further could be done about establishing a medical school. Hobson left Hong Kong a month later on leave and did not work in Hong Kong again after he came back to China in 1848, instead, he went to Guangzhou to open another hospital. He ended up eventually in Shanghai and left China in 1859.

When it was announced that a Medical College for the Chinese would be established in Hong Kong, certain objections were raised. Doubt was expressed as to whether the Chinese would make good Western-doctors or not, and therefore whether the money and energy would be worth spending. It was also suggested that the College should be set up in Guangzhou or elsewhere in China instead since it was intended for the Chinese. But the scheme soon gained powerful support. As soon as the process of preparation started, the Governor, Sir William Des Voeux, accepted the office of President. A year later Li Hongzhang agreed to become its Patron. In his letter of acceptance, Li wrote as follows:

To the Authorities of the Hong Kong College of Medicine for Chinese:

Gentlemen, I am in receipt of your letter informing me that I have had the honour of being elected Patron of your College. I also thank you for your desire to perpetuate my name on your College walls.

I wish every success to your benevolent design. I learn that there are between 20 and 30 students in the College studying Medicine, and consider it most proper that they should also pay attention to the sister study of Chemistry, and understand how to compound and how to analyze, thus insuring greater accuracy in the diagnosis of disease and the preparation of remedies.

I remark that your countrymen devote themselves to practical research and base their scientific principles on the results of investigations, thus differing from those who rest content with theories.

The happy results which ever attend the treatment of disease on scientific principles are evidence of the advantage to be derived from the constant study of Anatomy and Chemistry and the consequent illumination of the dark path of knowledge.

There is no doubt that when your admirable project is achieved it will be appreciated and imitated, and that it will through your students be a blessing to China.

Trusting that you will prosecute your Scheme with unflagging energy, and wishing you my compliments, I subscribe myself on the accompanying card.

Li Hongzhang

These remarks might well be interpreted as an official declaration of acceptance of Western medicine. Coming from such a personage as Li Hongzhang, it certainly carried great significance.

Following the formation of a Senate, with Dr. J. Chalmers of the Union Church as its Chairman, Dr. Frederick Stewart was appointed Rector of the College, Dr. Patrick Manson as Dean, Dr. James Cantlie as Secretary.

Dr. Frederick Stewart, was originally recruited as headmaster of the Government Central School which was opened on 1 January 1862 (Chapter II). At that time he was Colonial Secretary (see Chapter X).

Dr. Manson, later Sir Patrick Manson (1844–1922) was, like Ho Kai, a graduate of the Aberdeen University, having taken his M.B.C.M. in 1865. A year later, he arrived in China, having joined the Customs Service as a medical officer. He was posted first to Formosa and then Xiamen. In the latter place, he studied the disease filariasis which was common in the region, and discovered that the parasite filaria was transmitted by the culex mosquito. He came to Hong Kong to enter private practice in 1883 and left in 1889. After he returned to England, he founded the London School of Tropical Medicine. Acknowledged as the father of tropical medicine, he was knighted for services to the specialty. Perhaps not many people in Hong Kong knew that he founded the Dairy Farm to provide the local European population with fresh milk.

Dr. Cantlie, later Sir James Cantlie (1851–1926), by sheer coincidence, was also an Aberdeen graduate. He came to Hong Kong in 1887 to join Manson's practice. He is remembered in the history of the Republic of China for rescuing his former student Dr. Sun Yat-sen when the latter was kidnapped and incarcerated in the Chinese Legation in London. The story is too well-known and need not be repeated, but the event must be considered as one of the big "Ifs" in history. If it had not been for Cantlie, Sun would be taken back to China and sentenced to death, then the history of China would have to be re-written. Cantlie left Hong Kong in 1896. Back in London, he helped Manson to found the School and the Royal Society of Tropical Medicine. During World War I, he was responsible for organizing first-aid and ambulance services for civilians and soldiers. For his contribution to the war effort, he was knighted.

After the departure of Mansion, Cantlie succeeded him as Dean until he himself left. Both of them maintained their interest in the College and continued to give it their support.

Ho Kai was present at the initial meeting at which members of a special committee decided to work towards the establishment of the College. He was the only Chinese on the Committee and he had equally strong convictions as the others that Western medicine must be taught to the Chinese. He became associated with the College when he was appointed as Honorary Secretary to the Court after this body was formed in addition to the Senate. He was also designated as the Rector's Assessor, meaning probably his deputy. Other notables who became members of the Court included Sir James Russell, the Chief Justice, and Mr. J. H. Stewart-Lockhart, the Registrar General, who acted as Treasurer.

It would appear that no additional building was necessary to house the College and that all teaching, including the pre-clinical lectures and practical classes, could be conducted in the hospital building. The cost of establishing the College was therefore not substantial. There was a statement by the Senate that the government should be asked to "place the College under the auspices of the Government". This could well be interpreted as a request to government for a subvention or financial assistance.

The course of study was set for five years to be taught in English. At the end of the course, and after passing a number of professional examinations, the diploma of L.M.S.C.C., Licentiate of Medicine and Surgery College for Chinese, would be awarded to the graduates. Negotiations for the recognition of the diploma by the General Medical Council of the United Kingdom was undertaken on behalf of the College by Mr. J. J. Francis, Q.C., who was appointed as standing counsel for the College. The application was not granted in spite of repeated appeals. The syllabus included all the usual subjects with an early emphasis on clinical practice. Thus, in the first year, botany, physics, chemistry, anatomy, physiology, materia medica, and clinical observation were taught. In the second year, in addition to anatomy and physiology, medicine, surgery, midwifery and diseases of women and pathology were introduced. Other subjects added to the third year were medical jurisprudence, public health and practical minor surgery. The last two years were spent entirely on the clinical subjects.

All teaching duties as well as patient care at the Hospital were given free by a number of practitioners. Manson taught medicine, Cantlie, surgery, Dr. William Hartigan, disease of women, Dr. J. C. Thomson, Superintendent of the Alice Memorial Hospital, pathology, Dr. G. P. Jordon, a private practitioner who was also port health officer, public health, Dr. P. B. C. Ayres, the Colonial Surgeon, anatomy and Dr. J. M. Atkinson, a government medical officer, physiology. The teachers of the basic science subjects were Charles Ford, botany, T. K. Dealy, physics and W. E. Crow, chemistry, also D. Gerlach, materia medica. Ho Kai also took part in teaching, his subject, medical jurisprudence. As he was both a medical doctor and a barrister, he was eminently qualified to teach the subject. Medical jurisprudence is also called forensic medicine which is the science concerned with the application of medical knowledge to certain branches of law, both criminal and civil, such as the investigation of sudden deaths, accidental deaths and murders, the examination of crime victims and the analysis of poisons. One cannot be certain that, in those days, when not only the circumstances in Hong Kong were different but the subject itself was still in its infancy, Ho Kai actually taught forensic medicine. He apparently lectured on that classic Chinese textbook of forensic medicine, *Vindications of the Wronged* (洗冤錄). In this work, post-mortem changes on the body after various kinds of poisoning were described and the action of these poisons explained. There was also a well-known chart showing the spots on the body which were vulnerable to trauma resulting in death. But there was no record that Ho Kai ever acted as a police surgeon, the title that would most likely be used for such a post if it had been established in the medical service. Presumably he was mostly concerned with medical ethics and the laws and regulations related to medicine and health. He also helped to teach physiology.

The first class of students were assembled six months after the Alice Memorial Hospital became operational. They had to pay a tuition fee of $60 a year. They went through four professional examinations during the five-year course. The first examination was on botany, chemistry, anatomy, physiology, materia medica, physics and clinical observation, the second on anatomy and physiology, the third on medical jurisprudence and public health, and the fourth and final on medicine, surgery, midwifery and diseases of women. To conduct the examinations a board of examiners was appointed, consisting of the lectures and others who acted as external examiners. Ho Kai was an examiner in physiology, a subject in the first and second years which he helped to teach, and medical jurisprudence, his own subject in the third year curriculum.

The occasion of the first professional examination held on 6 August 1888 was considered so important and significant that an editorial appeared in the local English newspaper, the *China Mail*. The editor wrote:

The first professional examination of the College was held during the past week, the written papers being submitted to the students on Monday, August 6th and extended over the four consecutive days. To a non-professional reader the questions seem of a very searching character, and we believe that they are of the same quality exactly as questions submitted to the Universities and Colleges of Surgeons and Physicians at home. Not only had the Board of Examiners the British examining boards to guide them but the German element present in the Board brought the improved medical educational system of Germany to assist. We would remark however that the number of subjects for examination, namely, seven, is much in excess of what first year students are subject to at home. We understand from the examiners, and as some of them have examined in our home universities they are well qualified to compare, that the Chinese students are quite up to the standard of home excellence and the best of the Chinese students could quite hold their own with the best students of England. We understand that this will be actually tested by-and-by as it is intended to send home the best students for a two-year training after they have finished here. We have heard a great deal about the medical education of the Chinese in the North, but we cannot understand a system of education where it is impossible to collect a staff of special teachers for the special subjects. This can be done in the Far East in Hong Kong only, and while yielding all honour to the doctors who have done so much for education amongst the Chinese, still an individual cannot profess to teach everything even if he had the time. The future of medical education in the Far East, unless a special university is started, is dependent upon the exertions of medical men in Hong Kong. Here at all times, we have from 20 to 30 medical men, navy, military, and civilian, from which the teachers and examiners can be recruited. In addition the important subjects of botany and chemistry are here taught by specialists, and military medical work is under the immediate supervision of the Army Medical Department. The viva voce examination open to the public was held in St. Andrew's Hall on the evening of Friday, 10th August. The examiners sat at tables with models, specimens, bones, plants, microscopes, etc. etc. before them and the students had to make the round of seven tables before they had finished their labours. As usual at all examinations there were good and bad men but the readiness with which some answered any and every question put to them seemed to reflect great credit on the teachers and honour on the pupils. We had not of course the written answers submitted to us but if they were on a par with the viva voce the percentages awarded those students who passed were well deserved. The work done by the students has been made as practical as possible and the numerous visits made by the students to the gardens showed what interest Mr. Ford took in his work. The lectures on chemistry by Mr. Crow were fully illustrated by practical work and the students have been put through a practical course of chemistry in the laboratory of the College during the summer. Altogether the work of the College seems to be conducted in a thoroughly professional manner, whether as concerns the lectures or examinations. We find there are 17 students in attendance at the College, but one or two are absent on family affairs and others have joined so recently that they are not yet available for examinations. The lecturers speak in the highest term of the disciplines of the students and report most favourably upon the smartness and ability of many of the pupils. We can see a great future in all this and we are convinced that the energy of those responsible for the working of the College will be amply rewarded by turning out properly trained medical men in a few years more, ready to carry our healing art and modern science into the dark chaos of Chinese imperialism.

The "German element" present on the Board of Examiners referred to was probably the two German teachers and examiners in materia medica, Dr. D. Gerlach and Mr. C. Niedhardt. It was really surprising that the viva voce examinations were held in public, with an audience watching the candidates perform. This arrangement, to be sure, would never be accepted by present-day candidates in any such examinations as the ordeal itself is already enough to make the candidates nervous, to have an audience watching would surely be much worse. As regards the subject "Clinical Observations", the editor explained that:

> This examination is a new feature in medical examinations. The students had to examine patients, write out notes of cases and were carefully examined in clinical chemistry and the institutes of medicine.

Following the report the names of the successful candidates with the marks gained by each were published:

J. Wong	82%
Kong Wing-wan	75%
Sun Yat-sen	71%
U. I.-kai	59%
Kwan King-leung	50%
Kong Ying-wa	55%
Lau Sze-fuk	50% (failed in botany)

There were in fact twelve students among the first class of 1887 admitted to the College. Head and shoulder above the others in academic achievement was Dr. Sun Yat-sen, founder of the Republic of China, forever the most famous and illustrious Licentiate of the Hong Kong College of Medicine. Dr. Sun went to Honolulu in 1879 at the age of twelve to join his elder brother who was a successful farmer. He studied at a missionary school there, and became attracted to Christianity and science during this period of his adolescence from 1879 to 1883. Two years after his return to China he received baptism. He lived in Hong Kong for a while, attending first the Diocesan School and later the Government Central School. In 1886 he went to Guangzhou and began his medical studies in the Guangzhou Missionary Hospital under Dr. John Kerr. As soon as the Hong Kong College of Medicine was founded in 1887 he returned to Hong Kong and enrolled as a student. He thought that he would receive better training at the College. By the time he took up the study of medicine he had already made up his mind to stage a revolution. He found that he could make use of the College as his venue to spread his ideas and the medical profession to hide his activities. After he became famous and a national figure, his biographers would quote the Chinese axiom: "If you do not become a good minister, be a good physician" (不為良相，當為良醫), to explain his initial choice of medicine as a career. The meaning of this axiom is that if one cannot save a nation, one should at least heal its sick people. Physicians enjoyed a good standing in Chinese society, being graded among the scholars, many of whom indeed were well versed in herbal medicine as well. The fact remains that after his graduation Dr. Sun practised medicine for only two years in Macao, first in the Keng Wu Hospital (鏡湖醫院) then in the Chung Si Pharmacy (中西藥房). Afterwards, he devoted his entire life to the cause of revolution in China. He kept fond memories of the College and Hong Kong. When he visited the Hong Kong University Student Union in February 1923, he admitted in his address that he got his "revolutionary and modern ideas" in Hong Kong.

Eventually only six out of the twelve finished their studies. Dr. Sun graduated in July 1892, so did Dr. Kong Ying-wa 江英華, Dr. Kwan King-leung 關景良 graduated in July 1893, while Dr. Lau Sze-fuk 劉四福, Dr.

U. I.-kai 胡爾楷 and Dr. Wong Sai-yan 王世恩 graduated in March 1895. The first graduate ceremony of the College was held on 23 July 1892, in the City Hall. It was officiated by the Governor, Sir William Robinson, in the presence of a distinguished gathering which included Mr. E. R. Belilios, Mr. J. H. Stewart Lockhart, Dr. Ho Kai, Dr. J. Chalmers, Mr. J. J. Francis, Q.C., Dr. J. C. Thomson, Mr. Hugh Macallum, Mr. Charles Ford, Major-General Gordon, Bishop Barden, Dr. G. P. Jordan, Mr. T. H. Whitehead and others.

In addressing the gathering Dr. Cantlie said:

The distribution of the certificates of licence to practise medicine, surgery and midwifery which Your Excellency on behalf of the College has now to deliver to the young men presented to you, is an event of more than ordinary interest. The Licentiates are the offspring of a work which several of us have been engaged in for the past five years and which only today reached its first day of development. But still more it marks an era in the institute from which these young men emanate in as much as they are the first recipients of the qualifications. Older institutions have the reward of yearly sending forth its young graduates but owing to our youth we have had no such satisfaction. For five long years we have had to plod on in determined silence with only this red-letter day looming some-what mythically in the future.

The lack of interest has not been with the students of the College. Anyone who knows the Chinese even but slightly is well aware that steadiness of purpose is perhaps their most constant characteristic. In their natural history be it in the overthrowing of usurping rulers or beating off their enemies their constancy of purpose has always prevailed. Time shakes them not from their intent nor weakens the ardour of their understandings. The passing away of one generation but includes the theme with the sacred fire of heredity; the riches of a century passed in any attempt but affords time for its development and growth and brings it to fuller fruition and purpose. It is with the sons of such a people that we have today, and, having once taken up a subject, be it science or war, it is not in their nature to retract.

Dr. Cantlie then went on to speak on the administration of the College, the teachers, the work of the students and teachers, and the Alice Memorial Hospital. He concluded by asking the governor to give away the diplomas and said:

> Therefore in presenting these licentiates to you today we come not humbly in an apologetic way asking to be forgiven for lack of opportunity in that we have not done better; but we present them to you and to the world with our heads erect and with no apologies. We have taught them without pecuniary reward or extraneous help and freely we hand our offering to the great Empire of China where science is as yet unknown, where the ignorance of our own medieval times is current, where the astrologer stalks abroad with the belief that he is a physician, where the art of surgery has never been attempted, and where thousands of women suffered and died by the charm potions of the witchcraft practices of so-called obstetricians. The general effect of the work done in the College therefore will be beyond this small island. Here and at the treaty ports human sufferings can be relieved by the most advanced methods known to the healing art, but these are but as chance flakes of ocean foams to the sands on the seashore in proportion to the work to be done. It is only at the door of this huge Empire that science knocks. Respectfully for she honours the occupants; decidedly for she knows that in her right hand she brings health, well-being and comfort. What hope has she of entrance? Will she be told to approach by the backdoor, not so, for the greatest man of the Empire is her well-wisher. Will she be allowed to practise her art on hirelings only, not so, for the Emperor himself has succumbed to her influence. For no other than Li Hung-chang [Li Hongzhang], the Bismarck of China, is her patron and within the sacred precincts of the Emperor's Palace European medicine is welcomed and appreciated in the person of one of the graduates of the College of Medicine at Tientsin [Tianjin]. Our Licentiates therefore go forth with the knowledge that the heart of China has been probed. With that fact before them let us hope that they will not fall by their way but carry their profession of which they may well be proud into the uttermost limit of the Empire.

In his address following Dr. Cantlie, the Governor Sir William Robinson said:

I think there can be no doubt there is no ministry so nearly connected with Christianity as that of the medical profession. For you know the characteristics of medical men and the characteristics which prevailed the Gospel of Christ are pity, sympathy and love, and those are feelings which I am sure induce or ought to induce these young men to undertake the difficult work on which they have entered today.

He went on to reply to Dr. Cantlie's appeal for an endowment of $40,000, which Mr. E. R. Belilios had promised to match with a gift of a site and a building. He said that it would be difficult to obtain an endowment of $40,000 from the Legislative Council because there would be a budget surplus of only $2,000 at the end of the financial year. Diplomas were then presented to the two graduates, Dr. Sun Yat-sen and Dr. Kong Ying-wa.

As the purpose of the College was to train the Chinese as Western doctors to serve their own people, let us examine the subsequent careers of the six students in the first class who graduated at different times. Of Dr. Sun, it could be said that medicine's loss was China's gain, for he succeeded in his avowed mission to topple the Qing dynasty and found a republic. Dr. Kong Ying-wa was a Cantonese but he went to practise in what was Sandakan in North Borneo where he remained for the rest of his life. The first graduate of the College to practise in Hong Kong was actually Dr. Kwan King-leung, otherwise known as Dr. Kwan Sum-yin 關心焉 (1869–1945), who graduated a year later than Dr. Sun and Dr. Kong. Dr. Kwan belonged to an old Christian family. His grandfather Kwan Yat 關日 was among the first batch of ten converts baptised by the London Missionary Society in Guangzhou. His father Kwan Yuen-cheung 關元昌 was the first Chinese dentist, although he was trained as a pupil-assistant by an American. After he graduated in 1893, Dr. Kwan served in the Guangzhou government for a few years until he returned to Hong Kong in 1897 to start his private practice. He became very popular and much sought after by patients. It was said that Sun Yat-sen left him some surgical instruments when the latter gave up practising medicine. Apparently Kwan was a sympathizer with the revolutionary cause and had kept in touch with Sun after leaving the College. He was one of the founders of the local branch of the Chinese Medical Association and the first private hospital for the Chinese, the Yeung Wo Hospital (養和醫院), the predecessor of present-day Hong Kong Sanatorium and Hospital. In Dr. Kwan Siu-sek's book *The Kwan Family and the Beginning of Hong Kong*, it was revealed that Kwan Sum-yin wrote a memorandum to help raising funds for the University of Hong Kong. Another interesting sidelight was that Kwan started the "Society for Cutting the Hair but Keeping the Dress" (易髮不易服會) in 1910. The idea behind it was that it was time the Chinese should cut off the queue to remove the Manchurian stigma but retain the national dress style in preparation for the arrival of a new era. Significantly, it was the Hong Kong Chinese who took the lead in this movement. Ho Kai had his queue cut off long before Sun Yat-sen.

Nothing is known about the subsequent career of Dr. Lau Sze-fuk. Dr. U. I.-kai was an apothecary's assistant or a dispenser in the Government Civil Hospital before he proceeded to study medicine at the College. His name was mentioned repeatedly in the Colonial Surgeon's Reports in which his progress at the College was followed. Instead of returning to the government service after he graduated, he became a house surgeon in the Nethersole Hospital. In 1898 he died of plague at the height of the epidemic. Dr. Wong Sai-yan left Hong Kong to practise in either Singapore or Kuala Lumpur. It must be admitted that the initial harvest was not very gratifying after all, as only two out of the six graduates actually started practising in Hong Kong after they became licentiates. On the other hand, one could suspect that the Hong Kong College of Medicine was in fact in the very early years a hot-house or nursery for young Chinese revolutionaries. Besides Dr. Sun, or perhaps because of his influence, some of his contemporaries were known sympathizers and supporters of his cause. Their teacher, Dr. Ho Kai, was also known to have strong views on reform.

It would appear that there was only one student who entered the College in 1888, but he did not graduate. In 1889 there was again only one, who also did not graduate. In 1890 two students enrolled, one of them finished his studies, Dr. Wong I-ek 黃怡益 who came from and presumably returned to Fuzhou. The other who did not graduate was Chan Man-shiu (陳聞韶) who as Chan Siu-pak (陳少白) was a great friend and follower of Dr. Sun, and a well-known figure in the revolutionary movement. After another lean year or two, more and more students were admitted, some of them subsequently became famous doctors in Hong Kong.

After 1902, students of other nationalities were admitted, the first among them was E. L. da Souza, from Malacca. Because of this change of policy, the name of the College was later changed by legislation to "Hong Kong College of Medicine", dropping "for the Chinese" and its diploma retitled as "Licence of Medicine and Surgery, Hong Kong" (L.M.S.H.K.). No more students were admitted after 1913, when the College was absorbed into the University of Hong Kong. The last batch of students graduated in 1916. One of the last to enrol was Dr. G. H. Thomas (1889–1975) who entered the College in 1907. After he graduated in 1912, he spent two more years at the University studying for the degree and became the first M.B.B.S., Bachelor of Medicine and Bachelor of Surgery, in 1914. He loved to tell the following story about himself:

> Three licentiates of the College of Medicine including me were admitted as advanced students eligible to sit for the degree of M.B., B.S. after a period of two years of further study at the University. At the end of the prescribed two years, seven candidates presented themselves for the Final Degree Examination. Lavish preparations, including a banquet, had been made for the first degree conferring ceremony in which the Chancellor and the Vice-Chancellor would officiate; but alas!, it appeared that none of the seven aspirants had been found worthy of the degree. The University authorities, faced with an awkward situation, apparently decided to produce one graduate for the ceremony according to plan. I believe they selected me on the mistaken assumption that I, who had already been holding the Government post of Resident Medical Officer to the Tung Wah Hospital since 1912, would probably be the one calculated to do the least harm to the community. I firmly believe that this is the true story of how I,

in May, 1914, obtained the coveted but undeserved distinction of being the first graduate of Hong Kong University.

In the 28-year history of the College, from 1887 to 1915, out of a total of 128 students admitted, 51 graduated. It was not a very impressive record but the graduates made considerable impact on the local medical scene. Some went into private practice, others joined the government and government-assisted hospitals, filling posts as district medical officers, medical officers in charge of clinics, and hospital superintendents.

As time went on, it was evident that separate buildings would be necessary. The accommodation in the Alice Memorial Hospital was stretched to the utmost limit as a result of increasing activities over the years. To relieve the pressure, some teaching was later carried out in the wards of the Tung Wah Hospital. It would seem that the problem was due to failure of the government and the College to agree whether to raise money by public appeal for donations or not. The College's main source of income was fees collected from the students. There was no endowment fund from which an income could be obtained and used for recurrent expenditure. It must be pointed out that the teachers all worked on a voluntary basis without any remuneration. But when the number of students grew it was felt necessary to pay the teachers an honorarium. In 1900 the College approached the government for an annual subvention of $2,500. In return, the College undertook to bind its students to serve the government for three years after graduation for a salary of not more than $50 a month if they were engaged in private practice but $100 if they were not. With the annual grant of $2,500 approved, the College decided to establish a dispensary to cater for the poor Chinese patients. This was the out-patients clinic where teaching sessions could be carried out. But any further development was still out of the question.

In about 1905, a friend of Ho Kai made an offer to erect the College buildings. The Court took the opportunity to introduce certain reforms. As mentioned above, the name of the College was changed to Hong Kong

College of Medicine, dropping "for the Chinese" in order to admit students of other nationalities. A site in the Tai Ping Shan district, scene of the famous bubonic plague epidemic, was to be obtained from the government. It was estimated that the general College building would cost $30,000 and the anatomy room and museum $15,000. A public subscription of $50,000 was to be raised so as to set up an endowment fund, while the government would be asked to increase its annual grant from $2,500 to $5,000. A renewed application would be made to the General Medical Council for the recognition of the new Licentiate of Medicine and Surgery, Hong Kong. Ho Kai was requested by the College to draft a bill for introduction in the Legislative Council for the incorporation of the College and changing the name to "The Hong Kong College of Medicine". This service was recognized by the Court by a vote of thanks to Ho Kai recorded in the minutes of a meeting in that year. Ho Kai's generous friend who offered $50,000 was Mr. Ng Li-hing 吳理卿, a prominent Chinese merchant. It was decided not to proceed with the public appeal, but meanwhile plans for the buildings would be drawn up and tenders called for.

By 1908 when planning had reached an advanced stage, an offer, this time for the amount of $150,000, was made by Mr. (later Sir) Mormasjee Mody, a local Parsee merchant and philanthropist, for a University. The Court of the College decided that it would join the University scheme if asked but since the buildings would in any case be required, its own building programme should continue to be carried out. However, the big donor did not like the site chosen for the College buildings because there was no room for expansion. Ho Kai undertook to seek the views of the past and present students and found that they were in favour of the new site proposed for the University at the junction of Pokfulam Road and Bonham Road. It remained for him to persuade his friend Mr. Ng Li-hing to agree to this new proposed site and the other conditions for the College to be incorporated into the University. All these details were discussed and settled at a meeting called by the Governor Sir Frederick (later Lord) Lugard, at which were present Mr. A. H. Rennie, representing Mr. Mody who wanted to be anonymous at that stage, Mr. F. H. May, then Rector of the College and Colonial Secretary, who later became Sir Henry May and Governor of Hong Kong succeeding Sir Frederick Lugard, Drs. Ho Kai, J. C. Thomson and R. M. Gibson, and Dr. J. W. Noble. Dr. Gibson was the Medical Superintendent of the Nethersole Hospital. Dr. Noble was an American dentist who took an interest in medical education in Hong Kong. His partner, Dr. Herbert Poate, an Englishman, was the first dentist to practise in Hong Kong. The Poate-Noble partners provided free dental service to the patients in the Alice Memorial Hospital. It was decided that the College would continue to issue diplomas to its students who qualified but cease to exist as a separate body as soon as it became wholly absorbed into the Faculty of Medicine of the new University. The formal agreement was later signed in 1912. As the Rector's assessor, Ho Kai was authorized by the Council of the College to represent the College.

In the official history of the first twenty-five years of the Hong Kong University, there was an interesting account of an episode concerning Ho Kai. Sir Frederick Lugard was apparently worried about the response of the general public to the appeal for donations. Ho Kai then suggested that the University should run secondary courses in the Chinese language leading to the award of licences or certificates, while degrees would be reserved for the primary courses in English. He thought that people in China would be more inclined to help if they knew Chinese was to be used in teaching. Lugard however considered it a retrograde step for a University to offer courses of different standards, besides, duplication of this kind would involve more staff and thus more expenditure. In the event Ho Kai's judgment turned out to be wrong. The public appeal met with great success, and an endowment fund was established with a principal sum of almost one and a half million dollars, collected from donations by the community.

Ho Kai saw the University open in 1911. A year later, he received a Knighthood for his public services. In view of the timing, his part in the founding of the University must have been taken into consideration.

Health Problems, the Sanitary Board and the Public Health Ordinance of 1887

H ong Kong was apparently a very unhealthy place in the early years of its history. A Colonial Treasurer, A. Montgomery Martin, drew a very black picture of Hong Kong in a document which he sent home in 1844. He described the formation of the island as of rotten granite strata and said that "the material excavated in the course of building operations appeared like a richly prepared compost; it emitted a foetid odour of the most sickening nature and at night must prove a deadly poison." He likened the town to the bottom of a crater, and stated that this formation effectually prevented the dissipation of the poisonous gases. "The Chinese", he said, "had never deemed Hong Kong as injurious to health and fatal to life. As for Europeans those who survived a brief residence in the climate generally got a lassitude of frame and an irritability of fibre which destroyed the spring of existence."

The severe effects of various illnesses, especially the dreaded "Hong Kong Fever", on the early settlers were described by E. J. Eitel in his book, *Europe in China.*

For in summer 1843 occurred an extraordinary outbreak of Hong Kong Fever, which, during the six months from May to October, carried off by death 24% of the troops and 10% of the European civilians. It was noticed that this virulent fever ravaged chiefly the extreme eastern and western ends of the settlement, while the central parts of the city and especially the gaol escaped almost untouched. At Westpoint Barracks (above Pokfulam Road) where the Indian troops had lost nearly half their number in 1842, sickness was so universal in 1843 that the European troops stationed there were hastily removed on board ship in harbour. In the year 1843, the total strength of the European and native troops was only 1,526, but as 7,893 cases were treated in hospitals during the same year it appears that on an average each man passed through hospital more than five times during that dreadful year. The deaths among the troops on the Island amounted to 440, out of 1,526, or 1 in 3.5, the causes of death being fever in 155 cases, dysentery in 137 cases, diarrhoea in 80 cases. The number of men invalided or unfit for duty was such that frequently no more than one half of the men of a company were able to attend parade and sometimes there were hardly five or six men out of 100 fit for duty.

In later years, "Hong Kong Fever" proved to be malaria, and the fatal cases were therefore most likely due to the malignant tertian type. Its transmission by the anopheles mosquitoes was not then known. The rains, especially after typhoons during the summer months, filled up the swamps and marshes to make them breeding grounds for the mosquitoes and other insects. Some prominent residents died of the fever, including John Robert Morrison, son of Dr. Robert Morrison, in 1843 when he was designated as Colonial Secretary and the wife of Dr. Benjamin Hobson who died on board ship on her way home in 1845.

The year 1843 was thus a particularly bad one. At that time, the early settlers were in fact thinking of abandoning Hong Kong. Besides the prevalence of diseases, there were other difficulties which they had to face, for instance, the insecurity of life and property from robberies and piracies, the unattractive business profits and poor investment prospects. The notion of finding a healthier colony was even known to Queen Victoria who asked Lord Aberdeen, the Foreign Secretary, to keep her informed. However, the state of health and other conditions improved somewhat thereafter. The death rate among the European population in 1871 was 303 per thousand as compared with 684 per thousand in 1860, a considerable drop by half. Sayer, in his book *Hong Kong, Birth, Adolescence and Coming of Age*, quoted

Sir Hercules Robinson, Governor from 1859–65, as saying, on his retirement, that the healthiness of the place was so improved that it was rapidly acquiring the reputation of being the sanitarium of China. That was too optimistic as worse was yet to come.

The first ever annual report on the state of health in the Colony was written for the year 1845 by Dr. F. Dill who by then had succeeded the first colonial surgeon Dr. Anderson. There had been a rapid succession of four colonial surgeons in five years owing to illness and death between 1843 and 1847. Judging from present-day standards, there were gross deficiencies in the annual reports of the early years. For instance, they did not contain vital statistics such as the crude birth rate, crude death rate, infant mortality rate, maternal mortality rate etc. The incidence of diseases and the principal causes of death were not recorded separately and could only be roughly determined from the morbidity and mortality data of hospital admissions. It must be admitted however that statistical methods were not yet used at that time for the compilation and analysis of public health data. Since Ho Kai returned to Hong Kong in 1882, the Colonial Surgeon's Report for that year will be singled out for study, as it is relevant to have some idea of the medical and health conditions at the time when he started his career. It was written by Dr. P. B. C. Ayres who served for 24 years from 1873 to 1897. In 1882, the population, though not recorded in the Report, was 160,402, 99 per cent being Chinese.

The first section of the Report was on the Police. The number of admissions to the Hospital was 549 as compared with 498 in the previous year 1881. Of these 549 admissions, 92 were Europeans, 230 Indians and 227 Chinese. The actual strength of the force was 588: 103 Europeans, 171 Indians and 314 Chinese. The sickness rates among the three contingents were therefore 89.32 per cent, 134.50 per cent and 72.29 per cent respectively. There were 3 deaths due to illness and 5 due to other causes.

The second section was on the Troops. Of a total strength of 1,011, consisting of 845 whites and 166 blacks, 794 whites and 225 blacks, a total of 1,019, had been admitted into the Military Hospital.

The third section was on the Government Civil Hospital. The total number of admissions was 1,458 with 68 deaths. The patients were divided into six categories and the number in each was given as follows: Police 549, Board of Trade 116, Private Paying Patients 268, Government Servants 88, Police cases 207, Destitutes 230. The number of Chinese patients among 1,458 admissions was shown to be 494 or 33.88 per cent, Europeans 602 or 41.28 per cent and Indians 362 or 24.85 per cent. The incidence of diseases could be found in a table showing the admissions and mortality in the Government Civil Hospital in that year. Of the 1,458 cases admitted, there were 100 cases diagnosed as "febricula" which probably included mild cases of fever of unknown origin, or "influenza", as no death was recorded. Significantly, there were 60 cases of remittent fever with 1 death, and 35 cases of intermittent fever with 1 death. These could all be cases of malaria, totalling 95 with 2 deaths. Venereal diseases were common, there being 61 cases of syphilis of various types and 51 cases of gonorrhoea. Chest diseases were also common, bronchitis, asthma, pneumonia and pleurisy altogether accounting for 95 cases. There were 29 cases diagnosed as phthisis and another 5 with the symptomatic diagnosis of haemoptysis. Under diarrhoea and enteritis were 95 cases. There were 25 cases of dysentery, divided into 20 acute and 5 chronic. Also recorded were 8 cases of typhoid fever with 2 deaths.

The fourth section was on the Smallpox Hospital. Not a single case of smallpox was admitted that year but there were 7 in the previous year. The existence of this Hospital was a reminder that smallpox was endemic in Hong Kong since the beginning, with occasional epidemic outbreaks.

The fifth section was on the Victoria Gaol. The total number of prisoners admitted was 3,498 and there were 356 admissions into hospital, of which 301 were Chinese.

The sixth section was on the Lunatic Asylum. There were only 8 admissions, 2 being Chinese patients.

The seventh section was on the Tung Wah Hospital (see Chapter VIII). The total number of admissions was 1,454, among these 628 died, or 43.19

per cent. An interesting finding was that there were 250 females among the 1,454 patients. The number of out-patients treated was 67,158. Regarding the high mortality rate in the Tung Wah Hospital, the Colonial Surgeon, Dr. P. B. C. Ayres, offered the following explanation: "The Chinese rarely enter a hospital unless they are so ill as to be unable to work to support themselves, or are in the last extremity of disease, having a great dislike to any restraint upon their freedom of action; it is this that accounts for the large percentage of deaths in this institution." The number of cases of smallpox admitted during the year to the Tung Wah Hospital was 10, of these 3 died. Apparently, traditional practitioners performed vaccinations. The Colonial Surgeon wrote, after recording that 1,763 vaccinations were performed by the "native doctors" in the City of Victoria and the villages of Hong Kong, that "these vaccinations were efficiently and carefully performed on European principles and tubes of lymph are taken from well selected healthy children. This is one of the great benefits this Hospital confers upon the Community of Hong Kong."

The eighth section was on the Temporary Lock Hospital for the treatment of venereal diseases. The number of admissions was 99, all being females. Under the provision of Contagious Disease Ordinance, 10,441 examinations on prostitutes were carried out. Men suffering from venereal diseases were admitted into the Military, Naval, Police and Government Civil Hospitals.

The Report ended with a section on the Health of the Colony and Sanitation, in which Dr. Ayres commented on the Chadwick Report (see later) and supported its criticism of the overcrowding living conditions in the Chinese districts. In fact, an earlier Colonial Surgeon Dr. W. Morrison already drew attention to the unsatisfactory living conditions in the Chinese quarters when he wrote about smallpox in his Report in 1851.

Among the Chinese the mortality from smallpox has been very excessive. The disease has acquired intensity by the dirty and gregarious habits of the people and the pestilential defects in the construction and situation of their dwellings. I regret to say that the infamous resorts of vice so abundant in this City have more than all other places harboured the disease and diffuse it on the most extensive scale.

It was clear that, at the back of their minds, successive Colonial Surgeons were afraid that besides diseases which were endemic some other catastrophe might happen. It was to be bubonic plague in the year 1894 (Chapter VII).

As early as 1843, in view of the heavy toll of lives taken by diseases, Sir Henry Pottinger, the first Governor of Hong Kong, appointed a Committee of Public Health and Cleanliness with authority to enforce rigid sanitary rules amongst all classes of the community. In 1844 the first health ordinance was enacted, under the title of "Nuisances". In the following years, several amendments to the first Nuisances Ordinance had been made and a number of other ordinances related to public health and sanitation passed by the Legislative Council. A qualified medical practitioner was appointed by the Government as Medical Inspector of the Colony to supervise the administration of these health ordinances. He did not have any staff under him until 1873 when a Chinese was appointed as scavenger under the Survey Department, the forerunner of the Public Works Department. This was in due course followed by the appointment of European inspectors. It was only as a result of the Chadwick Report that a Sanitary Board with local government functions was set up to deal with matters concerning public health.

Mr. Osbert Chadwick, an Associate Member of the Institute of Civil Engineers, was sent out to Hong Kong to investigate the overcrowding conditions and bad sanitation arrangements, largely as a result of the repeated warnings by the Colonial Surgeons to the government to take action, as the insanitary conditions were a serious threat to the health of the inhabitants. He published his report in 1882. The Chadwick Report was divided into three parts. Part I consisted of a description of the existing state, under six headings: (1) general description; (2) house construction and drainage;

(3) formation of streets; (4) public sewers or drains; (5) water supply; (6) scavenging and removal of night-soil. In Part II, after a preliminary discussion on the health condition of the Chinese, the defects of the existing state of sanitation were dealt with in seven sections: (1) principle of sanitation and examination of the dry-earth system; (2) house construction and drainage; (3) street formation; (4) street sewers and intercepting sewers; (5) water supply; (6) scavenging and removal of night-soil; (7) sanitary staff. Part III was devoted to the villages and Kowloon Peninsula.

In his Introduction, Chadwick referred to the health condition of the Chinese. He said that Hong Kong had escaped the epidemics which had afflicted other places in the neighbourhood, but the officially published death-rate of the Chinese varied from 26 to 30 per thousand, which was far too high to permit the assumption of a good state of public health. He pointed out that the mean age at death of all men, women and children who died in 1881 was 18.33, while the mean age at death of those who died at over 20 years of age was 43. Having made these observations, he then went on to show that the unsatisfactory and insanitary conditions were responsible for the poor health statistics and should therefore be rectified.

In the letter which prefaced his report, Chadwick summarized some of his important findings and recommendations, which are reproduced as follows:

On the dry-earth system for the removal of refuse:

Complete sanitation demands the immediate and complete removal of all organic refuse. The dry-earth system facilitates the removal of human excreta and abate nuisance, in so doing it does not effect the removal of the remaining and far larger amount of refuse for which purpose drains are required. It does not do away with the necessity for proper drainage owing to difficulty of obtaining proper earth; it is inapplicable to Hong Kong.

On the water supply:

The present water supply is inadequate but this is about to be remedied. Unless waste of water be prevented neither the proposed works nor works many times larger would satisfy the want of the city. To provide powers for the prevention of waste a new waterworks ordinance is required, also to provide a new scale of charges of water. The present water rate is unequal and unjust in its incidence. To improve the present intermittent supply and render the distribution more uniform and effective it would be desirable to lay down certain new water mains. This would also be required for the distribution of the augmented supply when the new works are finished.

On buildings, drains and sewers:

Both the design and construction of existing dwellings is defective. The Building Ordinance requires complete revision. The amended law must be enforced with more vigour and intelligence than the present particularly as to alleys, lanes and open spaces. The system of house drainage is radically bad. The whole of the dwellings within the town requires re-draining and unless this is done but little health improvement would be made. The complete cheap and proper execution of this work can only be effected by the Government undertaking it. The cost of the work would be considerable even if carried out with the greatest economy. It is unjust to compel a landlord to pay a lump sum for remedying defects which have virtually received official sanction. The payment of these improvements should be distributed over several years. As the general public and the tenants are the principal beneficiaries by the expenditure of house improvements it will be just and expedient for the Government to pay for the execution out of general revenue. The construction of an intercepting sewer to divert the sewage from the harbour is desirable. The benefits to health derived from this work alone will be small compared to that derivable from the improvement of house drains and sewers. The determination of the best outflow is the best step to be taken. This requires the investigation of the tidal currents at different seasons of the year. The present sewers made by minor improvements should be made suitable for the conveyance of sewage as well as storm water. The sewage only should be diverted from them and the intercepting sewer by which it is conducted to a distant outflow; storm water must go direct to the harbour.

On scavenging and night-soil removal:

As to the scavenging and night-soil removal, to encourage the introduction of excreta into existing drains would be fatal. For the present at least some system of hand removal must be continued. The dry-earth system is inapplicable on account of the difficulty of obtaining a supply of suitable earth and the magnitude of the operations involved. Hence, the present bucket system must continue in an improved form. To this end the night-soil removal contract should be separated from that of street sweeping. The night-soil contractors should have the complete monopoly of that substance for which they would pay a large sum on account of its value; they would see that complete collection took place. In the end a system of water carriage will certainly prove more satisfactory when all is ready for its gradual introduction. The proposed house drains are suitable for this purpose also. Public latrines are most valuable means of sanitation. They should be required by Government to improve, the number increased, and they should be open to the public rates free. In towns having narrow streets complete scavenging is of the highest importance. This work when separate from the night-soil removal can be more completely carried out and supervised.

Chadwick also recommended the organization of a sanitary staff, with a special officer to supervise, and allocating the duty of enforcing cleanliness to the district watchmen.

In his Annual Report for 1882, the Colonial Surgeon, Dr. Ayres, commented on the Chadwick Report. He wrote:

[It] fully confirms all I have said in my reports from 1874 till now, and proves that if I have appeared to act the part of an alarmist it has not been without good and sufficient grounds. It can only be with regret that any colonist can look back on the past nine years that have been wasted, and the many great and valuable opportunities afforded for improved sanitation that in the last five years have not only been thrown away, but absolutely availed of to increase the number and size of the unwholesome dwellings so graphically described in Mr. Chadwick's Report…. A moment's consideration of the samples of the Chinese dwellings which I have given — examples not selected for badness but fairly representative — will show that overcrowding exists to a very serious extent, both as to the number of inhabitants within a given cubic space, and as to the provision of proper proportion of open space for light and ventilation, and for giving free access to the building. Other sanitary defects are equally apparent. The type of house in Hong Kong is quite different to that in use on the neighbouring mainland, and I am certain that the lower class population is more densely packed together in Hong Kong, and worse provided with appliances and cleanliness than they are in Canton [Guangzhou]. Now what has been argued of late years is that the unwholesome style of building in Hong Kong is peculiar to the Chinese and therefore though bad enough as one storied buildings, they have been permitted to make them three or four storied, and even to sub-divide each storey by cocklofts. For whose sake? Not for the sake of the Chinese population, but for the sake of a set of gambles on house property. The overcrowding has been represented as showing the prosperity of the Colony, which it is a well-known fact that crowds were procured by the speculators to fill these houses free of rent, in order that they might represent them to purchasers as being tenanted, and to this as much as anything we owe such an increase of the population living from hand to mouth as has appeared in the last few years, and the consequent overcrowding. In 1874 the houses that were more than two stories high could be easily counted. Now it would be much easier to reckon up those that are not more than two stories high.

Dr. Ayres continued to explain that though there were several large lots unbuilt in the east part of the town, the Chinese did not care for this locality, and small European houses were not such profitable properties as the unwholesome buildings in which Chinese were compelled to live, and also hundreds of Europeans. "These", he continued, "never got any repairs worth mentioning, however much they may be required." The Colonial Surgeon also agreed with Mr. Chadwick about the description of the defective drainage and bad sanitation. "These, among the numerous defects in these buildings are what for years the Surveyor General and myself have been protesting against, and which in defiance of our protests Chinese petitioners have received sanction from Government to perpetuate," he said.

It is quite clear that any proposals to improve the design of the existing buildings and provide proper drainage and refuse disposal had always been met by rebuff from the land-owners. They would rather build more substandard houses on an available plot of land to make a bigger profit. In other words, they were not primarily interested in health and sanitation, but only concerned with making money. On this point Mr. Chadwick wrote: "Few of the Chinese were permanent settlers but only residents coming to Hong Kong to avail themselves of the facilities offered by British rule for earning money with which they propose to return to their own country to end their days among their own people." Dr. Ayres was even more explicit. "Seeing the benefit that is acknowledged they receive from British rule, is it too much to expect that they should be required to conform to British laws, instead of British laws, against the interest of the British people, being made to conform to Chinese ideas? They do not come here with philanthropic ideas of benefiting the Colony any more than the Europeans, but with the same desire of realising a competence and clearing out as soon as possible."

Osbert Chadwick's name will always be associated with the early history of Hong Kong because of his famous report which however suffered the usual fate of such documents by being shelved for a very considerable time. In the last paragraph of his letter, Chadwick wrote:

> I trust that even should these suggestions be found undesirable or impracticable, my report will show the necessity for strong and complete measures of sanitation, and I trust that they will be undertaken for the immediate benefit of the public health, without waiting for the necessity to be demonstrated by the irresistible logic of a severe epidemic.

The plea for action was unheeded until the irresistible logic became a reality. Chadwick subsequently revisited Hong Kong in 1890. The government took an unusual step of appointing him to the Executive Council as the health situation had not improved since the publication of his Report eight years ago.

Following Chadwick's recommendation, it was decided to create a proper Sanitary Department under the Survey Department. This change was brought about gradually, first by the appointment of an inspector, and then by the constitution of a permanent Sanitary Board. In 1883 the post of Sanitary Inspector was filled by Mr. Hugh Macallum, who was the apothecary at the Government Civil Hospital. The Sanitary Board was formed with the following membership: the Surveyor-General as Chairman, the Registrar-General and the Colonial Surgeon. In the Order and Cleanliness Amendment Ordinance, No. 7 of 1883, the Board was given wide powers of inspection and control in accordance with a code of sanitary regulations. However, proposed measures to control infectious diseases, reduce overcrowding, clear the slums, protect food and water supply and others were again bitterly opposed by property-owners, both Chinese and Europeans. A draft Public Health Bill did not even get a first reading in the Legislative Council. Nothing in fact was accomplished for the next few years.

In 1886 while Sir William Marsh was Acting Governor (see Chapter X), to allay criticism the Sanitary Board was reconstituted under the Public Health Ordinance of that year. Six additional members were appointed to the Board, consisting of four unofficials, Mr. A. P. MacEwen, Dr. Patrick Manson, Dr. Ho Kai and Mr. N. J. Ede, and two officials, the Captain-Superintendent of Police and the Sanitary Inspector. Mr. MacEwen, a partner of a commercial firm, was an unofficial member of the Legislative Council elected by the Chamber of Commerce, while Mr. Ede was Secretary of the Union Insurance Society of Guangzhou. The new Board's first task was to revise the draft of the proposed Public Health Bill left over by the previous administration. This draft was ready by December 1886, and Ho Kai entered the arena in a fighting mood.

The sequence of events which followed the introduction of this draft bill to amend the Public Health Ordinance must first be related. It was submitted to the Colonial Secretary on 22 December 1886. As a member of the Sanitary Board, Ho Kai took part in the deliberations but he was generally opposed to the draft bill. He wrote a Protest or Memorandum of Objection which he sent to the Sanitary Board. This document was dated 2 December 1886 and was therefore written before the draft bill was submitted to the Colonial Secretary. The "Bill Entitled an Ordinance for Amending the Laws Related to Public Health in the Colony of Hong Kong", as the draft was subsequently called, had its first reading in the Legislative Council on 6 May 1887, introduced by the Attorney-General. It was published in the *Hong Kong Government Gazette* the next day on 7 May. On 11 May, Ho Kai led a deputation of Chinese members of the community to present their protest to the Acting Governor, Major General W. G. Cameron (see Chapter X). When the Legislative Council met on 27 May, Ho Kai's Protest or Memorandum of Objection was tabled by command of the Acting Governor but it was not published until after the Rejoinder by the Sanitary Board was received. This Rejoinder was dated 1 June 1887. On 8 July, the Bill was read for the second time in the Legislative Council. The Attorney-General proposed certain amendments and alterations including the relegation of a number of clauses to a buildings ordinance. An unofficial member, Phineas Ryrie, proposed that the second reading be postponed for a fortnight. He was seconded by Wong Shing. On 22 July, Ryrie again proposed further postponement but the motion was defeated by one vote, with the six official members saying "no" and the five unofficial members "aye". It was then decided that the bill should be published with the amendments and alterations indicated. Thereafter it went through a protracted committee stage which extended over several meetings, with many amendments proposed and made. Finally on 23 September 1887, the bill was given its third reading. On this occasion, A. P. MacEwen, an unofficial member who was also a member of the Sanitary Board, opposed its passage, seconded by Phineas Ryrie. At the division, the official members again defeated the unofficial members by one vote. The bill was therefore passed by a majority of one.

Apparently no further action was taken on it for some months after its stormy passage. On 7 May 1888, exactly a year after it had its first reading in the Legislative Council, MacEwen asked the following question: "What instructions the government have received from the Colonial Secretary regarding the Public Health Bill which was passed by an official majority last session and suspended from operation pending the receipt of such instructions?" The Governor replied but his words were not recorded. Shortly afterwards, the Ordinance, dated 30 May 1888, was published in the *Hong Kong Government Gazette* on 2 June 1888. It was designated as Ordinance No. 24 of 1887. This Ordinance must be regarded as the most important piece of public health legislation enacted in Hong Kong since it became a British Colony some forty years ago. Its provisions should be carefully studied because it could be said that in spite of it a bubonic plague epidemic broke out in Hong Kong six years later. Let us proceed to examine: (1) the first draft as published on 7 May 1887; (2) Ho Kai's Protest or Memorandum of Objection of 2 December 1886; (3) a report of the interview between the Acting Governor and Ho Kai's deputation on 11 May 1887; (4) the Sanitary Board's Rejoinder to Ho Kai's Protest dated 1 June 1887; (5) the amended draft as published on 23 July 1887; and (6) the Ordinance itself which was passed by the Legislative Council on 23 September 1887 and published on 2 June 1888.

The essential provisions of the bill, entitled an Ordinance for amending the Laws relating to Public Health in the Colony of Hong Kong, which was given its first reading in the Legislative Council on 6 May 1887 and published in the *Government Gazette* the next day, were as follows:

(1)   The Sanitary Board to consist of the Surveyor-General, the Registrar General, the Captain Superintendent of the Police, the Colonial Surgeon, and not more than five additional members, three of whom to be appointed by the Governor, one elected by the Chamber of Commerce and one by the Justices of the Peace.

(2)   The Board to have power to make, alter, amend or revoke by-laws with regard to twenty-six different sanitary measures, including drains, privies, light and ventilation of dwelling houses, scavenging and

removal of night-soil, protection of water-supply, prevention of overcrowding etc.

(3)   The Board to authorize its sanitary staff, consisting of a Superintendent, surveyors, inspectors and assistants to enter premises to inspect a nuisance and the Board to serve notice on the author of the nuisance to abate, remedy or remove such nuisance. In case of non-compliance of the Notice, the Board to authorize its officers to enter premises, forcibly if need be, to do whatever necessary to execute the Notice. The author of the nuisance to have the right to petition to the Board.

The rest of Part I was concerned with (1) seizure of unwholesome food; (2) Chinese cemeteries; (3) removal of infected persons; (4) night-soil and urine disposal; (5) the householders to provide dust-boxes; (6) the keeping of pigs, cattle and goats without a licence.

Part II of the Bill dealt with measures to be taken against epidemic diseases, such as proclamation, disposal of the dead, house-to-house visitation, destruction and disinfection of infected articles, and compulsory vacating of houses, and also other measures for prevention and mitigation. It will be seen that this part was of particular importance in the fight against the Bubonic Plague Epidemic in 1894 (Chapter VII).

In Part III, details regarding the construction of drains and their connection to the sewage system were defined. It included the following clause: "All works connected with the construction, disconnexion, trapping and ventilating of house-drains, shall be carried out at the cost and charges of the owner of the house, either by the Board or by persons approved of by the Board under the supervision of the latter."

Parts IV to VIII, if taken together, constituted in effect part of a buildings ordinance. In these parts details concerning windows, a basement, a kitchen, sub-soil drainage, privies, water-closets, spaces in front of and behind the building and living space were spelled out. A new building as envisaged by the Ordinance would have at least one window to every room to ensure proper light and ventilation. The basement of a building was not to be against the hillside and a distance of at least four feet should be maintained. A clear area between a building and the hillside was required in order to allow the laying of subsoil drainage, to be covered by concrete. Every building was to have a suitable privy of brick, at least three feet wide by four feet deep, opened into the outer air and not into the building, with proper ventilation. There would be an open space of at least seven and a half feet in width in front of a building facing a street, and also a backyard of at least ten feet in width, which should not be roofed. "Every domestic building or portion thereof found to be inhabited in excess of a proportion of one adult to every 300 cu. ft. of clear internal space shall be considered to be in an overcrowded condition and shall be deemed a Nuisance", the Ordinance stipulated. Also "Any person who shall not comply with the requirements of sections 81, 82 and 83 (which concerned overcrowding) shall be liable to a penalty not exceeding fifty dollars or in default of payment to imprisonment not exceeding one month."

Part IX began with the following clause: "All expenses incurred by the Board in consequence of any default in complying with any Order or Notice issued under the provisions of this Ordinance shall be deemed to be money paid for the use, and at the requirement of the person on whom the said Order or Notice was made, and shall be recoverable from the said person in the ordinary course of law at the suit of the Secretary to the Board duly authorised by the said Board." Thus, under this clause, owners of existing buildings would have to pay for amendments, alterations and additions in order to comply with certain provisions of a new Ordinance, although the buildings had in fact been erected and approved under the old one.

The first broadside which Ho Kai fired was in the form of a Protest or Memorandum of Objections submitted to the Sanitary Board on 2 December 1886. In the memorandum Ho Kai raised his objections to some of the essential provisions in the draft bill. He began by saying that "by this Ordinance and the bye-laws made hereunder, landed property in this Colony to the extent of millions of dollars will be sacrificed, vested interests greatly interfered with, and public confidence shaken to its foundation." He went on to deplore that the discussion of the draft bill by the Board had taken place behind closed doors, without consulting public opinion. He then queried the nature of the Sanitary Board:

> Is the Sanitary Board a scientific as well as practical body of men? Are we met together to discuss matters of sanitary science purely or practically? If purely, then I agree with every proposition of any scientific importance put forward to the meeting, and further, I would add much to the numerous provisions in order to render them more perfect and more scientific. I would advocate every poor family to have its three acres and a cow, a garden, a conservatory and what not, at the expense of the state or the princely merchants and rich landlords. But if practically as well, then I would oppose the many provisions which in my opinion are unnecessary, uneconomical and unconstitutional.

Following these remarks, he stated that some sanitarians were constantly making the mistake of treating Chinese as if they were Europeans.

> They appear to forget that there are wide constitutional differences between a native of China and one who hails from Europe. They do not allow for the differences of habits, usage, mode of living and a host of other things between the two. They insist on treating all nationalities alike however much they may differ from one another physically, mentally and constitutionally. Hence arise the several provisions in this Ordinance and Bye-laws in question which I have no hesitation in characterising as wholly unnecessary. One might as well insist that all Chinese should eat bread and beefsteak instead of rice and pork, just because the former articles agree better than the latter with an English stomach…. As long as we govern the Chinese according to our promise given while this Colony was yet in its infancy, viz., to govern them as much as possible in accordance with their manners and customs, and to respect their religion and prejudices, we must of a necessity modify our laws in order to meet their peculiar requirements.

Ho Kai was therefore literally saying that the Chinese should be left alone in their overcrowded and insanitary living conditions because they did not wish to have them improved by the application of European standards. He then went on to argue from the economical instead of the public health point of view.

> From an economical point of view, the idea of sacrificing the millions of square feet at an average price of $6 to $7 per square foot is even more ridiculous. What is this enforced sacrifice for? Simply for the sake of a theory that the Chinese public require all such sanitary improvements to promote their health and welfare. But I challenge the soundness of that theory. I say the Chinese in general do not require this sacrifice or even desire it. Let the Government ascertain the views of the Chinese public in this matter. I have often been told that I was almost always in a minority in the discussion of the various sections of this Bill, but I was and am confident that the public at large, without distinction of races, will support me in most of my contentions. I was often charged also with looking too exclusively after the interest of the landlords, but I always denied that charge. I do not only represent the interest of landlords, and personally I am not a landlord, I care for the tenants as much as the landlords, and the poor as well as the rich. It is not for the welfare of the poor to have a valuable space occupied by their small rooms narrowed, in order to provide for a model of a privy, a superb kitchen and a sumptuous backyard of 10 feet wide, while at the same time the wicked landlords continue to charge the same rent or even a higher one for improvements and increased capital necessary to effect such improvements.

Having said that the price of land per square foot in the populous districts around Queen's Road Central and Bonham Strand was something like $9 or $10 or more, and $3 or $4 in the more distant and less valuable quarters, he continued,

> Just fancy the position of the poor tenant if this Bill becomes law. He would be forced to pay an enormous rent for less space than before, plus all sorts of sanitary improvements which, however good in themselves from a European standpoint, they do not care for, and which they think at least their constitutions do not require.

Presumably Ho Kai meant that less houses could be built on a given piece of land under the new ordinance and to compensate for their loss the land-lords would have to raise the rent.

Having insisted that it was unnecessary to make improvements for the Chinese who did not want any change for the better, he protested that the Chinese should not be taught forcibly what was good for them just because they were considered ignorant. He gave three examples of measures which were good for the Chinese but should not be enforced by legislation: the establishment of the Christian religion, the abolition of traditional medicine and the prohibition of opium smoking. He did not agree with the argument that as habitable rooms got smaller and rents went higher in directly opposite proportions, wages would also be raised to com-pensate the poor tenants. His reason was that as the labour market was always in excess of the demand, those who wanted higher wages could easily be replaced, presumably by immigrants from China who would be willing to work for ten or twenty cents a day. "Now allow me to ask whether building four feet away from retaining walls, the leaving of a ten feet wide backyard and the establishing of a three by six feet brick privy and spacious kitchen, are more necessary than food and clothing, or more desirable than overcrowding?", he continued.

> I do not think it is a wise policy of any Government especially when it is not of a representative character, to legislate arbitrarily concerning the property of its subjects, and particularly when such measures involve so large a sacrifice of prop-erty. It shakes public confidence and drives away capital, a state of thing which may not affect those who have no permanent interest in the Colony, but it is sufficient to excite alarm the minds of those who are permanent residents and have the future welfare of the Colony at heart.

Finally, he touched on the argument that similar Bills had been passed in England. "In effect whatever laws that may pass at home we must also pass here. I protest loudly against this kind of indiscriminate and servile legislation." In conclusion, he agreed on the following: (1) overhaul of public drains and traps; (2) construction of good drains in every house; (3) a free and abundant water supply; (4) clearing the foreshore of rubbish and decayed matter; (5) confining building operations on virgin soil in the cold and dry months; (6) filling in all low and swampy grounds; (7) stricter system of removing filth and excreta; and (8) prevention of overcrowding not by compulsory and arbitrary legislation but by the extension of the town east and west.

After the Bill was published and the contents were made known to the public, Ho Kai led the fight in the second round of the battle. He was the spokesman of a deputation of Chinese who saw the Acting Governor Major-General Cameron on 11 May 1887. Among the gathering were Wong Shing and Wei Yuk, whom we have already encountered in previous chapters, and Leung On 梁安 who was then a member of the Tung Wah Board of Directors.

The interview was reported in the *China Mail* on 12 May as follows:

In the first place the Chinese desired longer time to consider the Bill than was likely to be afforded. They had read in the newspapers that His Excellency had said he wished to push the Bill on and bring on the second reading a month hence. They considered that a month is hardly long enough to have a public discussion and they would therefore ask His Excellency to postpone the second reading of the Bill to a later date. In the second place they would like the Ordinance to be translated into Chinese and published in the Gazette so that every Chinese would be in a position to discuss the provisions of the Bill. In the third place, Ho Kai touched upon the principal debatable points in the Ordinance itself, those he considered of vital interest.

He spoke of the great interference with vested interests contemplated by the provisions of the Bill and the great sacrifice of space and money which would be necessary if the present provisions of the Bill were put in force. Dr. Ho Kai in this connection referred to the clauses which dealt with the provisions for 10 ft. backyards, brick privies and kitchens and said he estimated that the sacrifice entailed by the enforcement of such provisions would amount to from ten to twenty million dollars.

He then spoke of the extreme hardship which would be inflicted on the poorer classes by the want of accommodation and the proportionate increase of rent. There was absolutely no provision at the present time for the sacrifice of so much space for backyards and other purposes, and the legislation against overcrowding would render a large number of people houseless, for there was no chance of any of the improvements being completed or the new houses constructed for years to come.

He then spoke of the interference with the domestic and social habits of the entire population by the provisions for privies and kitchens. These were to be for common use away from the house, and would necessarily lead to man and woman mingling together, a very serious objection in the eyes of the Chinese.

Dr. Ho Kai next complained that the Bill had made no provision whatever for compensating any person who might suffer. According to the Chinese view, the sacrifices which they were called upon to make were for the benefit of the public and Dr. Ho Kai asked His Excellency whether it was fair or not that the individual should be called upon to pay for what should be borne by the taxpayer.

He next touched on the constitution of the Sanitary Board. As at present constituted, there was only one Chinese Member on the Board and in the new Ordinance there was not even provision for him. As the Board was a municipal and not a legislative body he thought all ratepayers were clearly entitled to send a representative and that the Chinese should have at least two or three members on the Board.

The Acting Governor's reply according to the paper was as follows:

If a month was not long enough to consider the bill, he would grant longer time. The question as to the translation had already been settled. With regard to the sacrifice of vested interest, he said that in our country a certain amount of sacrifice of vested interests had at times to be made and generally they were gladly made. He himself was a house-owner in England and he had had to comply with certain regulations which might have interfered with the value of the property; and as Hong Kong was progressing as he hoped, to be a civilised place, he should expect the same readiness to make a sacrifice on the part of the inhabitants of

Hong Kong. It was all very well when a country or place is first opened up to do things in a rough and ready way, but as it matured and progressed it was to do as other civilised places had done. This Colony contained a mixed population and they must regard every class alike especially in a place like this, for if there was an epidemic in the Chinese quarter it would rapidly spread to the European quarter. Therefore they had to legislate for both classes alike to prevent such a calamity. With regard to overcrowding and the hardship which might result from the enforcement of the proposed law, the town was going to be divided into small sections for the purpose of carrying out the provisions against overcrowding, that the Government would clear out the sections one by one, and that no section would be compelled to discharge its surplus population until provision had been made elsewhere to receive it. He further explained that the reason why they had not proceeded with the opening up of new sites, extension of praya and so on was because it was useless to do these things if there was no law to compel the population to diffuse itself over the city. What was the use he asked of extending the praya, of reclaiming ground in Causeway Bay and elsewhere if there was no law to compel the population to distribute itself. Besides, if this law was passed, the continuation of the praya from East to West and all the other improvements would be absolutely necessary and would be available to get the Government at home to consent to the praya's scheme. Speaking of the amount of cubic space fixed as the limit for each person, the Acting Governor said 300 cub. ft. was to be allowed for each adult. At home, the sleeping space and the dormitories simply was measured, but here he believed under this Ordinance it was intended to include the whole of the clear space in the interior of the house whether dormitory or not, including the passages, etc. He was assured that this would be so. On the question of compensation, he wished to be very cautious and he would make no distinct promise on the very matter. If the Government thought that compensation was necessary in any case he had no doubt that it would be tendered, but at present the Government was not in a position to say anything on the subject.

Besides the report on the meeting, an editorial also appeared in the same issue of the paper. The editor wrote:

In matters of a special nature like those dealt with in the Building Ordinance which has recently been so deftly smuggled into the Sanitary Bin, we think that the home Government will give the most careful consideration and the greatest weight to the opinion of the Chinese. Some of the answers given by the Acting Governor are fairly satisfactory, that as to time being allowed for discussion and that as to a translation into Chinese being made of the Ordinance. His reply which refers to the duty of the native community to sacrifice themselves for the general good as a mark of advancing civilisation is rather a happy if a bold state-ment, but it leaves out of calculation the conditions upon the Chinese which were originally invited to come to Hong Kong, the reluctance of the Chinese to assent to an unknown quantity and also the laws and regulations which they have hitherto obeyed while they have resided here. What His Excellency said about carrying out the provisions of the Bill and the completion of schemes for meeting the difficulty of overcrowding is curious and not a little ingenious. He hints that if the published Bill can once give power to the executive here to turn out the residents from the congested district of Tai Ping Shan the executive would then be armed with an important weapon with which to fight the War Office and Admiralty authorities on the subject of the praya extension. Without desir-ing to compete with His Excellency in the tactical phases of warfare this looks very like arguing backwards. The Government here will have a good reason for passing the clauses to cure overcrowding so soon as they can show that they have made provisions for the population likely to be rendered houseless. Therefore as in the case at home the improved scheme of dwellings ought to come before the pressure which turns out the inhabitants from the overcrowded districts. One of the points of Dr. Ho Kai's remarks will be admitted by most of our readers, that is, a municipal body like that of the Board of Health should certainly contain a few Chinese members. Indeed when we consider the enormous executive powers that are proposed to be given to this Board it is a matter of grave question whether it should not be made far broader and more representative in its character than this. The secret manner in which this Health Ordinance and Building Bill have been welded together and the utterly unsatisfactory nature of the so-called minutes now published of its proceedings conclusively proves that the more open that its deliberations are made the better it will be for the welfare of the common interest of all sections of this community.

We now come to the Rejoinder, prepared by the Sanitary Board at the request of the Acting Colonial Secretary, to Ho Kai's Protest or Memorandum of Objection. Signed by J. M. Price, Patrick Manson, P. B. C. Ayres, A. P. MacEwen, T. C. Dempster, J. H. Stewart Lockhart and Hugh Macallum, it was dated 1 June 1887. The members said that Dr. Ho Kai began by stating that the Bill would sacrifice property to the extent of millions of dollars, that it would greatly interfere with vested interests and shake public confidence to its foundations, but as a careful perusal of his paper failed to disclose how these disastrous consequences were to be brought about, the statement, being a mere assertion, called for no comment from them. As regards the accusation that the Sanitary Board was wrong to legislate for Chinese as for Europeans, the members wrote:

These accusations we presume refer to the provisions in the Bill for light and ventilation, and for the limitation of overcrowding. In respect of the overcrowding clauses we desire to explain that the minimum cube of 300 feet for each adult person was adopted by us in view of that rudimentary principle of sanitary science which lays down that a minimum of 2,000 cubic feet of fresh air per head must be provided every hour in order to prevent the air from becoming fouled by putrescent organic matters exhaled from the lungs and skin of the persons living in it. With so reduced an allowance as 2,000 cubic feet per hour it becomes necessary to change the air at least once every hour in order to enable it to support life in health. In these circumstances less than 300 cubic feet could not be prescribed by any sanitary authority. We submit therefore that no home, whether European or native, can be a healthy home without the light and the facilities for ventilation sought to be secured by the Bill. These we reiterate fall far short of European sanitary provisions on the one hand, while on the other hand, nothing has been adduced to warrant the assumption that the constitution of the Chinese is so far different from that of the rest of the human race, that his dwelling may do with less light, less air and less ventilation, than the minimum provided in the Bill. Nor has the question of class legislation at all pre-occupied us in the framing of the measure under criticism. We have simply recommended, after the most careful consideration of local conditions and peculiarities, the least cube of space and the least ventilation which any habitation may have without becoming unhealthy under normal circumstance or without becoming a focus of infection in times of epidemic disease.

The members next discussed Ho Kai's remark about sacrificing millions of square feet of land averaging $6 or $7 a square foot for the sake of a ten-foot backyard, and his objection that the tenant would be forced to pay the landlord an enormous rent for less space. They wrote:

This sacrifice of landed property was to have been suffered by the landlords, but now, from the theory of enormous rents for less space to be paid by the tenants, we gather that the landlords are to recoup themselves from the tenants and that after all there is to be no sacrifice of millions on the part of property owners. The two statements are clearly antagonistic, and one or the other must fall to the ground. A great many Chinese tenements in Hong Kong actually have back-yards of smoke-holes as they are called, five feet wide. In many tenements these places are six feet wide, and in some they are actually seven and eight feet wide. The provision of the minimum of ten feet for the width of a backyard is not therefore of the enormously exaggerated importance made out by Dr. Ho Kai, for the extra width prescribed is only five feet more than the minimum dimension mentioned above, and two or three feet more than the maximum dimension adopted by the Chinese themselves of their own initiative, and the certainty is that the landlord who has pulled down an old house with a five-foot backyard and substituted it by a new house with a ten-foot yard, will be no loser by the alteration as regards rent. Should there be however in certain cases of extremely small lots actual loss by the provision of a ten-foot backyard, we have given opportunity for the special consideration of such cases on exceptional grounds.

The members did not regard the Bill as "unconstitutional and arbitrary" because in the matter of compensation, the colonial government should

follow the line of action adopted by all English municipalities of late years
in their endeavours to improve the dwellings of the people. They also said
that they had not copied the sanitary legislation of the mother country
with regard to local conditions and idiosyncrasies and had they followed
the English enactments more strictly their recommendations might then
possibly have warranted Ho Kai's protest. As to a number of propositions
recommended by Ho Kai to supersede the Bill, the members felt that the
Bill which they had drafted had already provided either directly or by bye-
law for the realization of nearly all of them or such of them as required
legislative sanction. They said:

> Dr. Ho Kai assisted at our meetings, took part in our discussions and was aware
> that we sought to give effect under the authority of the Bill to the programme
> which he has reproduced. Practically therefore we may say that the Protest winds
> up by advocating the adoption of the self same provisions so inconsistently con-
> demned in the preceding sentences.

Thus, Ho Kai was the only one among the members of the Sanitary Board
who opposed the Bill. His Memorandum of Objection was in effect a
minority report although he had taken some of the provisions in the draft
as his own recommendations. He stood against two other members of
his profession, Dr. Patrick Manson and Dr. P. B. C. Ayres, the former an
authority in tropical diseases, the latter the head of the local medical and
health service, who could certainly be regarded as better qualified to discuss matters concerning public health than Ho Kai.

In the event, an amended Bill was presented to Legislative Council and
published in the *Hong Kong Government Gazette* on 22 July 1887. One of
the major alterations proposed was the composition of the Sanitary Board,
consisting of the Surveyor-General, the Registrar-General, the Captain
Superintendent of Police, the Colonial Surgeon, and no more than six
additional members, *four* of whom (*two* being Chinese) to be appointed by
the Governor and *one* elected by the Chamber of Commerce and *one* by
the Justices of the Peace. Another concerned the issuing of a notice by the

Board through its secretary to the author of a nuisance to abate, remedy, and remove such nuisance within no less than twenty-four hours or more than one month. In the new Bill, the author of a nuisance was re-defined as "the person by whose act, default or sufferance the nuisance arises or continues, or, if such person cannot be found, the owner or occupier of the premises on which the nuisance arises." Provision was made that "where there is no occupier of the premises, notice under this section shall be served on the owner", and that "where the person causing the nuisance cannot be found, and it is clear that the nuisance does not arise or continue by the act, default or sufferance of the owner or occupier of the premises the local authority may themselves abate the same without further notice." The section which followed in both the old and new version, provided the sanitary staff the authority to enter people's premises, "forcibly if need be", in performing their duties. However, these three sections on the issue of notice, the abatement of nuisance and the provision against noncompliance with notices, were recommended for further consideration by the Executive Council. The most significant change in the new or amended bill was to relegate all sections concerning windows, privies and space in front of and behind buildings to the Building Ordinance. A concession was made regarding the paying of expenses by the person on whom notice was issued by the addition of the word "reasonable" before "expenses".

In the final version of the Bill which was passed by a majority of one and which eventually became Ordinance No. 24 of 1887, there were further amendments. The constitution of the Sanitary Board remained the same but the two elected members were to be elected by "such rate-payers as are included in the Special and Common Jury Lists and also by such rate-payers as are exempted from serving as juries on account of their professional avocations." As regards right of entry into premises for the purpose of inspection, a notice was to be given in writing not less than six hours before hand. The Sanitary Board was to serve notices for the abatement of nuisance and the compliance with the bye-laws. It would review such notices in case a petition was lodged. But on noncompliance with any notice the case would be brought before a magistrate who would then issue a summons. Similarly a magistrate was given the power to make orders to deal with nuisances and to prohibit the use of houses unfit for human habitation. This was an important change, transferring the power of dealing with contravention of the provisions and bye-laws regarding nuisance from the Sanitary Board to a magistrate who could impose a penalty in the form of a fine not exceeding twenty-five dollars. The clauses dealing with windows were entirely deleted but standards to be used for the erection of a new building remained in the Ordinance. It was not permitted to abut a house against the hillside and an intervening space of four feet was required. Water closets were not allowed to be connected to underground sewers, while privies must be provided in factories and other industrial establishments. A building on new Crown land was to have a backyard ten feet wide for a one-storey structure and fifteen feet wide for a two-storey structure. The definition of overcrowding was still less than 300 cubic feet of living space for an adult individual, and to prevent reduction of this standard sub-letting was not allowed. A common kitchen was not allowed to be used as a sleeping room. A magistrate was to be given power to make orders for the inspection of overcrowded premises and to take steps to abate overcrowding. In connection with the standard laid down of 300 cubic feet living space, two children under the age of ten years would be regarded as one adult, so would anyone over the age of ten.

It has been suggested that the Public Health Ordinance of 1887 was very much "emasculated" when it was finally passed, on account of the many amendments and alterations. The pity of it all was that the proposals to amend and alter some of the clauses and regulations were based on economic considerations and not health and sanitary standards. It has also been suggested that the difficult passage of the bill through the Legislative Council was due to the absence of a governor while it was debated (see above) but there were no grounds to blame the two acting governors, Marsh and Cameron, in fact, Ho Kai could not be regarded as having been too helpful, to say the least.

Following the amendment of the Public Health Ordinance, an ordinance to amend the Laws relating to the Construction of a Building was enacted in 1889 as Ordinance No. 15 of that year. The clauses in the original draft of the Public Health Bill concerning windows, ventilation under floors, privies and a space in front of buildings were all incorporated into the amended Buildings Ordinance. The standard measurements for privies, of 3 feet by 4 feet and the front space of 7.5 feet were maintained.

Also enacted was the "Ordinance to Resume Crown Lands under Lease and to Give Compensation Therefor and Other Cognate Purposes", No. 23 of 1889. In the preamble it was explained that should dwelling houses on certain portions of land under lease from the Crown be of insanitary construction as regards conditions of air and light, the Governor should be empowered to acquire or resume such lands and buildings compulsorily with a view to erect improved houses. The duty of determining the value of lands resumed for such purpose and of fixing the compensation to be awarded was to be transferred from the Surveyor-General to a Board of Arbitrators to be approved for the purpose.

Was the Public Health Ordinance effective enough after having been amended and altered in so many places, and were the provisions and bye-laws carried out effectively? The answers to these questions could be found in the comments by the Colonial Surgeon, Dr. Ayres, in his annual report for 1894, the first year Hong Kong was affected by the bubonic plague epidemic which went on for nearly thirty years.

By the Chadwick's recommendation a Sanitary Board was appointed in 1882 relieving me of a burden which I had borne for 11 years. In 1887 Mr. Chadwick was again sent out and expressed much surprise at the little that had been done in 6 years since his previous visit, and by his advice the Sanitary Board was re-constituted and enlarged, the Public Health Ordinance revised and enlarged as regards its powers and also the Buildings Ordinance, and since that many other amendments have been made with accompanying bye-laws and a Lands Resumption Ordinance sanctioned, and others in connection with sanitation, water supply, drainage etc. The water supply has been nearly completed but the quantity is found to be insufficient, the quality of the supply has been proved by monthly analysis to be superior to that of most English towns. The main drainage is nearly completed, but as regards house drainage is still far from being complete. The Buildings Ordinance refers only to new buildings, and existing buildings previous to this Ordinance remain the same. The Land Resumption Ordinance until 1894 remained a dead letter.

The Sanitary Board as reconstituted meets fortnightly and at times of alarm, as in the case of the smallpox epidemic and the cholera scare, holds frequent emergency meetings. Voluminous reports have been made, and some of them published by Sub-Committees and (various officers). The Board's officers have had some praise sparingly given, but one and all have been severely and at times censured in no measured terms by some members of the Board for having in their zeal for the service, done things which required immediate attention and common sense sanctioned being done, and on being reported at the next Board meeting received the censure as their reward for doing things without the previous sanction of the Board. The Official Members of the Board in their several capacities have had metaphorical missiles thrown at them in unstinted supplies. The want of a Medical Health Officer as Superintendent, many times insisted on by me from the beginning as being an absolute necessity, but from economical motives ignored till Mr. Macallum's health broke down completely from the overwork of doing the double duty which necessitated his being out and about the greater part of the day and doing his office work at night. The necessity of a Medical Officer of Health then began to dawn upon them generally and was fully recognised when the plague began. Long wordy, windy, desultory, rambling discussions are held by the Board at their fortnightly meetings ending in nothing being done.

Sub-Committee's reports, called for in many cases as a means of delaying action, and in abortive attempts at action, as in the case of the Sub-Committee's report on overcrowding when threats of riots and strikes, amongst the Chinese, moderated the tone of the majority of the Board when it appeared that the mercantile community and the general public would be seriously inconvenienced, and things were relegated to the future for further consideration, as in the case of the Sub-Committee appointed to enquire into the Fat Boiling Nuisance. The Unofficial Members of the Board appointed to this Subcommittee, after inspecting some premises situated on First, Second, Third and High Streets, sent in a report in which they said: "Nearly the whole of the houses are in a most dilapidated condition. The floors were reeking with filth. The drainage was very bad, smell abominable. In some of the houses were dark holes in which there were quantities of decomposing and putrid meat, fat and bones and one of them filled with maggots. The stench from these places was unbearable." I inspected these houses also and found them in the same condition I had reported twenty years ago; fat boiling was going on there, but, with the assistance of the Registrar-General, I had them cleared out and suppressed that business in the neighbourhood of the hospital. It had begun again of late years and I have often reported them before with result that the nuisance has abated for a time. When this report was read before the Board I stated that these houses were in as disgusting a condition as many of the worse slums of the Central District of Tai Ping Shan independently of the fat-boiling, that many other houses in the same streets where no fat-boiling was done were in the same filthy and insanitary condition, and that these houses were, in my opinion, unfit for human habitation. The Board then recommend — "that the tenants should be called upon to abate the nuisance", — which was done. The Board also recommend — "that the landlords should be notified to put these houses in proper order". That the notices were served is proved by the papers attached to the documents which had been before the Board but there is no record to show that the landlords paid any attention to the notification, and no further steps appear to have been taken in the matter and it ended in nothing being done. The houses in these streets, next to the walled-up portion of Tai Ping Shan, were the worst centres of the plague-stricken districts; scores of them were closed as unfit for human habitation and remain so to this day.

Thus Dr. Ayres made it quite plain that sanitary conditions remained as bad as ever, and quite justifiably he considered them factors which contributed towards the outbreak of the plague epidemic.

The Bubonic Plague Epidemic of 1894–1923 and the Discovery of the Plague Bacillus

The Bubonic Plague Epidemic 1894–1923

P lague is a disease of great antiquity which was mentioned frequently in the Old Testament, and in the early medical literature of Rome, Greece, Egypt, India and China. Perhaps the most famous, but certainly the best described, plague epidemic in history was the one which occurred in the fourteenth century. Known as the "Black Death", it decimated about one-quarter of the total population of the civilized world and half that of London. Commencing in Central Asia, it spread to Europe by 1348. After Italy, France, England and Germany it finally reached Russia in 1352. It was spread all over the world almost certainly by ships or other transports carrying plague-infected rats. In nature, plague is present among rodents. It is transmitted from infected rodents to healthy ones by their fleas and then to men by infected fleas. The causative organism is located in the gullet of the fleas, and discharged into the wound of the human victim after he has been bitten. The adult flea could live for a year or two. The relationship between the disease and poor hygiene is an obvious one as rats infest as well as multiply in filth and dirt. There are two clinical types of plague: bubonic, in which the lymph glands are affected, and pneumonic, in which lung tissue is mainly involved. The latter is capable of being spread by droplet infection, that is, from man to man through sneezing or coughing. In China, plague was endemic in certain parts, with epidemics breaking out from time to time. Bubonic plague occurred in the southern provinces, and pneumonic plague in the north. The last time a pneumonic plague epidemic ravished Manchuria was in 1910.

The incubation period of plague ranges from two to ten days, and averages three to four days. The onset is sudden, with the victim initially complaining of severe headache and backache. Following rigors, the temperature may reach 104°F or higher on the first day. In bubonic plague the affected glands become swollen during the next few days, being painful and tender, and proceed to suppurate and rupture. In over 70 per cent of the cases, the lymph glands in the groins are affected. In pneumonic plague, instead of glandular enlargement, the predominant feature is a severe chest infection with frequent coughing productive of at first watery and then blood-stained sputum. The disease has been called "Black Death" on account of the discolouration of the skin which becomes dark after haemorrhage has occurred underneath it, a sign of severe septicaemia. Both types usually ran a fatal course until the introduction of antibiotic therapy in recent years.

The starting point of the bubonic plague epidemic which affected Hong Kong was Yunnan province where the disease was first detected probably in 1850. An epidemic occurred there in 1860 and recurred nearly every year up to 1893. Early in 1894 the capital city of Guangdong province, Guangzhou, became infected. Because of the proximity and the constant traffic by land and sea between the two cities, Hong Kong was hit in May that year. The first case was seen and diagnosed as plague by Dr. J. A. Lowson on 8 May. The patient A. Hung was a ward boy in the Government Civil Hospital, of which Lowson was acting medical superintendent. He died shortly after lapsing into a coma. There were then three medical officers in the government: Dr. B. P. C. Ayres, the Colonial Surgeon, Dr. J. M. Atkinson and Lowson. Atkinson happened to be on leave so Lowson was in charge. After the news of an outbreak of plague in Guangzhou reached Hong Kong Lowson was sent there a few days before to see if it was true and he was able to confirm it from what he saw. His diary was a record of the events that took place during the first few months of the epidemic, and a source of much information.

As soon as it was realized that plague had broken out, the government took immediate steps to deal with the situation, such as disinfecting the affected areas, isolating the patients, disposing the dead bodies and enacting legislation to enforce such measures.

In the Tai Ping Shan District (太平山) where many cases were found, the Chinese lived together in appallingly overcrowded conditions without proper ventilation, water supply and drainage and even with their pigs and poultry in their make-shift houses, a perfect breeding ground for the infected rats. The place was at once disinfected but cases continued to be prevalent. To eradicate this focus of infection, the government resumed all lands in the entire district and demolished all the structures, estimated at some three hundred, involving seven thousand inhabitants. The authority was provided by the Tai Ping Shan Resumption Ordinance of 1894 (see Chapter IX). To replace the old ones, new houses were built according to new standards laid down by law, such as the provision of windows and privies and space in front and behind. The rest of Hong Kong was subjected to a thorough cleaning-up of its environments to rid the territory of filth and rats. Throughout the epidemic and thereafter, cleansing operations were regularly carried out in the native quarters during which streets, lanes and backyards were swept with a quicklime solution and tanks filled with Jeyes fluid were placed in central positions for people to disinfect their beddings, furniture and utensils by soaking them. When the relation between rats and the disease was realized in later years, people were encouraged to catch rats by the offer of a reward of two cents each, later raised to five cents. This gave some enterprising citizens the idea of importing rats from elsewhere to boost their income. After this trick was discovered, tin boxes were provided, attached to lampposts and filled with kerosene, for the dead rats to be put into but the monetary reward was withdrawn.

Patients were at first sent to a hospital ship, the *Hygeia*, which was anchored in the harbour for the isolation of infectious diseases such as cholera and smallpox. The ship was soon filled to capacity with patients removed by force despite the objection of the Chinese who also complained of the inconvenience for the relatives to visit. Ho Kai suggested an alternate place on shore but the government doctors insisted that the *Hygeia* was more suitable. However, as the situation worsened within a matter of days, a number of temporary hospitals were opened by using a police station, a glass factory and even a pig and cattle depot. Later, in July, another hospital was opened in Lai Chi Kok in Kowloon, with a grave yard nearby. Cases were also admitted into the Tung Wah Hospital, of this more later. In all these facilities, herbal medicine was used as insisted by the Chinese, but without proper attention to hygiene and sanitation. The conditions in them "defied description", as observed by Lowson, who also wondered how anyone could come out alive. As an alternative to isolation in hospital, the Chinese requested that the patients should be sent back to Guangzhou but the government at first did not approve (see later). As regards burial of dead bodies Lowson laid down specifications such as disinfecting the site with lime and how deep the grave should be dug to prevent the coffins from being exposed in case of flooding after heavy rainfall. Again the Chinese objected because they would prefer private burials in chosen sites for feng-shui purposes, or to have the bodies sent back to their village homes.

The strongest objection by the Chinese was against the compulsory house-to-house search for patients and dead bodies. Three hundred British soldiers under eight officers of the Shropshire Regiment were deployed to carry out the operation. After the patients or the dead bodies were removed, the houses would be disinfected by spraying or fumigation. The inmates had to hand over their clothes, beddings and other personal items for disinfection. The Chinese considered such measures as unwarranted intrusion into the privacy of their homes. They were afraid that their womenfolk would be tampered with. They said that they could not allow strangers who were foreigners as well to enter the boudoirs of their wives and daughters or subject them to the staring eyes of passers-by when they had to stand outside in the street while waiting for their houses to be searched. They were also afraid that the government might demolish their houses and force them to move to another district, thus causing them loss of property and goods. A signature campaign was launched to register their objections and to petition the government to withdraw the operation, which, after a time, was suspended. It was only after the Chinese realized that the epidemic had come to stay that they were more aware of the importance of personal and environmental hygiene and became more co-operative to comply with the sanitary regulations.

During the first few months Drs. Ayres and Lowson worked hard to deal with the situation and it was a wonder that they did not come down with the infection. They were given assistance by the medical officers from the services. In Lowson's diary, the names of Dr. Penney, a naval surgeon, and Dr. James, a major in the army medical corp, appeared a few times. Dr. Cantlie whom we have met in Chapter V, also gave help. As dean of the College of Medicine, he offered the use of the medical students but Lowson regarded them as useless. Lowson was apparently a very strong-willed person who did not get on well with people. In his diary he made very scathing remarks about everybody from the Governor down to other officials and non-officials. He deplored the ignorance of members of the Permanent Committee of the Sanitary Board which was formed to co-ordinate the efforts of various bodies to fight the epidemic. This committee was chaired by J. J. Francis, Q.C., who has appeared in Chapter V as counsel for the College of Medicine. He was admitted first as a solicitor in 1869, then as a barrister in 1877, and became a Queen's Counsel in 1886. He had held the posts of police magistrate and puisne judge. But two members were said "to know something", they were Dr. Ayres and Mr. F. H. May, the Superintendent of Police. Lowson made no mention of Ho Kai in his diary. Ho Kai was not concerned with the medical aspect of the epidemic, but he made his contributions as a member of the Legislative Council and the Sanitary Board and also as a bridge between the Chinese community and the government as we shall see in the following chapter on the Tung Wah Hospital.

The epidemic caused serious disruption and damage in Hong Kong. In the words of the Governor, Sir William Robinson, "as far as trade and

commerce were concerned, the plague assumed the importance of an unexpected calamity". In fact, not only the economy but all aspects of life
were affected. People, both Chinese and Europeans, panicked and left Hong
Kong in large numbers. The death rate was understandably highest amongst
the Chinese because they accounted for 95 per cent of the population.
Other nationals did not escape altogether, including Europeans in spite of
their better living conditions and cleaner personal habits. Among those
exposed to the disease, a number of British soldiers, including an officer,
Captain Vessey, who took part in the house-to-house searching operation,
and a few nurses working in the Government Civil Hospital died in the
epidemic.

The health authorities must have found it very difficult to keep accurate
records during the first few years of the epidemic. They were able to count
the number of admissions into the Hospital (except the Tung Wah), and
the number of dead bodies found to have the disease at autopsy in the
public mortuary. But there must have been a fair number of Chinese
victims who died at home and were buried without notifying the authorities. Others might even have left Hong Kong after contracting the disease.
However, some statistics could be compiled from figures recorded in
official documents.

A table showing the incidence and mortality of notified cases from 1894
to 1923 appears in Appendix VI. Two sets of data obtained from two different sources were used in compiling this table. The incidence was taken
from the Colonial Surgeon's Reports covering the period and the mortality
from *Historical and Statistical Abstract of the Colony of Hong Kong 1841–
1930*. Two striking features of the epidemic are clearly shown in this
table. Firstly, the incidence of the disease fluctuated from year to year.
Characteristically, recrudescences occurred in between bad spells. One can
imagine that hopes were raised in the years when the incidence fell to such
low figures as 21, 25, 38, 39 and 44, only to be shattered by a sharp rise in
the following years. As late as 1922, there were as many as 1,181 cases, but
in 1923, only 148 cases were reported. Then the epidemic ended as abruptly

and dramatically in 1924 as it started in 1894. After 1924 there had been some sporadic cases, 4 in 1926 and 12 in 1929. Since then Hong Kong has remained free of plague. Secondly, the very high mortality rate reflected the uselessness of the then available methods of treatment. The serum used by the Western doctors was certainly no more effective than the herb medicine prescribed by the traditional practitioners. As a final reckoning, it could be seen that the total incidence of plague cases in twenty-nine years was 21,867, and the total number of deaths 20,489, a mortality rate of 93.7 per cent.

According to Lowson, who wrote a report on the first year of the epidemic, there were 2,679 cases in 1894 with 2,485 deaths, a mortality rate of 92.76%. The distribution of these cases among different nationalities is given in Appendix VII. The victims were mostly Chinese, but it must be conceded that the majority of the population was also Chinese, whether their living conditions were worse or not.

An analysis of the age and sex incidence of 2,050 well-documented cases from among 2,679 affected cases in Lowson's report appears in Appendix VIII. There were 1,368 males and 682 females, with the majority in the younger and middle-aged groups.

Some rather exaggerated claims had been made in Chinese works on the history of Hong Kong concerning the effect of the plague epidemic on the state of the population. It was alleged that at one time, half of the population had fled. In Appendix IX is a table showing the total population in Hong Kong during the years 1894 to 1923. It increased steadily from 246,006 to 667,900 in the course of twenty-nine years, a gain of 421,894 or 171.5 per cent. There was no significant decrease during the period except a loss of 10,000 among the Chinese in 1896 which was made up the next year. It should be pointed out that the figures might not be entirely accurate in the non-census years because of the inconsistent inclusion or exclusion of military personnel.

To commemorate this unprecedented catastrophe, a medal was struck "in honour of those who assisted in the cleaning up of Tai Ping Shan". The ribbon was red in colour, with four vertical yellow stripes. On the obverse side of the medal was engraved a scene of the epidemic. On the reverse side was inscribed: "For services rendered during the Plague of 1894", and in a circle around the periphery, "Presented by the Hong Kong community".

The Discovery of the Plague Bacillus

Two bacteriologists, a Japanese and a Swiss respectively, arrived in Hong Kong soon after the outbreak of the epidemic with the purpose of studying the disease. Shibasaburo Kitasato (1852–1931) was Director of the Institute of Infectious Diseases in Japan. He was trained by Robert Koch and had been accredited with the isolation of the tetanus bacillus while working with Emil von Behring. Alexandre Yersin (b.1863) was from the Pasteur Institute in Saigon. He had done some pioneer work under Emile Roux in Paris on the diphtheria bacillus and its toxin and could claim to be a pupil of Louis Pasteur. He was at 31 in 1894, the younger of the two.

Kitasato arrived in Hong Kong on 12 June 1894 and discovered his bacillus on 14 June. He immediately sent a wire to the medical journal the *Lancet* besides making a public announcement. Later he addressed a public gathering and sent a further report to the *Lancet*. His talk was reported in the *Hong Kong Weekly Press* on 15 July. "In the first day he was able to discover the bacillus in the bubo, lungs, liver and spleen of dead patients and he immediately made a culture in agar, on the same day he took with all precautions some blood from the finger tips of patients suffering from the disease in a severe form and again found the bacillus. He then inoculated mice, guinea pigs and rabbits with the virus, and in every instance the animals so inoculated displayed the symptoms of the disease and died".

Yersin arrived on 15 June 1894 and made his discovery on the 20 according to his diary. Because he refused to work in the same laboratory matshed used by Kitasato, another one had to be erected for him. He also accused Kitasato of putting obstructions in his way. Apparently he was not allowed to perform autopsies and he had to resort to bribery in order to obtain some buboes from dead bodies before they were buried for examination. After he made his discovery, he sent a report and some material back to Paris without any fanfare.

These discoveries were known to Lowson, who wrote in his diary: "June 14th: Kitasato discovered bacillus" and "June 23rd: Got microscopes again out. Yersin got his bacillus".

Much discussion followed the publication of the findings of Kitasato and Yersin, to decide on which of the two bacilli was the real discovery as they appeared to have different characteristics. The details were summarized in a paper written by Dr. E. Larange in English entitled "Concerning the Discovery of the Plague Bacillus" which was published in 1926. He was at one time an assistant of Yersin in Indo-China, or nowadays Vietnam.

In an editorial in the 11 August 1894 issue of the *Lancet*, Kitasato was quoted as having written that: "The organism, which is a bacterium resembling the bacilli found in the haemorrhagic septicaemias, except that the ends are somewhat rounded, when stained lightly appears more like an encapsulated diplococci, but when more deeply stained, it has the appearance of an ovoid bacillus. When, however, it is focused more accurately, it is still possible to see the diplococci form". This was Kitasato's first description of his bacillus. In the 25 August 1894 issue, the *Lancet* published Kitasato's further description of his organism. "The bacillus is found in the blood, the bubos, the spleen and the viscera. It is a rod with rounded ends with bipolar staining. I am at present unable to say whether or not Gram's double staining method can be employed. The bacilli show very little movement". This description prompted Larange to comment that: "On this Kitasato's claim rests, it is the only basis of his priority. But the fact that he could not decide upon the reaction to the Gram stain and he observed motility of the bacterium, shows that he was in doubt between several bacilli which were present in his slides and cultures and that he could not separate or distinguish them apart". He concluded that it seemed that Kitasato was in a hurry to publish his first results.

Others also expressed their doubts, notably Dr. Aoyama, a member of

Kitasato's team who actually did the autopsies. In fact he caught the disease after nicking his finger while doing an autopsy and he was lucky to have survived. In his paper, "On the Plague Epidemic in Hong Kong in the Years 1894 to 1895", quoted by Larange, he wrote in German: "As the bacilli present in the blood differ in size and staining properties by the Gram method, I think that they are not the same as those present in the glands. When the streptococci are broken from their chains and are liberated, they may produce the appearance of the blood bacilli. As the streptococci are mostly present in the blood vessels of the lymphatic glands. I think Kitasato's bacilli need to be considered as streptococci circulating in the blood". It was rather extraordinary that with his experience and expertise Kitasato could have made such a careless mistake.

Yersin described the characteristics of his bacillus in his diary. The following is quoted from Larange: "June 20: … a film is prepared and put under the microscope; at the first glance, I see a real mass of bacilli, all identical. They are very small rods and lightly coloured (Loeffler Blue)". Excerpts of his original paper, translated from French into English, has been reproduced in a book entitled *Plague and Other Yersinia Infections* written by Dr. Thomas Butler. Yersin wrote as follows:

It seemed logical to start first by looking for a microbe in the blood of patients and in the pulp of the buboes. The pulp of the buboes always contains masses of short, stubby bacilli which are rather easy to stain with aniline dyes and are not stained by the method of Gram. The ends of the bacillia are colored more strongly than the center. Sometimes the bacilli seem to be surrounded by a capsule. One can find them in large numbers in the buboes and the lymph nodes of the disease persons. They are seen in the blood from time to time, but less abundantly than in the buboes and the lymph nodes, and only in very serious and rapidly fatal cases.

The pulp of buboes, seeded on agar, gives rise to transparent, white colonies with margins that are iridescent when examined with reflected light.

Growth is even better if glycerol is incorporated into the agar. The bacillus also grows on coagulated serum.

In broth, the bacillus has a very characteristic appearance resembling that of the erysipelas culture: clear liquid with lumps deposition on the walls and bottom of the tube.

Microscopic examination of the cultures reveals true chains of short bacilli interspersed with larger spherical bodies.... As the cultures get older, swollen and abnormal forms become more common, and these do not stain easily.

The differences between Yersin's and Kitasato's original descriptions of their bacilli and the modern concept of the bacterium Yersinia pestis have been summarized by Butler in a table. The bacillus is now described as "a small oval bacillus, Gram negative, non-motile and non-sporing, staining heavily at both ends but lightly in the centre with Giemsa or Wayson's stain". This bipolar staining is regarded as almost diagnostic. On culture it becomes pleomorphic as pointed out by Yersin.

After he returned to Japan, Kitasato did not do any further work on his bacillus. Yersin continued to study his bacillus under Roux back in Paris, in October 1894. He made an attenuated live vaccine and an antiserum. According to Larange, he succeeded in immunizing small laboratory animals and horses with the vaccine. Also according to Larange, after he got back to the Far East in 1896, Yersin tried the antiserum on human beings. He cured his first case in Guangzhou with 30 c.c. of the serum, in less than 24 hours. Then in Xiamen, he treated 23 cases with a cure rate of 21.

The controversy ended with Yersin's bacillus declared the real discovery. The bacillus was initially known as Bacillium pestis until 1900 when it was renamed Bacillus pestis. After 1923 it was known as pasteurella pestis. The generic name Yersinia in honour of Yersin was proposed in 1944, and so his bacillus has become Yersinia pestis. And because he found it here, we should thank him for earning Hong Kong a place in medical history with it.

To complete the story, Yersin noted the large number of dead rats in the affected areas but the discovery that the bacillus was transmitted by the bite of an infected flea carried by rats was not made until 1897 in the Indian epidemic, three years after Yersin's discovery of the bacillus.

The Tung Wah Hospital and the Introduction of Western Medicine

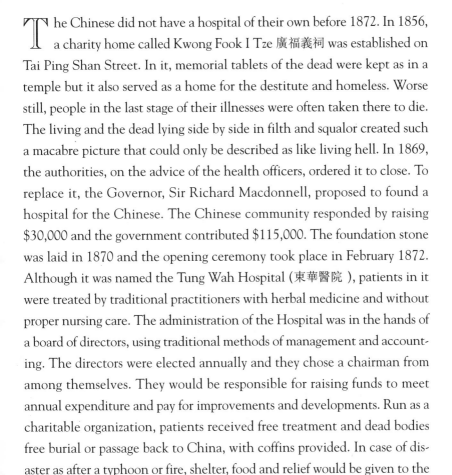

The Chinese did not have a hospital of their own before 1872. In 1856, a charity home called Kwong Fook I Tze 廣福義祠 was established on Tai Ping Shan Street. In it, memorial tablets of the dead were kept as in a temple but it also served as a home for the destitute and homeless. Worse still, people in the last stage of their illnesses were often taken there to die. The living and the dead lying side by side in filth and squalor created such a macabre picture that could only be described as like living hell. In 1869, the authorities, on the advice of the health officers, ordered it to close. To replace it, the Governor, Sir Richard Macdonnell, proposed to found a hospital for the Chinese. The Chinese community responded by raising $30,000 and the government contributed $115,000. The foundation stone was laid in 1870 and the opening ceremony took place in February 1872. Although it was named the Tung Wah Hospital (東華醫院), patients in it were treated by traditional practitioners with herbal medicine and without proper nursing care. The administration of the Hospital was in the hands of a board of directors, using traditional methods of management and accounting. The directors were elected annually and they chose a chairman from among themselves. They would be responsible for raising funds to meet annual expenditure and pay for improvements and developments. Run as a charitable organization, patients received free treatment and dead bodies free burial or passage back to China, with coffins provided. In case of disaster as after a typhoon or fire, shelter, food and relief would be given to the victims. Altogether it was a most public-spirited and highly commendable

effort. The chairman and members of the Board, who were usually prominent merchants from prestigious firms, were in the eyes of the community
their leaders. Originally there were sixteen of them, their standing in
society was such that they wielded considerable influence outside of the
Hospital. Almost any question affecting the welfare of the community, even
matters regarding the relationship with the government, could be referred
to them. The first chairman of the Board who took office in 1869 was Leung
On or Leung Wan-hon 梁雲漢, comprador of Gibb, Livington & Co. Among
the directors of the first board was Wong Shing, who later became the
second Chinese Legislative Councillor in 1884 (see Chapter II).

The Tung Wah Hospital came under severe criticism by the health
authorities for its failure to give them effective assistance and co-operation
in the fight against the plague epidemic. It did not matter that herbal medicine was used in treatment but from the point of view of public health it
was essential that such measures as isolation of the patients and contacts,
disposal of dead bodies and accurate reporting of cases should be carried
out. The Hospital Board failed to comply because of their ignorance and
resistance against changes. Dr. Ayres, the Colonial Surgeon, had always
been against the Hospital. He once wrote in his annual report the following remarks:

> The existence of this hospital in which it appears that more than four-fifths of
> the inmates are treated by so-called Chinese methods, is somewhat anomalous in
> a British Colony. It is not for me to discuss the matter from the point of view of
> the statesman, who, doubtless, has to consider the desirability of humouring to
> some extent the prejudices of the Chinese population, who in this Colony out-
> number the Europeans by the proportion of twenty to one. It is my duty to look
> at the matter from the point of view, and there can be very little doubt from that
> point of view, that the so-called Chinese medical methods are really nothing but
> empiricism and quackery.

A series of events involving the Hospital happened as soon as the epidemic broke out. On the third day after the onset, 10 May, Dr. Lowson was

sent there to see if there were any cases. He found twenty but they were not diagnosed as such by the traditional practitioners. In spite of the insistence of the government authorities, the Board of Directors refused to let medical officers enter the Hospital again. Meanwhile, ten thousand copies of a circular written by a traditional practitioner, in which he appended a prescription said to be an effective cure for plague, was distributed to the public by the Man Mo Miu Committee. The Man Mo Miu 文武廟 was a temple situated near the Hospital where the directors worshipped and offered their spring sacrifices. The Committee was in effect a branch of the Board, consisting of some of the directors. By turning out this circular, the Committee was literally advising the public that it was not necessary to enter hospital for treatment.

As the epidemic had come to stay, the government took action to remove by force cases found by house-searching to the isolation hospitals and dead bodies to the public mortuary for post-mortem examination. The Chinese were strongly against those moves and blamed the directors for not protesting to the government on their behalf. Matters came to a head when the Chinese made a counter-proposal to have patients and corpses sent back to China. On 20 May, a meeting was convened which was held in public and chaired by a director, Lau Wah-chuen 劉渭川. In attendance were the Superintendent of Police, F. H. May (later Sir Francis May, Governor of Hong Kong, 1912–19) and Dr. Ayres, the Colonial Surgeon. May said that the Guangzhou government would not give approval to the proposal. The statement was received by the gathering with shouts and angry words. To calm their feelings, Lau offered to negotiate personally with the Guangzhou authorities, but in the midst of the commotion, report came that Lau's shop was being ransacked. So Lau left the meeting in a hurry but as he got outside, he was stoned and his sedan chair was overturned. To escape injury, Lau ran back to the Hospital for cover, having lost tremendous face. He was then comprador of the Hong Kong and Shanghai Bank, a position that made him the doyen of the corps of compradors. The meeting was then adjourned without a resolution. The hostile and ugly mood of the mob outside the Hospital prompted the government to despatch a gun-boat, H.M.S. *Tweed*, to Possession Point which was within range of Po Yan Street (普仁街), where the Hospital was situated, with its gun trained at the mob, ready for action. Under the threat, the mob finally dispersed. The matter of sending cases back to Guangzhou was resolved later when the government, in deference to the wish of the Chinese community, changed its mind. In his diary, Lowson wrote on 13 June: "loaded 45 patients for Guangzhou in junks. 3 died". Again on the 15: "loaded junks for Guangzhou, 36".

An impasse then prevailed, without further improvement in the relationship between the Board of Directors and the government. In time, feelings against the Hospital were so strong that the government decided to appoint a Special Commission to inquire into its working. The Commission was chaired by J. H. Stewart-Lockhart, the Colonial Secretary, with the following as members: A. H. Thomson, Ho Kai, C. P. (later Sir Paul) Chater and T. H. Whitehead. A. H. Thomson was a government official in the Colonial Secretariat. The other three were unofficial members of the Legislative Council. Sir Paul Chater (1846–1926) was the first unofficial member of the community in Hong Kong to receive a Knighthood which was awarded him in 1903. A wealthy merchant and philanthropist, he gave generously to many charities in his lifetime and bequeathed his famous collections of porcelain and oil paintings, including many by that famous artist of the China Coast in the nineteenth century George Chinnery, to the Hong Kong government. Besides sitting on the Legislative Council from 1887–99, he also served on the Executive Council from 1896 to 1926 as its first unofficial member. Mr. Whitehead was the chief manager of the Chartered Bank of India, Australia and China, who served on both the Legislative and Executive Councils. The terms of reference were whether the Hospital was fulfilling its object and purpose, if so, whether the organization and administration could be carried out more effectively, and if not, whether its object and purpose could be fulfilled by any other organization.

The Commission sat between June and July, 1896. Many witnesses, both Chinese and Europeans, were called. Although it was not included in the terms of reference, inevitably they were asked whether Western medicine should be introduced into Hospital or not. As a result of the deliberations, although there was no consensus of opinion, certain conclusions were reached. It was conceded that the Hospital was established to take the place of the I Tze which was thought to be undesirable, and to admit the sick, and even more, dying Chinese, the administration of the Hospital should be in the hands of the Chinese and that the Chinese way of treatment should be given as many Chinese who would rather die than receive treatment in the Government Civil Hospital should be induced to be treated in the Tung Wah Hospital. The Commission further recommended that it would be of advantage to the Hospital, would facilitate its relations with the government and the public and would secure continuity and uniformity in its arrangements, if there were associated with the annually elected Committee some Chinese residents of long standing who had experience of the Hospital and whose advice would carry weight with the Chinese community. Thus, the permanent Advisory Board was born. Another important recommendation made by the Commission was that a Chinese registered doctor be appointed as Medical Superintendent whose salary was to be paid by the government. The Medical Superintendent would investigate the cause of death and supply accurate returns on those who died to the government, a task unable to be accomplished by a herbalist. It was added that the doctor should not treat patients with Western medicine unless requested. A Chinese steward was also to be appointed to supervise the sanitary maintenance of the hospital buildings.

These recommendations found support from enlightened members of the Chinese community, notably Fung Wah-chuen, Ho Kai's friend who had lent him money and whom we have met in Chapter II. A member of the Sanitary Board and one time Tung Wah director, he was another comprador, first with the National Bank and then the firm of Shewan, Tomes and Co.

With the acceptance of the recommendations by the Board of Directors, the door was at last opened for a Western doctor to be appointed to the Hospital. Dr. Chung Boon-chor 鍾本初 became its first medical superintendent "at a salary of $150 a month with no private practice", minuted the Governor. Originally he was given only the duties of a health officer, as mentioned above but a breakthrough was finally achieved when he performed an amputation of the thigh, the first ever operation done in the Hospital. The date given was 1899, if correct, it would mean that he had to wait for three years before he could introduce Western medicine into that stronghold of conservatism. It was said that he also insisted on treating all cases of malaria with quinine. Chung was probably a graduate of the College of Medicine but his name could not be found in Professor Lo Hsiang-lin's book on Sun Yat-sen's University Days; he was house surgeon at the Alice Memorial Hospital when he received his appointment. In time he was followed by other Western doctors, mostly graduates of the College of Medicine and later the University. He himself was succeeded by Dr. Jeu Hawk, an American graduate. And so, as Dr. Elizabeth Sinn wrote in her book *Power and Charity*, "The Chinese hospital offering purely Chinese treatment was no more". As a member of the Special Commission, Ho Kai played an important role in toning down the objections to the Tung Wah Hospital so that it could continue to exist. Consequently, Chinese medicine remained available at the Hospital for a long time and patients had a choice between it and Western medicine. In Dr. Jeu Hawk's fifth year as superintendent, which would be about 1907, it was recorded that of 3,200 in-patients, 1,815 opted for Western medicine against 1,385 for Chinese. Dr. G. H. Thomas whom we have met in Chapter V, completed fifty years of volunteer service as honorary consultant in surgery to the Hospital in his life time.

The conversion of Tung Wah Hospital had far-reaching consequences, signifying that the Chinese had come to accept Western medicine. At the turn of the century, aside from attending the public hospitals, Tung Wah, Alice Memorial and the Government Civil, the Chinese could consult their own Western doctors in private practice. In *20th Century Impressions of Hong Kong*, five Chinese doctors were included in the "Social and Professional Biographies" section, presumably because they had achieved eminence. They were: Drs. Kwan Sum-yin, Wan Tuen-mo 尹端武, Ho Ko-tsun 何高俊, Ho Nai-hop 何乃合 and Coxion To 杜國臣. It could therefore be said that they had succeeded when Ho Kai failed twenty years ago. Dr. Kwan has been introduced in Chapter V, his surgery was in No. 18A Stanley Street in Central District. Dr. Wan Tuen-mo was otherwise known as Wan Man-kai 尹文楷. He was a graduate of the Tianjin Medical College although he was born and received his early education in Hong Kong. He served in the Chinese Navy after graduation, later he went to Guangzhou to work in the Pok Chai Hospital under Dr. John Kerr, Sun Yat-sen's old teacher, before returning to Hong Kong. The other three were graduates of the Hong Kong College of Medicine. Dr. Ho Ko-tsun (L.M.S.C.C. 1901) taught anatomy at the College after graduation, and was a medical officer in the Tung Wah Hospital, the Alice Memorial Hospital and the Chinese Public Dispensary, Eastern District, before entering private practice. It was mentioned by Professor Lo Hsiang-lin that in 1911, after the Republic of China was established, he was briefly a deputy director of public health in Guangzhou. Dr. Ho Nai-hop (L.M.S.C.C. 1899) had the distinction of being the only resident doctor in the New Territories at one time when he was a medical officer in the Government Service. Dr. Coxion To also known as 杜應芬 (L.M.S.C.C. 1899) was house surgeon at the Alice Memorial Hospital and later the Nethersole Hospital for twenty-three years. Dr. Jeu Hawk, the second medical superintendent in the history of Tung Wah Hospital, later also went into private practice. Not all graduates of the College of Medicine became private practitioners. The most notable exception was Dr. Wang Chung-yik 王寵益 (1889–1930, L.M.S.C.C. 1908) who achieved eminence by being the first Chinese to be appointed to a chair, of pathology, in 1920, in the Faculty of Medicine, University of Hong Kong.

The circumstances under which Western medicine was introduced to the Chinese in Hong Kong, a British Colony, were therefore different from what transpired in China. There, the medical missionaries had an earlier start. The Chinese were shown the skill of these doctors in performing surgical operations to excise disfiguring tumours, remove bladder stones and repair hernias, and above all, treat eye diseases, using the couching method to extract cataracts thereby restoring eyesight with dramatic effect. As expected they met with opposition and prejudice, but the traditional practitioners were distinctly at a disadvantage when faced with such competition. So, with patience and tact, the missionaries gradually won the confidence of the people. In fact, they were more successful in healing the sick, their primary objective, than making conversions among their patients, their second. They too had the idea of training young Chinese as Western doctors to treat their own people and from the pupil-assistant system, eventually, medical schools were established all over the country with missionary funds. Interestingly, the first was one for women named the Hackett Medical College for Women established in Guangzhou in 1899.

In Hong Kong, Benjamin Hobson's efforts soon expired. Missionaries were never as active as their colleagues in China because the government had provided a medical service for the general public though on a limited scale. The skills of Manson and Cantlie, the two most eminent doctors were available, more to the Europeans than the Chinese. They were not missionaries but they worked without remuneration in a missionary hospital, the only one of its kind. They were Christians, so was Ho Kai who found himself in a supporting role and not a fellow practitioner. In the Government Civil Hospital there were not only no big names on the staff but few Chinese used it because of the high charges and restrictions. The idea of establishing a medical college came from Manson, Cantlie and others, it could only be considered as a missionary effort because the Alice Memorial was used as a teaching hospital. The government never took the lead in either healing the sick or initiating medical education although some medical officers helped to teach. It had to be a plague epidemic to give the government the opportunity to act. But it acted in such a way that it would be unacceptable nowadays. The government doctors used more force than persuasion to try to introduce Western medicine, for instance, they did not use health education methods to teach the public hygiene and sanitation. Against the circular issued by the Man Mo Miu Committee, no counter measure was undertaken to enlighten and placate the Chinese and thus to get their co-operation. The government doctors acted most high-handedly in dealing with the situation. From their writings, one could see that both Ayres and Lowson were brash and impatient and certainly did not understand the value of public relations as we know it today.

In the midst of all this was the Tung Wah Hospital, called an anomaly by Ayres, considered as should be abolished by Dr. J. C. Thomson as a witness before the Special Commission, but peculiarly placed to play a significant role in the chains of events, sparked off by the plague epidemic and ended with its own conversion. The Directors of the Board were regarded by the Chinese as their representatives although there was a Chinese member on the Legislative Council. Not that Ho Kai was not respected or trusted but one would suspect that he was probably less in touch with the grass-roots as we call them nowadays. It could be the image of him as an anglicized professional man which made him perhaps less revered than the directors robed in the mandarin style complete with peacock feathers on their hats and strings of beads around their necks. In any case, Ho Kai was the lone voice on the Legislative Council at that time and opposition by him of any unpopular legislation would not carry much weight. The government chose to get messages through to the Chinese community by using the directors, likewise, members of the public sent their complaints and objections through the same channel, in matters related to the plague epidemic as well as others. The Special Commission did not take immediate steps to introduce Western medicine into the Tung Wah, in fact discussions on the medical aspect were not included in the terms of reference. Ho Kai as a member agreed with the others that Chinese medicine should continue to be used and no Western medicine should be used unless agreed by the patient. But it was inevitable that once a Western doctor was appointed to the staff, even though his duties were originally as a health officer, sooner or later Western medicine would be introduced. It would not be in character if a Western doctor worthy of his training did not keep trying. Did Ho Kai foresee this would happen and so he went along with maintaining the status quo first? Had it not been for the plague epidemic would an inquiry be held into the operation of the Tung Wah resulting in Western medicine being introduced? Was there any other way to introduce and popularize Western medicine, for instance, could the young graduates of the College of Medicine achieve the same results in private practice? These were questions one might raise even though no satisfactory answers could be found.

The Legislative Council 1890–1914

Ho Kai was a member of the Legislative Council for twenty-four years from 1890 to 1914. He took an active part in the proceedings of the Council, speaking often in its debates. For the first six years, he was the only Chinese member until he was joined by Wei Yuk. Some laws passed during Ho Kai's tenure will be discussed in this chapter, they were chosen either because of their significance or being topical at the time and amusing in retrospect, but first a brief history of the Council.

With the formation of an administration in 1843, the Governor of Hong Kong was given full authority to make laws with the advice of a Legislative Council subject to three limitations. The authority had to be exercised in accordance with any instructions given by the Secretary of State, it was subject to the power of disallowance by the Crown of any Ordinance either in whole or in part, and Parliament was to retain the power of concurrent legislation over the Colony. During Ho Kai's time, the Legislative Council consisted of ex-officio members and official as well as unofficial members who were nominated by the Governor. It was the nearest thing to an assembly or parliament although the unofficial members were not elected by the people. However, certain groups like the Chamber of Commerce and the Justices of the Peace could elect members from among themselves for nomination by the Governor to the Council. Otherwise the nomination of unofficial members was entirely the prerogative of the Governor and did not follow any procedure or system. To be appointed to the Legislative Council was regarded as an honour and for the duration of their appointments members were styled as "the Honourable". There was a higher body, the Executive Council, also presided by the Governor. It could be regarded as his cabinet, consisting of ex-officio members and unofficial members appointed by the Governor. Most of the unofficial members either had served or were currently serving in the Legislative Council. Big business such as the Hong Kong and Shanghai Bank and Jardine, Matheson and Co. was usually given a seat. However, Ho Kai was never appointed despite his prestige. The Executive Council was a decision making body which was concerned with all policy matters and current issues. Bills in draft form were first approved by the Executive Council before they were sent to the Legislative Council where they were passed into law after three readings, at the second of which there could be a debate. Amendments were then made at this committee stage.

The Legislative Council which was formed in August 1843 consisted of only three members: A. R. Johnston, J. R. Morrison and W. Caine. Johnston was the Deputy Superintendent of Trade. Morrison, the son of Robert Morrison, succeeded his father as Chinese Secretary and Interpreter to the Superintendent of Trade after the latter's death in 1843. In June 1843, he was appointed as Chinese Secretary and Interpreter in the new Colonial Government. Caine was an army officer who had judiciary experience elsewhere now occupying the post of Chief Magistrate in Hong Kong. But the Council never met because Johnston left for England on sick leave the following month and Morrison died of the dreaded Hong Kong fever only a week after the announcement of his nomination. In January 1844, the General Officer commanding the garrison, Major-General G. C. d'Aguilar, was appointed to the Council. In February the same year, the Council, consisting of Pottinger, d'Aguilar and Caine, passed the first ever ordinance which prohibited slavery in the Colony. It was however disallowed by the home government because the Slave Emancipation Act of 1833 applied to all British possessions. Sir Henry Pottinger resigned shortly afterwards and was succeeded by Sir John Davis in May 1844. Davis wanted a Legislative Council of five, viz. the Major-General, the Chief Justice, the Colonial Secretary, the Colonial Treasurer, and the Chief Magistrate, with himself as Chairman. However, he was overruled by the Secretary of State. Eventually he went back to the original number of three, and appointed the Major-General, the Chief Justice and the Attorney-General. Somehow final approval was not obtained until September 1845. It had taken just about two years to get the membership of the Legislative Council settled.

The Council was gradually enlarged in subsequent years with the addition of official and unofficial members. In 1850, when Sir George Bonham was Governor, two unofficial members were appointed to the Legislative Council for the first time, they were David Jardine of Jardine, Matheson and Co., and James Forrest Edger of Jamieson How and Co. Since then the "taipans" (chief managers) of the big "hongs" (firms) were predominant among unofficial members in the Legislative Council and later the Executive Council. By the time Ho Kai was appointed in 1890, the Legislative Council had a membership of eleven, viz., six official members: the Governor, the Colonial Secretary, the Attorney-General, the Colonial Treasurer, the Surveyor-General and the Registrar-General, and five unofficial members: Phineas Ryrie, A. P. MacEwen, C. P. Chater, J. J. Keswick and Ho Kai himself. MacEwen and Chater have already been introduced in previous chapters. Phineas Ryrie was the head of the firm of Turner and Co., and J. J. Keswick was of Jardine, Matheson and Co. Ho Kai took the place of Wong Shing who had served for six years.

From the Hansard Reports of the period 1890 to 1914, one gets the impression that in those day the atmosphere in the Legislative Council Chamber was much more relaxed and the exchanges much more lively and spontaneous. The Chairman, who was of course the Governor or the Officer Administering the Government in his absence, made rather long speeches in some sessions besides his review of events every year. He entered into the discussion at almost every session by asking questions and making comments. Sometimes he even had to answer questions which were raised after notice was given at the previous sitting. There were cries of "hear, hear", and applause in the middle or at the end of speeches. Laughter was allowed and even interjections. Another unusual feature noted was the appearance of counsel when some bills were discussed. For instance, when a Bill to Amend the Law in respect of the Sale of Shares in Companies Registered under the Companies Ordinance and another concerning the Sale of Arms and Ammunitions were read, the stockbrokers and arms dealers engaged Mr. J. J. Francis, Q.C. to present their views on both occasions. Admittedly some speeches could well be prepared beforehand, but the language used by every one was distinctly more parliamentarian. As a barrister, Ho Kai's style was also somewhat legalistic. He certainly showed that he had a perfect command of English, at times using phrases and expressions that were both elegant and flowery.

Laws dealing with sanitation and health matters will be discussed first. At the session held on 5 March 1890, at which Ho Kai was sworn in as a member, amendments to the Public Health Ordinance No. 24 of 1887 were discussed. It was therefore on this Ordinance that he spoke for the first time. It is not intended to follow the many amendments of the Public Health Ordinance through the years since its enactment in 1887. Some significant changes were introduced during the period of the bubonic plague epidemic, mostly by strengthening the bye-laws and enforcing their execution. On the occasion when an amendment in relation to regulations governing common lodging houses was made in the 1894–1895 session, a strike by the coolies in Hong Kong was sparked off. They thought that the purpose was to introduce a poll-tax so that they all would have to pay something to the government after a head-count. Ho Kai admitted in his speech that he was unable to convince the coolies that the amendment was not meant for that purpose. During this period, the Tai Ping Shan Resumption Ordinance 1894 was also introduced. An area of some 400,000 sq. ft. or 10 acres was to be resumed because of the notoriously insanitary conditions which existed in that district. Opposition came from the residents because they would lose their houses and properties. Compensation was to be offered to them, the amount required being estimated at some $800,000. Ho Kai was not against the resumption but he objected to government's proposal to float a loan in order to get the estimated amount for paying out compensation.

In the same 1894–1895 session, a Medical Officer of Health Ordinance was introduced in Legislative Council. This official was to be a member of the Sanitary Board and given power to enter premises, etc. Ho Kai thought that the power and duties of the officer would soon bring him into collision with the Sanitary Board. Eventually it was agreed that he should be the adviser to the government on all sanitary matters through the Sanitary Board to which he should be attached and on which he should occupy a seat, but he should have no vote, it being inadvisable that he should enter into discussion on points on which he should be called upon to advise.

In 1906, the then Governor, Sir Matthew Nathan, constituted a Commission of Inquiry with the following terms of reference: "(1) whether the administration of the Sanitary and Buildings Regulations enacted by the Public Health and Building Ordinance of 1903 as now carried out is satisfactory and if not, what improvements be made, and (2) whether any irregularity or corruption exist or has existed among the officials charged with the administration of the aforesaid regulations." The Commission consisted of H. E. Pollock, K.C., an unofficial member of the Legislative Council, E. A. Hewett, another unofficial member, Fung Wa-chun 馮華珍, Lau Chu-pak 劉鑄伯 (who later succeeded Ho Kai), Henry Humphreys and A. S. Hooper. In their report which was submitted a year later, they said that they were forced to the conclusion that irregularities, corruption and bribery were rampant in the Sanitary Department, not only amongst the native subordinates but also the British inspectorate staff. It was pointed out that owing to the hardship inflicted by many of the regulations much injury was wrought to the property, and that consequently the general prosperity of the Colony was retarded. Stress was laid on the fact that the "open spaces" section, under which vested rights were sacrificed without compensation, had been in a large measure responsible for causing the property owners of Hong Kong excessive losses. It was further shown that by placing the whole control of the administration of the Sanitary Department in the hands of the Principal Civil Medical Officer, the Board was reduced to something even less than a consulting committee. The Commission recommended that the administration of the Public Health and Building Ordinance should be entirely separate from the Public Works Department, that water supply, public roads, sewers, etc. should remain under the control of the Public Works Department but all matters related to sanitary affairs, nuisances and the actual construction or alteration of buildings should be wholly transferred to the proposed Sanitary and Building Board, to be divided into four sections: secretarial, medical, engineering and veterinary, and composed of four officials and six unofficials.

On 1 June 1907, Ho Kai asked the following questions at a meeting of the Legislative Council:

(1) What steps does the government propose to take, and when, in regard to carrying out the recommendations of the Public Health and Building Ordinance Commission,

(2) If the government does not propose to carry out the recommendation of the Commission in toto, which of such recommendations does the government propose not to carry out,

(3) Will the government make a statement of what they propose to do with regard to the recommendations of the Commission.

The Colonial Secretary replied that a précis of what steps the Government would take was laid on the table, a Bill to Amend the Public Health and Building Ordinance was being drafted, and the recommendations would be carried out after the amendment was made. The bill to amend the Ordinance in the light of the recommendations made by the Commission was passed in 1908. The principal changes were:

1.   a slightly increased electorate by substituting the word "persons" for rate-payers who were entitled to vote, and giving members of the Council a vote for the representatives on the Board;

2.   the Principal Civil Medical Officer who was head of the Sanitary Board and thereby ex-officio President of the Board was removed and

his place taken by a specially appointed officer devoting the whole of his time to these duties. The Captain Superintendent of the Police was also removed and his place on the Board taken by the Medical Officer of Health;

3. the transfer of practically all building matters from the Sanitary Board to the Building Authority;

4. power given to the authorities to cause the owners to pull down the upper storeys of houses which were too dark and thereby insanitary, and where the work benefited the adjoining owners they were to pay the cost of reconstruction, but the compensation to the owner of the property pulled down was to be paid by the government;

5. the right of appeal from the discretion exercised by the Sanitary Board or Building Authority to the Governor-in-council, the applicant to have the right of appearing in person or by his representative, and be heard at the Council, or the right of appealing to the Council in lieu of the Governor-in-Council.

At the committee stage of another sanitary bill, Ho Kai managed to persuade the Council to agree with his view. This was the Bill to Amend the Cattle Diseases, Slaughter-Houses and Markets Ordinance of 1887, introduced in October 1890. The main object of the bill was to make adulteration of food for either men or animals punishable. Ho Kai said that it was hard to impose a fine of a hundred dollars on someone who would feed a dog with tainted or adulterated food, because he would have thought that animals could easily find such food even without being fed with it. He also pointed out that some items of food eaten by the Chinese were in fact tainted, for instance preserved eggs or hatched eggs, and "fried duck" which was regarded as unwholesome by the Europeans. A European member actually supported him by saying that he had eaten such tainted food without any ill effect. The Chinese would certainly be deprived of certain delicacies if their sale was punishable by law by the passing of this Bill.

During the 1900–1901 session, on 14 March 1901, a sanitary bye-law was discussed. Ho Kai once again demonstrated his reluctance to allow sanitary officials or measures to disturb people. The bye-law stated that "any house or part of a house in the villages of Quarry Bay, Shaukiwan, Stanley, Aberdeen and Aplichau which is occupied by members of more than one family shall, unless specially exempted by the Sanitary Board, be cleansed and lime-washed throughout by the owner, to the satisfaction of the Sanitary Board, not less than twice a year, namely during the months of May and June, and of November and December." Ho Kai opposed the measure as unnecessary, expensive and troublesome. "If a bye-law to compel the villagers to clean their houses twice a year were introduced", he said, "I would support it, but I oppose their being asked to clean their houses either by lime-washing or using disinfectants of any kind, because I do not believe lime-washing is absolutely necessary to enable people to keep their houses clean." He estimated that if it cost $5–$10 to clean a town house, it would be $2–$4 for a village house.

Having dealt with the essential amendments of the Health Ordinance, we proceed to examine three bills which were related to the needs of the community for open space, transport and water respectively.

On 25 June 1898, the Legislative Council discussed a petition from the public for more open space outside the city limit. There was already an area within the racecourse in the Wongneichung Valley for the use of the general public as a recreation ground but this was considered insufficient. Another area in Causeway Bay, between Jardine's Bazaar and North Point, was suggested. This was agreed. To commemorate Queen Victoria's Diamond Jubilee which was celebrated in 1897, the year before, it was decided to name it Queen's Recreation Ground. Ho Kai made a further suggestion on 3 August that another area in the vicinity of Sung Wong Toi 宋王台 in Kowloon be used as a public playground. He explained that there was a large rock commemorating the brief stay of the last boy emperor of the Sung dynasty in the Kowloon Peninsula when he and his entourage were being pursued by the Yuan 元 or Mongol troops along the coast. The entire party later committed suicide by drowning themselves in the sea further up the coast when they realized that they could no longer escape. It would, Ho Kai pleaded, be a suitable spot which was also a historical one. The legislature agreed. The Queen's Recreation Ground has become Victoria Park, much used today to stage demonstrations and protests besides sporting activities, while the rock commemorating the last emperor of Sung has been preserved though reduced in size and moved to a small park which is adjacent to the original site.

The Tramways Bill was read in the Legislative Council on 29 July 1901. It was for the purpose of allowing a company to run trams from one end of the Island of Hong Kong to the other. Ho Kai said that a tramway would be most useful as it would furnish a cheap means of travelling for the poorer classes, and would enable them to spread themselves out as it were, thus relieving overcrowding in the towns. But at the same time unless the question of the fees to be charged to the labouring class were settled, he would not give his support. Ho Kai argued that a coolie had to pay fifty to sixty cents a night for his lodging, and if he had to spend say three cents twice a day for trams, he would have little left from his daily wage for food. The point was taken by the Council and the Bill passed.

As regards water, Ho Kai's views were somewhat unconventional. On 23 June 1902, the Water Bill was discussed. He pointed out that the allowance of daily consumption was too small. For a house with $100 a month rental, water allowance was fixed at $4 a quarter at 50 cents per 1000 gallons, i.e. 8000 gallons per quarter. When this amount was divided by the number of people in the household, it would be too small. He pointed out that a Chinese household would invariably be much larger than a European's, there might be as many as twenty to thirty persons against ten, including servants. He also said that the allowance was not only for potable purposes but for washing as well. If there was not enough water, the houses could not be kept clean, he added. This remark was meant to remind the government that in debates on the Public Health Ordinance and Regulations, the official members always talked about keeping the Chinese residential quarters clean. He understood that charges would be made by a meter in order to prevent wastage but thought that the installation of the meter would be too expensive for the owner of the house. He proposed postponement and when it was decided to proceed with the bill, he opposed its passage and threatened to petition the Secretary of State for the Colonies.

Matters affecting the Chinese community whether to improve their welfare or to regulate their activities were essential parts of the business of the Council. Though nominated and not elected, Ho Kai called himself a representative of the Chinese community and indeed he was addressed by the Chairman of the Council and his fellow members as such. Many issues affecting Chinese customs and habits and the status of the Chinese were discussed during his time. Perhaps the most important was the Protection of Women and Children Ordinance and the related incorporation of the Po Leung Kuk 保良局 which literally means the Bureau for the Protection of the Innocent.

In the early years of Hong Kong, young girls were exploited for prostitution, concubinage and bondage. Because of the Chinese preference for male children, the daughters of the poorer families could suffer either one of the three fates. Some of them were lucky enough to have been treated well after they were bought as a concubine or a servant girl, called *mui tsai* 妹仔 in the Cantonese dialect. As the latter, some might even be luckier still by getting married off to a decent young working husband. Others might be forced into prostitution against their will. But even as a concubine or a *mui-tsai* they could still suffer harsh treatment because of jealousy or a cruel streak in their masters or mistresses. For those who succeeded in escaping, a home was founded for them as well as abandoned girls and others recovered from brothels in 1878. This was the origin of the Po Leung Kuk which at the beginning was under the management of the Tung Wah Hospital. For the sake of stamping out prostitution and forbidding the sale of girls generally, the Protection of Women and Children Ordinance was enacted in 1887. Obviously, some of the provisions were regarded as contrary to Chinese customs. For instance, the age limit of girls to be afforded protection was set at sixteen and below and the Chinese protested because this would interfere with their custom of taking concubines who might be under that age. Apparently Ho Kai, though not yet a Legislative Councillor, sided with the Chinese on this issue which became the subject of a memorial to the Secretary of State for the Colonies. The reply was hardly palatable, for it was said that no undertaking could be given that Chinese taking concubines under that age would not be prosecuted. Like the Public Health Ordinance, the Protection of Women and Children Ordinance was frequently amended whenever loopholes were found and new illicit practices discovered. It became also the legislation which dealt with the establishment and keeping of brothels.

In the 3 July 1891 sitting of the Legislative Council, a very amusing exchange took place when an amendment of the Protection of Women and Children Ordinance was introduced. The purpose was "to impose penalties for the detention of women and girls for the purpose of prostitution, also if kept by threatening legal proceedings for the recovery of any debt or alleged debt or by using any threat whatever that should also come under the penalty." The Registrar-General, as protector of the Chinese, was to be given the power to inspect brothels and arrest the keepers without a warrant. The Attorney-General had to explain to the Council the practice of "flying the pigeon" (放白鴿) as follows: "Persons could part with their children often more than once for a sum of money and then going to claim them as their natural parents and trying to get them back from persons who had paid a sum of money for them under threats of bringing a charge of kidnapping or unlawful detention." In other words, they made use of the law to regain legal possession of the children after getting money for the transaction. Ho Kai supported the amendment which would deal with persons practising "flying the pigeon". He said that girls were sold to purchasers as servants and kept till they were twenty by Chinese or eighteen by European reckoning, when they would be given in marriage for a certain sum of money, but attempts to regain the girls could then be made. In other words, the natural parents would sell the girls first, have them brought up at the expense of the foster parents, and then reclaim them to get more money by marrying them off.

In a more serious vein, an Ordinance for the Establishment and Incorporation of the Chinese Society for the Protection of Women and Children was brought before the Council on 25 April 1892, but the Chairman, Sir William Robinson had to withdraw it. In his speech, he said: "I was certainly under the impression that this Bill would have been well received and thoroughly approved of by the community as well as the unofficial members of the Council, but I regret to say that it appears the Bill does not recommend itself to the community or to all of the unofficial members." After referring to the good work done by the Po Leung Kuk, the Chairman continued:

> The Bill, I think has been thoroughly misunderstood. It is not only a Bill to give the Society legal status. The real intention of the Bill is to place the Society more under the control of the Government than it has ever hitherto been. This view appears not to have been taken by the gentlemen who have opposed the Bill or by the community who are stated to have strong objections to it. I may say that had the Bill come on for the second reading to-day I was perfectly prepared to modify it in certain particulars. I should have amended the Bill so that the meetings of the Society and the buildings and establishment of the Society should be open at all times to any Justice of the Peace, and so have removed it from the odium of the charge brought against it by the member for the Chamber of Commerce (Mr. Whitehead) namely that it was a secret society.... Since the last meeting of the Council, when the Hon. Member for the Chamber of Commerce stigmatised the Po Leung Kuk as a secret society, very serious charges against the operations of the Society have been made to me. One of them is that the subordinate members of the Society are not disinclined to exercise what is known as the practice of squeezing if an opportunity occurs. Another is that of the $30,000 which is mentioned by the Registrar-General as the amount of subscription gathered in aid of the Society, a certain portion of the amount has been obtained by means which could hardly be called justifiable. I think as such very grave

charges are hanging over this Society, a Society which has done very good work,
it would be the wish of the members themselves that the matter should be
thoroughly investigated into.

The Governor then appointed a special commission, consisting of the
Registrar-General, Ho Kai, C. P. Chater and T. H. Whitehead, to consider
the Bill and report. The Commission's report was published before the
second reading of the Bill took place on 2 June. In the introductory speech
the Attorney-General said: "The grave charges pending over the Society
have been thoroughly enquired into and to-day the Po Leung Kuk stands
clear entirely of all unjustifiable amputations which were cast upon its
character and good faith." He explained that the Kuk had already been in
existence for thirteen years, and in the four and a half years up to 1891,
2,751 cases had been dealt with. He said that as the Kuk was now to receive
funds it should be independent of the Tung Wah Hospital and become
incorporated. He agreed to have a permanent committee of advisers. Ho
Kai supported the motion, saying that an endowment of $20,000 was now
available. He also traced the history of the Kuk, which was established in
1880 to assist the government in prevention of the crime of kidnapping
and kindred offences, and rescuing women and children from being the
victims of crime and degradation, furthermore to dispose of these women
and children in the best manner possible, having regard to their lifelong
welfare and happiness. On some points, however, he did not agree. The
Permanent Board of Directors was to consist of no less than five and not
more than ten persons including the Registrar-General who should be ex-
officio the President, and also the Member of the Council for the time
being representing the Chinese who should be ex-officio Vice-President.
Then the first Permanent Board of Directors was to consist of persons whose
names were contained in the schedule to the Ordinance, with vacancies
occurring from time to time to be filled by the Governor who might call
upon the continuing members of the Board for recommendations. Ho Kai
did not like the Permanent Board to be an elective committee at the same

time, nor did he think the Registrar-General should be the President of the Permanent Board of Directors rather than a Chinese member. After the passage of the Protection of Women and Children (Amendment) Ordinance 1894, the Secretary of State for the Colonies instructed that the registration of brothels and inspection of inmates, being contrary to the recognized policy of Parliament, should be abolished. Ho Kai duly protested.

To the satisfaction of all concerned, on 18 January 1896, Sir William Robinson laid the foundation stone of a new home under the auspices of the Po Leung Kuk Society, for which $20,000 was granted by the Government and $30,000 subscribed by the Chinese community. The ceremony was performed with a silver trowel and a silver-mounted mallet, handed to the Governor by Ho Kai.

Ho Kai was deeply concerned with gambling in Hong Kong. Shortly after he was appointed, on 13 October 1890, he asked a question for the first time: "What steps have been taken or are being taken by the Government (1) to suppress or diminish public gambling in this Colony, (2) to regulate, register or suppress the hundreds of gambling clubs that have sprung up into existence during the last few years." He attempted to explain his motive by making a speech which was interrupted by the Chairman who pointed out that it was out of order. Surprisingly Ho Kai started arguing. The Attorney-General gave the conventional reply that a draft ordinance dealing with the question of gambling had been prepared and was under consideration. But when the Bill was presented on 5 December, Ho Kai said that it was a very drastic bill, and a bill that would no doubt suppress gambling in a particular way but it was totally different from what was expected. His complaint was that it made no difference between social clubs properly so-called amongst the respectable Chinese and those that were simply gambling houses. One effect, he said, would be to increase the power of the police enormously for good or for evil. "It is not for me to say anything about corruption or bribery in connection with such a useful body as the police but one cannot help thinking that to increase their power so enormously is a serious thing," he concluded. One could deduce from these remarks that even then corruption in the police force was already in the minds of legislative councillors. The debate went on for a few sittings, until March the following year, 1891. Corruption was again cautioned, and Ho Kai continued to oppose the registration of Chinese social clubs for the purpose of the Ordinance. He finally made the suggestion that gambling should also be suppressed in Kowloon.

Also in the year that he was appointed, in discussing an item in the Appropriations Bill of a sum of $140,000 for the extension of the gaol, Ho Kai objected to the provision of separate cells or solitary confinement for Chinese prisoners. The unofficial members were of the opinion that it was unnecessary, but the officials thought that solitary confinement could be used as additional punishment for the prisoners. The proposal was eventually withdrawn. In opposing the official view Ho Kai made the following speech:

Talking about separate cells and other punishments, I am afraid the members were far from accurate in speaking of solitary confinement as a punishment to the Chinese. Every one knows the Chinese are a very patient race and I know some members of the lower classes or criminal classes will sit down for days by themselves and take no notice of the people. They are not active; they do not care for outdoor exercise and solitary confinement to them, I am afraid, would be rather a comfort. As to overcrowding and the fear of epidemics, that is also without foundation. There has been no epidemic in the gaol and the Chinese herd together themselves outside the gaol quite as much. Then I say that there is an enormous difference between the Europeans and the Chinese constitution. Of that the Legislature never takes any notice, they simply say that what Europeans require the Chinese must require and consequently they make the mistake of treating the Chinese like the Europeans. And now you ask for a very large sum for gaol extension because you think Chinese prisoners require as much accommodation as European prisoners and that they should have a separate cell and so on, and of course you give them a great deal of nourishing food and everything else you may go extending the gaol indefinitely, and by and by it will cover the whole colony. I am sure that there are other means that could be devised to make the punishment more salutary and prevent the lower class of Chinese desiring to rush into gaol as a comfortable boarding-house where they can have a lot of amusement and pay nothing.

It might well be a waste of time and effort but an ordinance to prevent certain nuisances which was enacted in 1872 was to be amended in 1900 by adding *chai mui* 猜枚 as a nuisance. This is a finger game which is still played in drinking parties by two opponents. They each shout out a number and using their fingers make a sign for another number. The one who happens to have given the number which turns out to be the sum of the two numbers indicated by their fingers, wins the game and the other has to drink up. It can be imagined that because the shouting becomes louder and louder as more and more liquor is consumed, it is a very noisy game. It is a form of noise pollution comparable to the banging of the tiles on a hard table in a game of mahjong but perhaps much worse as it is produced by the human voice. It certainly is a nuisance which disturbs the neighbours. The proposal was to ban the game from 11 p.m. to 6 a.m. Ho Kai argued that the hours should be extended in the Chinese quarters because the Chinese usually would not mind noisy parties. He might as well say that they should be allowed to make as much noise as they liked so long as they did not disturb the Europeans!

Besides Chinese customs, the treatment of the Chinese themselves was occasionally the object of legislation. In the 1897–98 session, on 8 November 1897, an amendment to the Chinese Extradition Ordinance of 1889 was discussed. In the Bill, which was proposed by the Attorney-General, "six-months immediately prior to the date of his so being brought before the Magistrate" was stipulated as determining the period of residence in the Colony that would render depositions inadmissible in proceedings against a person whose extradition was applied for. Ho Kai objected to the words "immediately prior to" which would deprive every Chinese of his claim of Hong Kong residence if he "happened to leave the

Colony temporarily, no matter how long he might have resided in the Colony". The Chinese mandarins could wait for an opportunity until the man they wanted went back to China on family or personal business, and would pitch upon that time for the commission of the alleged crime. All Chinese merchants, no matter how long they might have resided in the Colony, would forfeit the residency claim once they returned to China for any purpose for a short period of time, because "immediately prior to" the date of his being brought before the Magistrate he had stayed that short period of time in China and had disrupted his six-months residence in the Colony. Ho Kai proposed deleting the words "immediately prior to" and amending the provision to "the person has not resided in the Colony more than six months during the twelve months previous to the date of his so being brought before the Magistrate", i.e. if he could prove that during the twelve months he had resided in the Colony continuously and had only left for a month or two, then in that case the Chinese government would have to secure their extradition in the old way and bring the witnesses down from Guangzhou. This was considered as the necessary safeguard against depositions which were thought to be liable to abuse. The Council accepted Ho Kai's point as the lesser evil between possible abuse of depositions and possible abuse of residency claim. The Attorney-General warned that people could "reside seven months in the colony and then commit crimes on the mainland during the remaining five months of the year", but endorsed the proposed amendment.

At a sitting on 21 December 1899, a Bill entitled an Ordinance to Provide for the Summoning of Chinese Before the Registrar-General was introduced. The Registrar-General would have the power to summon before him any Chinese whom he desired to question upon any matter of importance connected with the New Territories and affecting the Chinese in Hong Kong. The date should be noted as the administration of the newly leased New Territories was then in a somewhat confused state. Although the real object was not clearly stated, Ho Kai offered no strong opposition. However he said that the Registrar-General would have such very great power not possessed by even the Chief Justice or the Governor. He advised the Registrar-General to exercise great tact and discretion and suggested a period of twelve months after which a review should be carried out. In the end it was agreed to give the Ordinance a run of two years before reviewing and for further periods to be determined from time to time by resolution of the Legislative Council.

There were obviously many problems arising from land transactions in the newly leased New Territories. The Chinese became deeply involved as they began to buy up land. A Bill entitled an Ordinance to Amend Ordinance No. 18 of 1900, which in turn was entitled an Ordinance to Facilitate the Hearing, Determination and Settlement of Land Claims in the New Territories, to Establish a Land Court, and for Other Purposes, was read for the first and the second time on 20 July 1903. On 31 July it reached the committee stage. Ho Kai's main objection was the retrospective character, pointing out that "under Ordinance 47 of 1902, a claimant whose claim to land has been allowed by the Land Court had a permanent heritable and transferable right of use and occupancy in his land". The Attorney-General, in establishing the principle of the Bill, said that "the Crown was the proprietor of the land in the New Territories by virtue of the arrangement made between Her late Majesty the Queen and the Emperor of China". The Crown was therefore "a party" in reality to every case before the Land Court". The Bill was made retrospective "to enable Government to use the power of appeal which by inadvertence had not been given in the principal Ordinance to the Crown while it had been given to ordinary claimants". The Bill provided that the Chief Justice might at any time, upon good cause shown, grant to the Crown leave to appeal to the Full Court of the Supreme Court from any decisions of the Land Court which affected the rights of the Crown as proprietors of New Territories land. Ho Kai's objection was voted down. On 10 August, at the third reading, Ho Kai again reiterated that the retrospective Bill if passed into law "will cause great hardships and do injustice to certain claimants and also unsettle the title and rights of those who have acquired them from the original claimants, and have already paid the purchase money upon the faith that the claim, once having been admitted by the Land Court, was all sufficient". But the Attorney-General said that hardship would be felt by speculators only. He gave the example of a man who established a claim before the Land Court, then sold it for $100. The buyer sold the land again for $50,000. By and by the land was sold for $500,000. Meanwhile the Land Court considered the matter slowly, allowing the claim of the original claimant who paid $100. Then the Governor-in-Council must decide whether to grant a title, the Land Court having allowed a claim. The Attorney-General emphasized the distinction between the two. If the government decided not to grant a title but retain the land for public benefit, the compensation paid would be $100, therefore no hardship would be caused to the original claimant or the public. The Bill was passed.

All residents in Hong Kong know that at one time no Chinese was allowed to live on the Peak which was reserved for the Europeans. This was the object of an Ordinance for the Reservation of a Residential Area in the Hill District introduced in the Legislative Council on 14 April 1904. The explanation was that such a restriction was necessary in order to prevent overcrowding. To make the Bill more acceptable, it did say that the Chinese were not restricted from building houses on the Peak but they would have to get approval from the Governor-in-Council. Ho Kai said that it had a decided savour of the nature of class legislation but having consulted members of the Chinese community he found that they had no strong feelings or objections if they were not allowed to live on the Peak. He suggested however to change the phraseology so as to make it less blatantly obvious that the Chinese were to be excluded. The first Chinese to have a house on the Peak was Sir Robert Ho Tung 何東 (1862–1955) who bought the "Chalet" in 1906, not long in fact, after the passage of the above ordinance. Sir Robert never sat on either the Legislative or the Executive Council. He first joined Jardine, Matheson and Co. as a clerk, rose to be its comprador, then started his own business, and became one of the richest men in the Far East. In his life-time and in his will, he gave away a great deal of his wealth to many charities and public institutions. He was the acknowledged doyen of the Eurasian community in Hong Kong, another new breed resulting from mixed unions, usually of European fathers and Chinese mothers in the first generation.

In the 1908–1909 session, presided by Sir Frederick Lugard, An Ordinance to Amend the Magistrate's Ordinance 1890 and to Effect Certain Other Amendments in the Criminal Law was tabled in the Legislative Council. Its main object was to control, by legislation, the Chinese habit of spitting in and out of doors. The two Chinese members, Ho Kai and Wei Yuk dissented strongly on the ground that to penalize a universal and almost involuntary habit would antagonize the whole Chinese population. Ho Kai put up a good fight in the acrimonious debate which followed. "The Chinese", he said, "like other people, prefer to be led rather than driven. The Ordinance would either be a dead letter, which was bad for the law, or the whole population would be liable to fines or imprisonment." Lugard stated that he meant to stick to his principles and drove his clause through against repeated amendments. Thereafter the Chinese started a signature campaign and presented him with a petition signed by 8,000 persons, but could have contained another 80,000 signatures. In it, they said that their feeling was stirred to its depth and the very existence of the Colony as a loyal dependency was threatened. Lugard had to give way but he announced that the Chinese had decided to set up an Anti-Spitting Committee for the total suppression of the habit by persuasive and educative means instead. In proposing that the legislation should therefore be repealed, he said that "methods of co-operation are in every way to be preferred to methods of coercion".

During Ho Kai's time, the Legislative Council enacted Ordinances related to the registration of doctors, dentists, pharmacists and midwives and also the Hong Kong College of Medicine and the Hong Kong University Ordinances. He had an interest in all these ordinances, particularly the last two as he played an important role in the establishment of the two institutions.

The Medical Registration Ordinance of 1884 was amended in 1892. In the original, it was stated that "This ordinance shall not operate to limit the rights of the Chinese practitioners to practise medicine or surgery and to receive, demand or recover reasonable charges in respect of such practice." To improve the language, it was thought that this sentence should be re-written as follows: "This ordinance shall not be deemed to prohibit Chinese practitioners from practising medicine or treating surgical cases according to Chinese methods or for demanding or recovering reasonable charges for services rendered by them in respect of such practice." Another point was that applications for registration from colonial or foreign practitioners should be referred to the Medical Board instead of the Colonial Secretary, but the case of the graduates of the Hong Kong College of Medicine for the Chinese was different. The Attorney-General said: "At the present moment I am sorry to say that the examination through which they go there is not equivalent to the minimum course required in England and therefore for the present they cannot be registered under the Ordinance but I hope thereafter that their qualification may be so far improved as to admit them as medical practitioners." In other words, these graduates of the local medical school were not registrable under the Ordinance along with other "Western-trained" doctors. In reply, Ho Kai made the following speech:

> I wish to move leaving out the words "according to Chinese method". If passed, the result would be that those who have studied Chinese medicine would have a free hand in dealing with Chinese patients whereas those who have had a far better training in Western medicine and yet who are not considered by their fellow professionals of the Western world as having attained such a high standard as they themselves, would be driven from the Colony and be unable to exercise their craft after many years' study even among their own fellow countrymen. I do not think that the Government have exercised an unwise discretion in allowing the Chinese to practise their own system of medicine and surgery among their own people. In the present state of the Colony I think it would be

dangerous to provide otherwise. The Chinese should be exempted from the operation of this ordinance for sometime longer. I hope the time may come when we may be able to pass an ordinance that all Chinese practitioners here, whether practising among the Chinese according to the native or European methods, should be men who have proved themselves to have studied the subject and not merely holding themselves out as medical practitioners without having gone through any course of study whatever. At the present moment I wish the Government would consent to delete these few words to enable those students who have studied European medicine in the Hong Kong College of Medicine for the Chinese for the past five years and also the Manson Memorial Hospital at Formosa or at Tientsin [Tianjin] or anywhere else to practise.

Ho Kai's objection was quite clear, that the local graduates were not provided for if only those who practised according to Chinese methods were exempted. The Attorney-General said that he was advised by the Medical Board that as there was no such thing as surgery in the practice of Chinese medicine, the proposal was to put "treating surgical cases according to Chinese methods" instead of "Surgery". This was precisely Ho Kai's point that the local graduates would therefore not be allowed to practise, because they would not be treating cases according to Chinese methods. Finally, at the sitting on 11 January 1893, it was agreed that the original clause: "This Ordinance shall not operate to limit the right of Chinese practitioners to practise medicine or surgery or to receive, demand or recover reasonable charges in respect of such practice", should be retained. Under it the local graduates would be able to practise their profession as "Western doctors", The Medical Registration Ordinance of 1892 was further amended in 1914 to accommodate the medical graduates of the Hong Kong University whose degree was recognized by the General Medical Council.

The Dentist Registration Bill was also a rather complicated affair. In 1906, this was brought before the Legislative Council. The Bill provided for the registration of dentists who qualified from various dental schools, including some in the United States. But no exemption could be made for

Chinese dentists because there was no such thing as Chinese dentistry as opposed to Chinese traditional medicine. If the Bill was allowed to pass, then every one in Hong Kong would have to go to the registered or "high-class" dentists, and the poorer classes would suffer as no "street" dentists could practise any more. After Ho Kai explained these circumstances, the Bill was withdrawn. A Dental Registration Ordinance was eventually passed in 1914.

A Pharmacy Ordinance came into being in 1908, and in 1910 it was extended to allow medical practitioners to dispense for their own patients. A Midwives Ordinance was passed in 1910, and a Nursing Ordinance much later in 1931.

It must have given Ho Kai much pleasure to see the enactment of the Ordinance for the Incorporation of the Hong Kong College of Medicine. At the sitting on 16 May 1907 the Council was informed that hitherto the College had existed on only the fees paid by the students, while the teachers were serving in an honorary capacity without pay. But now that government was to give $2,500 a year as a subsidy and Mr. Chau Chuk-kai 周竹楷 had left a bequest of $10,000 as an endowment, the College would have to be incorporated so as to be able to acquire property and manage the funds. For similar reasons, when the Hong Kong University was established in 1911, an Ordinance to Incorporate and Regulate the Hong Kong University was enacted.

On account of its historic origin, opium-smoking was allowed in Hong Kong. Among the earliest ordinances passed were several for the purpose of regulating the sale of opium, the control of opium farms and the operation of opium divans. These included Ordinances No. 21 of 1844 for licensing the sale, No. 5 of 1845 to make better provision for licensing, No. 2 of 1858 for licensing and regulating the sale of opium, No. 23 of 1887 for the better regulating of the trade, No. 21 and No. 22 of 1891 entitled Prepared Opium and Raw Opium respectively, and others.

Although opium-smoking was regarded as yet another Chinese social custom rather than drug addiction, Ho Kai showed signs of impatience and intolerance with the subject in later years. In the 1896–97 session, on 26 August 1896, the Prepared Opium Ordinance of 1891 was amended. Opium dens were under control of the government, and every person who opened or carried on a divan had to obtain a licence from the Colonial Secretary. It was stipulated that only males would be allowed to be in charge of divans, not females. Ho Kai as a lawyer thought that entry into a divan would therefore be restricted to the keeper himself and suggested to allow "a bona fide member of such keeper's family to enter or remain" in an opium divan. In 1904, another discussion took place on opium. It was then discovered that opium had been added to pills and wines, which the Council regarded as distinct from opium itself and decided to ban them from being sold in the open market. In 1901, when the Opium Ordinance to repeal the ordinances of 1891 was discussed, Ho Kai said that he wished all opium farms, opium divans and public houses where opium was smoked would be closed. At the very last session that he attended, on 26 February 1914, the Opium Ordinance was again brought up, this time to allow transhipment for importation and exportation. A permit was to be obtained every time opium was transferred from a ship to another, from a ship to a warehouse and from a warehouse to a ship. One could well imagine that Ho Kai really had had enough.

An interesting complication arose when it was discovered that some people were receiving morphine either by injection or oral administration from persons not being registered doctors who could use the drug for the treatment of patients. It was thus necessary to have a Morphine Ordinance to prohibit the administration of morphine unless by medically qualified men. This was done on 29 August 1893. The motion was seconded by Ho Kai, who, in his speech, drew the distinction between opium-smoking and morphine injection. He was aware that morphine could be a substitute for opium and used for the treatment of opium addiction but it was itself a habit-forming drug. The Morphine Ordinance was rather comprehensive and virtually a precursor to the later Pharmacy and Poisons Ordinance or Dangerous Drugs Ordinance because it spelled out the circumstances

under which morphine could be sold, kept and administered. It was somewhat puzzling to read that two unofficials, T. H. Whitehead and E. R. Belilios,
asked for an adjournment in order to study reports but Ho Kai voted with
the officials against them and so the bill was passed.

In addition to legislation for opium and morphine, liquor also came under
control by Ordinances No. 8 and No. 11 of 1844, the former prohibiting
the distillation of spirits, the latter for licensing public houses and regulating the retail of fermented and spiritous liquor. On 16 September 1901 the
question of collection of duties on liquors was discussed. The Attorney-
General said that it was "for the purpose of raising the revenue necessary to
carry on His Majesty's Government in the Colony". He continued:

> The principle is, shortly, the imposition of duties upon liquor as being after con-
> sideration, deemed to be the article most properly subject to duty in the occasion
> which has arisen. It is the abandonment of the last of the revenue obtained
> hitherto from opium which we have every reason to believe will not come here
> in such a large volume in the future as in the past, that has compelled those
> responsible for the finances of the Colony to look about for some source that will
> give the supply of ready money needed for carrying on the Government of the
> Colony.

On the reference to the drop in opium revenue and the suggestion to
augment it by taxing liquor, Ho Kai expressed his views as follows:

> However much I approve of the principle of levying duties on intoxicating
> liquors I do not approve of the principle — the drastic principle — of enforce-
> ment and especially of detection. These sections (31, 35) give power to the Gov-
> ernment to order a search of the baggage of all persons landing in this Colony
> and also to enter every business place and every domestic home in the Colony.

He thought that the former provision was unnecessary in connection
with the working of the law. As regards the latter, he said: "Once liquor is
imported into the Colony without paying duty it is almost impossible to
detect, and to bring the crime home to the smuggler."

As a barrister, Ho Kai was able to assist in matters which concerned the legal profession. Rather unexpectedly he crossed swords with E. R. Belilios over the laws relating to solicitors on 13 March 1909. One of the clauses read as follows:

> No person shall have been admitted as a solicitor of the Supreme Court of Jurisdicature in England or as an attorney or writer in one of the Courts of Dublin or Edinburgh shall be admitted to practise within the Colony as a solicitor otherwise than as a clerk to a solicitor or a firm of solicitors practising in the Colony until he shall have actively resided in the Colony for a period of six months next preceding such admission and unless he shall have previously given six months' notice in writing to the Registrar of the Court of his desire and intention to apply to be so admitted; but any person who may have been admitted to practise as a solicitor within the Colony as a clerk to another solicitor or firm of solicitors, shall, after having so practised for a period of six months, be deemed to have been admitted to practise within the Colony as a solicitor and shall be entitled to so practise upon his own account unless precluded from so doing by any lawful agreement or undertaking.

The motion proposed was to delete this clause but strangely enough, Belilios objected. He gave three reasons for retaining the clause. Firstly, it would restrict the influx of lawyers of unknown characters and dispositions, secondly, it would protect the interest of the old-established solicitors and attorneys, and thirdly, it would safeguard the Colony from being victimized by unscrupulous men. Ho Kai said he was a member of a committee of lawyers who considered the bill and he voted against the retention of that particular clause. "At the end of this 19th Century", he went on, "it is very curious to hear one speak of the vested interests of a profession or a trade and to argue that those who happen to have been in the locality for some little time should in consequence have the field to themselves, and that a sort of monopoly should be created in their favour and the door shut against others." To counter the three grounds Belilios gave for retaining the clause, Ho Kai said that one or more solicitors would not increase the number of litigations in Hong Kong, vested interests were totally at variance with the idea of free trade and opportunities for all, and as to being cheated by unscrupulous men, common sense should be used. Not satisfied, Belilios had more to say:

> A solicitor who comes as a clerk to a firm of solicitors comes on the recommendation of people of England who have probably known him from childhood. They have studied him, they have studied his character and recommended him to a firm of solicitors in the Colony. Consequently there is some safeguard in regard to him but it is quite different in a full-blown solicitor coming here and starting a practice within a fortnight of his arrival.

At the division, every member of the Council, except Belilios, voted in favour of the motion to delete the clause.

Ho Kai had definite views on certain political issues, for instance, he was for a representative assembly and against substantial military contributions. In the early years, under the governorship of Sir John Davis and Sir George Bonham, attempts had been made to grant some form of municipal autonomy to the residents. The instructions were from the Home Government but the local government was unable to carry them out successfully. The reason given was that the influential residents, including the Justices of the Peace did not wish for a representative municipal institution as a matter of constitution conviction. They had neither the time nor the inclination to assume the duties that were expected of them. With the nomination of unofficial members to the Legislative Council, there was no more talk of a municipal council. But some unofficial members pleaded in 1894 for free election of representatives of British nationality on the Legislative Council. The petition was signed by T. H. Whitehead, C. P. Chater, Thomas Jackson (who was the manager of the Hong Kong & Shanghai Banking Corporation) and Ho Kai. In the sitting on 14 December 1895, Whitehead asked the following question:

> Will the Government lay upon the table a copy of the correspondence which has passed between the Government and the home officials and between the latter

and the Colonial Government, concerning the petition from the ratepayers of
Hong Kong to the Commons in England praying for reform in the constitution
of the local Government, as well as copies of all communications on the subject
of the appointment of two unofficial members to the Executive Council and two
additional members of the Legislative Council?

The motive behind this question was that Whitehead had heard that
the Colonial Secretary, J. H. Stewart-Lockhart, openly boasted of having
squashed the petition by writing a long memorandum to the Secretary of
State. In the ensuing exchange of questions and answers, the Colonial Secretary denied the allegation. Whitehead further pointed out that in other
colonies such as Mauritius and Honduras, there was unofficial majority in
their legislative assemblies whereas the official members outnumbered the
unofficials in Hong Kong's Legislative Council. No reform resulted from
this petition. In 1896, the first unofficial member was appointed to the
Executive Council, this was C. P., later Sir Paul, Chater. The number of
unofficial members of the Legislative Council was increased in subsequent
years, but the officials remained in majority. It was on the Sanitary Board
after its reconstitution in 1887 that elected representatives sat eventually.

It was interesting to find that even in the early days the unofficial
members of the Legislative Council were unanimous in regarding Hong
Kong's contributions to the maintenance of the garrison as excessive. Ho
Kai participated in discussing an Appropriations Bill for the first time on 1
December 1890. The proposal by the Financial Secretary was to double the
sum to $233,572 for the year 1891. Chater took the view that it should
remain at £20,000 as in the previous year. Ho Kai supported him. When
the motion was put to vote, the unofficials lost by five to six. There was
another discussion on 7 May 1891, when Ryrie, Whitehead and Ho Kai
again protested. They said that the additional amount would affect a
proposed increase in salary for the Government Civil Service.

A bill which must be of particular interest to Ho Kai was that entitled
"An Ordinance to Prevent the Publications of Seditious Matter" which

was read for the first time on 26 August 1907. The second reading took place on 3 October 1907. As a known sympathizer and supporter of the revolutionary movement in China however, he had to sit through the proceedings in silence. Introducing the Bill, the Attorney-General said, "There has been an amount of seditious matter published in this Colony for some time past, which in the opinion of the Government may have the effect of inciting to crime in China, and the object of this Bill is to prevent Hong Kong being a place where seditious pamphlets may be printed and circulated with a view to distribution in China." He went on to say that the subject had created a great deal of criticism of the press in Hong Kong against the action of the Chinese government. He told the Council that he would move the elimination of some words in a particular clause, which read: "or to excite enmity between His Majesty's subjects and the Government of China, or between that Government and its subjects". The proposal was to delete "or between that Government and its subjects" so as to make it clear that there was no intention to interfere with affairs in China. The Attorney-General said that the two Chinese members (Ho Kai and Wei Yuk) suggested that it might be desirable to insert a short preamble to the Bill to explain its provisions and he had prepared one which had met with their approval. In seconding the motion, the Colonial Secretary said that for some years past the incontinence of the native press in the Colony towards the reigning dynasty in China had been a serious source of embarrassment. He gave the examples of some recent publications which he considered as "inciting persons to deliberate rebellion against the great and friendly empire which lies so close to our border". When another member suggested that the provisions should apply to Chinese papers only, Ho Kai made his one and only remark: "That is class legislation."

Finally, as unofficial members could introduce "private bills", usually for the purpose of incorporating charitable bodies or religious institutions, Ho Kai as a member of the local Christian Church was responsible for "The Bill for the Incorporation of the Senior Missionary in Hong Kong of the London Mission Society" and "Chinese Congregation Church Ordinance".

Ho Kai retired from the Legislative Council at the end of February 1914. The last sitting which he attended was on the 26th. The Chairman, Sir Henry May delivered a eulogy. "It is with much regret that I have to announce to you", he said, "that owing to indifferent health the Senior Unofficial Member, whose fourth term of appointment as a member of the Council expires on the 25th instant, has been compelled to intimate to me that he would not be prepared to accept an invitation to continue his services upon the Council." After referring to his period of twenty-four years as the longest in history except for Phineas Ryrie's of twenty-four and a half years, he continued.

> During that exceptionally long period, he has rendered extremely efficient service not only as a representative of the Chinese community but as an independent member of the Council. Gifted in a thorough knowledge of the feelings of his fellow countrymen, with a clear intellect, sound judgment and fluent command of the English language, he has always been of the greatest assistance in the deliberations and debates held in this chamber. Moreover, he has earned our admiration for the ungrudging manner in which, both inside and outside this Council, he has devoted his intellect and his energies to the advancement of the best interests of the Chinese community and for the good of the Colony as a whole. The 24 years during which he has served have been very busy ones. During them the population and the trade of the Colony have increased enormously, its boundaries have been enlarged, pestilence has necessitated stringent legislation to preserve the public health, unrest and disturbance in China have rendered necessary strong measures for the preservation of public peace and education has claimed special attention.

Following the eulogy, the Council passed the following resolution:

> This Council desires to record its heartfelt thanks to Sir Kai Ho Kai for the assistance which he has at all times ungrudgingly rendered in the work of the Council and its deep appreciation of the valuable services rendered by him to the Colony throughout the 24 years of his service as a member of the Legislature.

The resolution was seconded by H. E. Pollock, Q.C. In his reply, after thanking his colleagues for the sentiments they had expressed, Ho Kai said, "There is one thing, and one only, that I can claim for myself, and that is that I have always tried during the past period to do my best in the discharge of my public duties, and in no instance have I permitted my personal inclination or self-interest to interfere in the discharge of my public duties both inside and outside this Council."

The retirement of Ho Kai from the Legislative Council was the subject of an editorial in the *China Mail* on 27 February 1914. It said:

The approaching retirement of Sir Kai Ho Kai from participation in the work of the Legislative Council is a matter of much regret, particularly as it has been necessitated by failing health. Yesterday, His Excellency the Governor expressed, in most felicitous terms, the regret of himself personally and that of the Council on their loss. That regret, we feel sure, is felt by all interested in the welfare of the Colony. Sir Kai Ho Kai, as His Excellency pointed out, has been associated with the many and varied duties that fall to the lot of a member of the Council for the long period of 24 years which constitutes almost a record for an unofficial member. During those years Sir Kai Ho Kai has rendered the Council and the community valuable aid in many directions, and only those who actually participate in such work can fully realise what its conscientious fulfilment entails. To enumerate even the most important duties that Sir Kai Ho Kai has taken part in while a member of the Legislative Council would necessitate a very long albeit very interesting narration of most of the important events in the history of the Colony during a period covering nearly half a century — a period during which, as His Excellency stated, "the trade of the Colony has increased enormously ... and education has claimed special attention".

Through such transition the duties of Sir Kai Ho Kai particularly as a representative of the Chinese community, must have been very arduous, calling for uncommon ability, patience and tact. It is especially gratifying to know that on two occasions Sir Kai Ho Kai received signal acknowledgment from His Majesty the King of the appreciation of his services. Sir Kai Ho Kai and his colleagues in

Council afford an admirable illustration of the excellent qualities that have done so much towards building up the British Empire and all that has made and continues to make for its honour, its power and its success. All will hope that with more leisure Sir Kai Ho Kai's health will benefit and thus enable him to take some active part in our civic affairs, for the Colony can ill afford to lose one whose experience has been so extensive and who has been ever ready and willing to respond to the many calls made upon him.

That hope was not fulfilled, for only five months after this editorial was written, Ho Kai died.

Government and Administration of Hong Kong 1886–1914

⸻⸻⁊⁊⁊⸻⸻

In 1843, the Secretary of State, in consultation with Sir Henry Pottinger after the latter had taken up the post of governor, decided on the following principal administrative officers for the government of Hong Kong: Governor and Chief Superintendent of Trade, Colonial Secretary, Colonial Chaplain, Chief Justice, Attorney-General, Chief Magistrate, Colonial Treasurer, Surveyor-General and Harbour Master. They became heads of departments, with a small staff under them. A Colonial Surgeon was added to the establishment later. In 1844, the post of Registrar-General was created, and in 1845, the post of Superintendent of Police. Gradually, other officers were appointed, for instance, an Inspector of Schools in 1847, an Auditor-General in 1857, and a Postmaster-General in 1860. The government underwent further expansion as time went on. Parallel with the development of the administration was the constitution of the Legislative Council and the Executive Council which has been described in the previous chapter. The three most important officials were the Governor, the Colonial Secretary and the Registrar-General.

In such an administrative structure, the Governor was in fact the head of the government, being responsible for both external and internal affairs. Externally, he had to deal with diplomatic and trade problems between Hong Kong and China, indeed, the earlier Governors were concurrently Chief Superintendents of Trade until that post was abolished altogether. Internally, he had to formulate policies concerning all aspects of the administration, for example, finance, law and order, public health and sanitation, education, public works and land disposal. In all policy decisions, he had to give some indication as to how the natives should be treated, an important issue with not only social repercussions but economic consequences. It could be readily appreciated that the Governor's own outlook and philosophy could well influence the thinking of the government as a whole. Though he had to take advice and delegate, he was not just a mere figurehead. Eitel would probably not agree with the above assessment of the Governor's role. His was as follows:

> Each man begins the world afresh and the last man repeats the blunders of the first. However it is remarkable how little depended upon the character, wisdom and energy of any of these exalted individuals…. What makes and mars the fortunes of Hong Kong is not the wisdom or foolishness, the goodness or badness of its Governors. There is an indomitable vitality within and a Supreme Governor above this British Colony, and these powers irresistibly push on and control the evolution of Hong Kong until its destiny be fulfilled in accordance with a plan which is not of man's making.

If Eitel were to go on writing the history of Hong Kong up to the later periods he would have to withdraw these remarks.

A list of governors from 1843 to 1919 is given in Appendix I. Captain Charles Elliot, the man on the spot, was designated as administrator, not governor, in January 1841. In any case, he was recalled in August because Lord Palmerston did not approve of what he had done. Sir Henry Pottinger succeeded him as administrator until he was appointed governor in June 1843, thus becoming the first. He was an East India Company official and had been Chief Superintendent of Trade, so were two others who followed him, Sir John Davis and Sir John Bowring, both reputed to be brilliant linguists and sinologists. The rest were from the colonial service, having had experience as governor elsewhere. Ho Kai began his community service when he was appointed to the Sanitary Board in 1886. For nearly thirty years he was adviser to six governors, from Sir George Bowen to Sir Francis May, in his various capacities, particularly as a member of the

Legislative Council. The parts played by these six governors in the events which have been described in the previous chapters and related issues will now be discussed. Before Sir George Bowen, his predecessor Sir John Pope Hennessy will first be introduced for reasons which will be understood.

Sir John Pope Hennessy, Governor, 1877 to 1882

In Chapter II it was mentioned that when news of Ho Kai's success at the bar examination reached Hong Kong, Hennessy considered it as an event worthy of special mention at a Legislative Council meeting. The two probably never met, as Hennessy was about to depart or had departed when Ho Kai came back. Hennessy was the first Governor to appoint a Chinese to the Legislative Council, thus paving the way for Ho Kai to succeed his brother-in-law Ng Choy and Wong Shing in due course. Hennessy had been described as "brilliant, impatient, with left-wing ideas", and "having combined this idealism with great polemical skill which masked his administrative inefficiency and lack of common sense". In his previous posts in Borneo, the Bahamas and the Windward Islands, he had been noted for these characteristics as well as his tendency to side with the natives. In Hong Kong, he was accused of being too pro-Chinese by the European community, with which he was on bad terms. For allowing Chinese to be admitted into the Hong Kong Museum at other hours instead of restricting their entry in the morning only, he incurred the wrath of William Keswick, Jardine Matheson's taipan. Hennessy's point was that as ratepayers, the Chinese had paid for the building as well. Other examples of his concern for the Chinese were stopping the brandishment and public flogging of criminal offenders and the establishment of a home for girls and women, the Po Leung Kuk in 1878 (see Chapter IX). Some blame for the bad sanitary conditions in Hong Kong had been put on Hennessy, but it was during his governorship that Osbert Chadwick was sent out as adviser and investigator in response to the attacks and complaints by the Colonial Surgeon, Dr. Ayres, in his annual reports. Hennessy's grandson, James Pope

Hennessy, wrote a book entitled *Verandah* on the tempestuous life and career of this unusual colonial administrator.

Sir George Bowen, Governor, 1883–1885

Sir George Bowen arrived in Hong Kong in March 1883 and left in December 1885. He had been Governor of Mauritius. Although Ho Kai did not serve under him, Bowen should be included because he was responsible for the implementation of the recommendations of the Chadwick Report which was published in 1882 (Chapter VI). He adopted the constitution of the Sanitary Board to consist of three members, the Registrar-General, the Surveyor-General and the Colonial Surgeon. During his time the scheme to build the Tai Tam Reservoir to supply water to the island was started. It will be recalled that water supply was one of the concerns of the Chadwick Report. Bowen re-organized both the Executive and the Legislative Councils. As a result, Wong Shing was appointed to the latter in 1884, two years after the departure of Ng Choy. The Government Central School, which Ho Kai and Sun Yat-sen attended in 1870 and 1884 respectively was replaced by the Queen's College. Pleading ill-health, Bowen asked to retire and left after only two years and nine months in office, at the age of sixty-four. He was described by Endacott as "perhaps the last of the old type of governor" as the colonial service had started to recruit by examinations, and "having adopted in Hong Kong the attitude of an elder statesman (who) resented the guidance of the Colonial Office". Sayer wrote that he was "self-assured, robust, setting much store by the pomp and ceremonial government, reserving himself for the broad lines of administration".

Sir William Marsh, Acting Governor, December 1885 to March 1887 Major-General W. G. Cameron, Acting Governor, April 1887 to September 1887

After the departure of Sir George Bowen there was an interval of twenty-two months before the next governor arrived. For the first sixteen months, the government was administered by the Colonial Secretary, Sir William Marsh and for the next six months by the General Officer in Command, Major-General W. G. Cameron. It was during these two years that the Public Health Ordinance was hotly debated. Marsh was appointed Colonial Secretary in 1879. He had once before acted as Governor between 1882 and 1883 after Hennessy's departure and before Bowen's arrival. He was transferred from Mauritius to Hong Kong, two years after Hennessy assumed office. Apparently he found it difficult to work with Hennessy and once requested to be transferred elsewhere. Apart from his involvement with the Public Health Ordinance, he continued with the implementation of some of the recommendations of the Chadwick Report such as the laying of a sewage system in the city and the construction of the Tai Tam Reservoir Scheme. To relieve the congested state in the Chinese quarters in the city, he appointed a land committee to find more building sites for houses. Marsh would have been present at the opening of the Alice Memorial Hospital which took place on 16 February 1887. He retired in April and Cameron took over until September. Cameron approved the enlargement of the Sanitary Board to include four ex-officios and six un-officials but had to face Ho Kai's objections to other provisions of the Public Health Ordinance (Chapter VI). He would have been consulted on the preparation work of the establishment of the Hong Kong College of Medicine which was done during his six months in office.

Sir William Des Voeux, Governor, 1887–1891

Sir William Des Voeux took up his post as Governor in October 1887 and left in May 1891. He had been Governor of Fiji and Newfoundland. It would appear that Des Voeux was not well most of the time. Sayer described him as "physically frail", and said that he was "intimate, industrious and interested in the details of public affairs". Much of what has been written of the public health administration and the Public Health Ordinance in Chapter VI took place during his governorship. It could be said that Des Voeux was very interested in the Public Health Ordinance of 1887, but in the face of so much public opposition, he could not be faulted for not having taken a firmer stand on its original provisions. That it was enacted at all after its stormy passage in the Legislative Council spoke well for Des Voeux's chairmanship. According to Sayer, Des Voeux made smallpox vaccination compulsory for all Chinese children, after having made sure that there would be no opposition from the Chinese community. Sayer also recorded that when Osbert Chadwick returned to Hong Kong in 1890, he was appointed by Des Voeux as an unofficial member of the Executive Council for the duration of his stay, a most unusual appointment which undoubtedly reflected the Governor's concern and interest in sanitary matters and public health. It was Des Voeux who appointed Ho Kai to succeed Wong Shing in the Legislative Council in 1890. He is best remembered for the praya reclamation scheme, resulting in a main road along the water-front which was named after him. Ho Kai did not have any direct involvement in this development which was proposed by his colleague, Sir Paul Chater. Chater bought large areas of the reclaimed land and formed the Hong Kong Land Company; as its chairman he was the richest land-owner in Hong Kong, after Des Voeux Road became the golden mile of Hong Kong, its banking and business centre. When Des Voeux went on leave in February 1890, he was presented with an address from the European and Chinese communities, represented by their respective senior unofficial member of the Legislative Council. In his memoirs, *My Colonial Service*, Des Voeux quoted a few passages from Ho Kai's address, after describing Ho's career briefly.

Sir William Robinson, Governor, 1890–1898

Sir William Robinson succeeded in December 1890 and held office until January 1898. He had spent some years in the West Indias before he came to Hong Kong. In appearance, his resemblance to King Edward VIII was remarkable as can be seen from Figure 6 in which he appeared with members of the Legislative Council, including Ho Kai. In the year 1891 Hong Kong celebrated its Golden Jubilee. Three years later, bubonic plague hit Hong Kong. Robinson therefore was much involved in the campaign against the epidemic, and as Chairman of the Legislative Council, he presided over many amendments of the Public Health Ordinance of 1887 and the enactments of new legislation and regulations related to the fight against the disease. In 1895 resumption of the Tai Ping Shan district was carried out and by 1898 the place had been cleared and rebuilt. Further resumption of other overcrowded areas in which the Chinese lived was also successfully accomplished. His leadership did not impress Dr. Lowson, who in his diary, accused him of indecision and of not visiting hospitals "to run into some danger". It must have been a most difficult period to govern Hong Kong, not only because of the epidemic but its effect on the economy and the population. Before Hong Kong, Robinson was Governor of Bahamas. Sayer said that "his entry to Hong Kong was ill-starred indeed, for he came from a land flowing with milk and honey, but almost from the day of his arrival misfortune after misfortune assailed it with swift succession". He proved to be an able administrator as he weathered the storm well and stayed in office for fully six years, the longest tour of any governor thus far. While facing the demand for reform in the government, he dealt with the problem with great skill. He added more unofficial seats in the Legislative Council, and a second Chinese, Wei Yuk was appointed in addition to Ho Kai. He also appointed two unofficials to the Executive Council for the first time; J. J. Bell-Irving of Jardine, Matheson and Co., and C. P. Chater. For the Sanitary Board, he agreed to a plebiscite which decided on an unofficial majority, thus averting the formation of a municipal council. Robinson was the first Governor of Hong Kong to have to deal with the reformists and the revolutionaries who sought refuge in Hong Kong. He took the decision to banish Dr. Sun Yat-sen from Hong Kong for five years in 1895. Dr. Sun then went into exile and it was while he was visiting London that he was kidnapped by officials from the Chinese Legation and imprisoned in its premises in Portland Place. In 1898 Kang Youwei came to

Hong Kong following the unsuccessful coup d'etat known as the Wuxu Year Coup which ended the Hundred Days Reform (Chapter XI) and, contrary to the treatment given to Sun, was received as an official guest. This reflected on the mentality of the British government, for whereas Sun was a revolutionary opposing the Qing dynasty and therefore a criminal, Kang still professed allegiance to the throne and remained a loyal subject.

Sir Henry Blake, Governor, 1898–1903

The next Governor, Sir Henry Blake, spent five years in Hong Kong, from November 1898 to November 1903. He was even more concerned with Hong Kong–China relations than his predecessors. China was then a chaotic state following the Boxer Rebellion and the occupation of Beijing by allied troops. On his arrival he was immediately involved in all kinds of problems arising from the lease of the New Territories which took effect on 9 June 1898. Measures required to administer the sale of land alone must have taxed the energy of Blake fully. (For more about the New Territories, see Sir Francis May and Sir James Stewart-Lockhart.) Ho Kai found in Blake a sympathizer of the revolutionary movement. A story concerning the involvement of the two in a political intrigue will be told in Chapter XI. The plague epidemic was still raging in Hong Kong. By now the association between rats and plague was being suspected. The award of two cents for a rat was started in 1900, part of a genuine attempt to combat plague made by Blake. His other efforts included further re-organization and strengthening of the Sanitary Board and new legislation to deal with insanitary properties. Still there was a public demand for a commission of enquiry into the state of sanitation in Hong Kong. For the third time Osbert Chadwick visited Hong Kong in 1902, accompanied by Professor W. Simpson of the London School of Tropical Medicine and Hygiene. Their recommendations included making all houses rat-proof and bacteriological examination of all rats. Yet more legislation was therefore enacted to augment existing buildings ordinances. Malarial survey was also included in the mandate given to the two experts, as the association between the anopheles mosquito and malaria had already been discovered by then. During his term of office, Blake appointed the Inspector of Schools, the Registrar-General and Ho Kai to report on local education. As a result of their deliberations, Ho Kai's old school, Queen's College, was put under the Education Department. It was further decided to close its door to European children and open it only to Chinese boys who had to pass a test in their own language before they were permitted to enter. Consequently, the Kowloon English School for which Sir Robert Ho Tung bore the cost, was established in 1902 for European children.

Sir Matthew Nathan, Governor, 1904–1907

An unusually young governor with a different background succeeded Blake. Sir Matthew Nathan was only thirty-three years of age when he was appointed. He arrived in July 1904 and stayed until April 1907. He had been an officer in the Royal Engineers. Nathan's legacy in Hong Kong was not so much the road in Kowloon which was named after him but the Kowloon-Canton Railway which connected Hong Kong to Guangzhou and hence to other parts of China and the East. The railway project must have appealed to the "natural financier" and "keen student of commerce" as he was called by Sayer as well as the engineer in Nathan, who saw that better communication between Hong Kong and the mainland would be of immense commercial value. During his governorship, in 1906, a commission of enquiry into the administration of the Sanitary Department and the Building Authority was set up because their efforts to apply the new Public Health and Buildings Ordinance of 1903 were not popular and the plague epidemic continued to take its toll. The Commission reported in 1907 by which time Nathan was about to depart so the task of implementing the recommendations was left to his successor. In the continuous battle against plague, a bacteriological institute was established, where not only bacteriological examinations were carried out but vaccines against other infectious disease were produced. Nathan, on account of his youth, advanced further in his career after he left Hong Kong, ending his service as Governor of Queensland. Again quoting Sayer, "nor was Hong Kong unconscious of the loss when he left and retained for many years the memory of the wisdom and compassion of her youngest and only bachelor Governor".

Sir Frederick Lugard, Governor, 1807–1912

Sir Frederick Lugard, Governor from 1907 to 1912, came to Hong Kong from Northern Nigeria. To him Hong Kong was only a brief interlude in a career entirely spent in Africa. It was for his services there that he ended up as Lord Lugard. The Sanitary Commission's Report of 1906 awaited his arrival. His solutions to the problems concerning the Sanitary and the Public Works Departments have already been discussed in Chapter IX. A memorable event during Lugard's governorship was the ban imposed on opium-smoking in Hong Kong. In 1907, the British government agreed to reduce the export of opium from India while the Chinese government undertook to reduce the acreage of opium growth within her borders. In the circumstances, the Hong Kong government closed all public opium-smoking divans but private smokers were free to indulge in their habits. To make good for the loss in receipts from the opium farms, a modest customs and excise duty was imposed on spirits and liquor. The British government also helped with two annual grants of £9,000 and £12,000 each for 1910 and 1911. By this time China had become a republic and its President, Dr. Sun Yat-sen, licentiate of the Hong Kong College of Medicine, welcomed the measures taken to free China from the harm and misery caused to the country by the obnoxious substance. Lugard's name will always live with Hong Kong University which was called his "pet lamb" in the early days of its inception, it was also Ho Kai's for he had put in an enormous amount of work and energy into the project. The University was opened on 11 March 1912, only five days before Lugard's departure on the 16th. On his last day in the Legislative Council, Ho Kai spoke on the financial success which marked

Lugard's regime and his achievements in winning the respect and confidence of the Chinese community.

Sir Francis Henry May, Governor, 1912–1919

Sir Francis Henry May was the first cadet officer in the Hong Kong Civil Service to become Governor of Hong Kong. He held office from 1912 to 1919. The training of a cadet included language studies, posting as a district officer to learn the geography and customs of the people of the territory while acting as the local magistrate, and then various appointments in the administration. At the top of the promotion ladder, the former cadet might become the Colonial Secretary of Hong Kong or elsewhere or Governor of another colony. May came to Hong Kong in 1881. He made his mark as the Captain Superintendent of Police, in which post he served for ten years. He was member of the Sanitary Board, and earned a grudging approval from Dr. Lowson for his performance during the Plague Epidemic (Chapter VII). Lowson who had not a good word for anyone, wrote in his dairy that "May knew something but others did not but complained and made idiotic suggestions". In the take-over of the New Territories in 1888, May led a small force to occupy Tai Po but met with demonstrations and abuse from the villagers before he eventually raised the Union Jack in the district. In 1902 he was promoted to become Colonial Secretary. In 1911 he was transferred to Fiji Island as Governor but within a year he was recalled to take over from Lugard as Governor of Hong Kong. After the arrival ceremony, while he was carried uphill to Government House from the water front in a sedan chair, an assassin fired one shot at him which missed in full view of the crowds which lined the streets on the procession route. Later, it was found out that it was the act of a lunatic or fanatic without political implications. It was thought that someone might want to settle accounts with him for what he had done as Superintendent of Police in expelling corrupt elements from the urban force. He was the last Governor under whom Ho Kai had served, in fact, Ho Kai retired from the Legislative Council one and a half years after May took office.

Next in importance to the Governor was the Colonial Secretary, then as now the head of the civil service in charge of administration and the Governor's right-hand man. He would act as Governor when the incumbent went on leave or before the arrival of the appointee. The post could be a stepping stone to a governorship elsewhere.

As list of Colonial Secretaries from 1843 to 1912–26 appears in Appendix II. The first Ho Kai would have contact with should be Sir William Marsh (see above). The next was Frederick Stewart and further down the list Sir James Stewart-Lockhart.

Frederick Stewart, Colonial Secretary 1887–1889

A graduate of the Aberdeen University, he was appointed Headmaster of the Government Central School in 1862 at the early age of twenty-five. Ho Kai was in fact one of Stewart's pupils as he entered the School in 1870, but not Sun Yat Sen who entered in 1884 after Stewart left the post. Stewart became police magistrate in 1881 and Registrar-General in 1883, and was appointed Colonial Secretary in 1887. Two years later, he died in Hong Kong. A stained glass window was erected in St. John's Cathedral in his memory. It was probably in the establishment of the Hong Kong College of Medicine that Ho Kai came closest to Stewart, who was Colonial Secretary in 1887. Stewart's period as Registrar-General was when Ho Kai was on the Sanitary Board but he played no prominent part in the Public Health Ordinance debates. Had it not been for his untimely death, he would probably have gone further as he was only fifty-three.

Sir James Stewart-Lockhart, Colonial Secretary, 1895–1902

Sir James Stewart-Lockhart must have been a very good friend of Ho Kai's because, as we have seen in Chapter II, he wrote to one of his sons to enquire after the family after Ho Kai's death. He arrived in Hong Kong as a cadet in November 1879 and stayed for twenty-three years. He spent his first two years learning Chinese and Cantonese as required in Guangzhou, and passed his final examination in 1881. After minor postings, he be-came assistant Colonial Secretary in 1883 and in 1887 was promoted to be Registrar-General. As he was proficient in Cantonese, it was said that he was very friendly with the Chinese. His friendship with Ho Kai must have started at this stage as they worked together in many committees, for instance, the Sanitary Board, the Tung Wah and the Po Leung Kuk. As Registrar-General, his conduct during the Plague Epidemic received some scathing remarks from Dr. Lowson. An entry dated 24 May (1894) read as follows: "Lockhart angry because he could not get himself in the limelight. He was of no assistance with the Chinese who distrusted him as the British distrusted him. He was simply pushed aside by Francis and the rest. His spite therefore landed on Ayres and me." In 1895, he finally achieved his ambition of becoming Colonial Secretary. After the leasing of the New Territories in 1898, Stewart-Lockhart was appointed Special Commissioner to survey the place and establish an administration there. Finally, he was appointed as the first Civil Commissioner in Weihaiwei after it was acquired by Britain in the scramble for bases in North China by foreign powers in the aftermath of the Boxer Rebellion. He remained at the post for twenty years.

The subjects the colonial officials had to govern were Chinese, account-ing for over ninety-five per cent of the population. The impression given by the Chinese to the Europeans had been described by Dr. E. J. Eitel as follows:

As regards the general attitude of the Chinese community, it seems that in pro-portion as the leading Chinese residents learned, towards the end of this epoch (up to 1882), to understand the principles of British communal liberty, there

appeared among them a tendency to retire to their own shell, deliberately refus-
ing any identification with the European community. The persistent refusal to
adopt European costume or English ways of living, the uniform aversion to
participation in local politics, coupled with a deep-seated anxiety to keep on
good terms with Chinese Mandarindom even when it blockaded the port to
throttle their trade, the steady increase of Chinese joint-stock companies from
which foreign investors were jealously excluded, the readiness of secret combination to retaliate against unpopular government measures by a general strike —
all these symptoms of Chinese clannish exclusivism, natural enough in people
whose just liberties have for centuries been invaded by despotic rulers, clearly
indicate that on the Chinese side there is, as yet, no desire to see the chasm that
still separates Chinese and European life in this Colony bridged over.

Dr. Eitel a missionary of the London Missionary Society, was the author of
Europe in China, a history of the early years of Hong Kong. A noted Chinese
scholar, he held the post of Inspector of Schools in the government.

The importance of gaining the trust and confidence of the Chinese was
well realized by the Governors. The post of Registrar-General was created
by Sir John Davis as early as during the period 1844 to 1848. In order to
keep law and order, Davis wanted to have all residents, Europeans and
Chinese, registered so that they could be tracked down in case they committed criminal offences. Initially the move offended both communities.
The Registrar-General was given the task of looking after all matters
concerning the Chinese. The post was sometimes called "Protector of the
Chinese" translated into Chinese as 撫華道, which designation remained
unchanged until 1913 when it became Secretary for Chinese Affairs (華民
政務司). Sir Hercules Robinson (from 1859 to 1865) started the cadet
scheme to train European officials in the civil service by first making them
learn the language so that later as district officer, assistant registrar general
and registrar general, they could deal with the Chinese directly without a
language barrier. The scheme however lapsed for twelve years until it was
revived by Sir John Pope Hennessy, 1877–1882. Robinson was insistent

that the Chinese should be fully and correctly informed of the nature, purpose and details of every government measure affecting their interests. He created a translation office and published a Chinese version of the *Government Gazette*. On the other hand, he would like to be accurately informed of what the Chinese really wanted, needed and wished to say, hence the Registrar-General's post was an essential one.

The job was also not an easy one. To make it a success, the official should be able to make friends with the Chinese and understand their customs and mentality. A distinct advantage was therefore proficiency in the language, hence the training in the cadet scheme. He would have to work closely with the Chinese members of the Legislative Council and those of the various boards and committees, especially the chairmen of the Board of Directors of the Tung Wah Hospital. These people, Ho Kai included as we have seen, would jealously guard the Chinese way of life against any kind of interferences and changes, hence, tact and diplomacy were required to gain their co-operation.

Sir John Pope Hennessy, who appointed the first Chinese to the Legislative Council, upgraded the post of Registrar-General to be an official member of the Council in addition to the Colonial Secretary and other senior officials. The Registrar-General was already an ex-officio member of such important committees as the Tung Wah Hospital, the District Watchman, the Po Leung Kuk and the Chinese Public Dispensaries Committees. The District Watchmen were members of a vigilante which the Chinese organized to patrol their districts during Sir Richard MacDonnell's governorship, 1866–1872. As expected, this matter brought the Registrar-General into conflict with the Superintendent of Police as each claimed to be the logical choice to command such a force. The Police was very much under fire at that time and in the end, the special Chinese constables remained under the control of the Registrar-General. The work of the Tung Wah Hospital and the Po Leung Kuk has been described in previous chapters. The Chinese public dispensaries were opened in order to provide the Chinese with the services of doctors. Initially, the scheme was part of the campaign against plague and other infectious diseases but later it was extended as a general outpatients clinic service. The Registrar-General was also a member of the Sanitary Board, the vicissitude of which has been described in considerable detail in Chapter VI.

From the list of Registrar-Generals in Appendix III, we have already identified Dr. Frederick Stewart (from 1883 to 1887) and Sir James Stewart-Lockhart (from 1887 to 1895) who was both Registrar General and Colonial Secretary for some years. They both had distinguished themselves in the post before they were further promoted.

Essays on Reform and Revolutionary Activities

———∞∞∞———

The Opium War of 1839–41 first exposed the weakness of the Celestial Empire. It was followed by a series of debacles which led to the gradual decline and ultimate demise of the Qing dynasty. The Taiping Rebellion broke out in 1850, and lasted until 1864. The leader Hong Xiuquan 洪秀全 was born into a poor peasant Hakka family in Guangdong in 1814. He grew up to become a village teacher. Though he had the ambition to do better, he failed in the state examinations repeatedly. It was said that in 1837, he lapsed into an unconscious state which lasted for several days. During the episode he saw the vision of an old man who appeared to him as his father and the old man's son as his elder brother. After coming around, he re-read a religious pamphlet distributed by a Protestant mission. It then dawned on him that he was the son of God and the brother of Jesus Christ, chosen by God for a special mission which was to destroy the demons on earth and set up the Kingdom of God. This became his *raison d'être* for wanting to overthrow the Qing dynasty and establish a new regime. The rebellion began in 1850, spreading from Guangxi to Hunan and Hubei and down the Yangzi valley. After a siege, Nanjing was captured in 1853. Continuing their way northwards with the object of capturing Beijing, the rebels only got as far as south of Tianjin where their communication lines broke down. Thereafter, they settled down in the areas they occupied. In their administration, they introduced certain reforms, notably a land distribution scheme. Gradually, internal strife developed among their leaders and moral decay began at the top. But they were able to last for a few more years until 1864 when Nanjing was recaptured from them by government forces. The man responsible for finally suppressing the rebellion was Zeng Guofan 曾國藩.

While the Taiping Rebellion was raging in the north, two incidents occurred in the south. One was known as the "Arrow War" of 1856. The *Arrow* was a lorcha, a boat with a Western hull and Chinese sails lying off Guangzhou, owned by the Chinese but flying the British flag. On 6 October, she was boarded by the Chinese who imprisoned the crew on a charge of piracy. They were alleged to have hauled down the British flag. When the demand for the crew's release was not met, British gunboats bombarded the forts guarding the Bogue and occupied the Guangzhou factories. The other was the murder of a French missionary Father Chapdelaine, by bandits in Guangxi in February that same year, 1856. Despite protest by the French government, the Chinese did not take any action. As a result of these two incidents, the British sent Lord Elgin and the French Baron Gros as heads of missions to extract compensation and assurances from the Viceroy of Guangzhou, Ye Mingshen 葉名琛 (1807–59) who however stubbornly resisted. Not getting what they demanded, an Anglo-French force bombarded and occupied Guangzhou in 1857. They proceeded to the north and were joined by American and Russian forces. Finally in Tianjin a treaty was signed in 1858, giving the foreign powers more concessions and privileges. But in 1860 the Chinese reneged on the treaty terms. The allies again gathered together an expeditionary force which occupied Beijing. The treaty was then rectified.

In 1884 the Chinese and the French were involved in a border war in Indo-China, which ended in Annam as it was then called becoming a French protectorate. Then in 1894 the Sino-Japanese War was fought by land forces on Korean soil and naval forces off the mouth of the Yalü River. It ended in defeat for China. By the Treaty of Shimonoseki, Japan at first obtained Taiwan, the Liaodong Peninsula and other concessions. Subsequently, the Liaodong Peninsula was returned to China after Russia, Germany and France intervened. Given the right to construct the Manchurian Railway and other concessions in 1896, Russia extended its influence into Manchuria, and in the following year occupied Dairen. In 1898, Emperor Guangxu (r. 1875–1908) issued an edict to institute reform in the government. Then followed the period of the Hundred Days Reform which ended after a *coup d'etat*, known as the Wuxu Year Coup. When the Dowager Empress Cixi resumed power, she ordered the persecution and punishment of the reformists, thus bringing to an end the movement. The final act was the Boxer Rebellion in 1899. Beijing was once again occupied by foreign powers in 1900 following widespread burning and looting of missionary settlements and slaughtering of Chinese Christians by the Boxers. The Dowager Empress and the Emperor fled, leaving Li Hongzhang to deal with the foreigners. There was little hope that the dynasty could continue to exist after all these defeats and humiliations.

The Reform Movement was initiated during this difficult period by a number of capable administrators and brilliant intellectuals. Prominent among the earlier advocates were the following:

Gong Zizhen 龔自珍 (1792–1841), wrote two long articles in 1820, one enumerating the advantages of making Turkestan into a province and the other a plea for a law forbidding foreigners to trade at Guangzhou. In the second article he showed remarkable foresight by saying that China would sooner or later get into conflict with foreigners over trade. In many articles written later, he attacked the authorities for their lack of statesmanship and self-respect. He also wrote to Lin Zexu 林則徐 (more later) when the latter was sent to Guangzhou, advising him to restrain foreign trade there.

Wei Yuan 魏源 (1794–1856) was noted for his work on the geography of foreign nations under the title *An Illustrated Gazetteer of the Maritime Countries* (海國圖誌) which first appeared in 1844. In the preface, he wrote: "Why is this book written? The answer is, it is written to attack barbarians by using barbarians, and to learn the superior techniques of the barbarians in order to curb the barbarians."

Mandarins such as Zeng Guofan, Zuo Zongtang 左忠棠, Li Hongzhang and Zhang Zhidong 張之洞, became aware of the necessity to introduce reforms, having seen the armed might of the foreign powers, and faced their plenipotentiaries. They remained loyal to the Emperor but hoped that changes would be made in the government. They realized that China would not be able to continue to exist unless some Western technology was adopted to modernize its administration and armed forces. They bought firearms, built arsenals and warships, encouraged Western studies and initiated the policy of "officially supervised and merchant managed enterprise" (官督商辦) for the development of industrial and commercial projects. Zeng, Zuo and Li are such well-known figures in Chinese history that even a short summary of their careers would not be necessary while Zhang will be encountered later. Another mandarin was Lin Zexu (1785–1850), who having served in the civil service for some years, rose to be Governor-General of Hubei and Hunan in 1837. In 1838 he memorialized the throne on the subject of opium suppression, which he enforced in his provinces. He was then appointed Imperial Commissioner with plenipotentiary powers to examine the opium situation at Guangzhou and put an end to the evil. In 1839, having confiscated large consignments of opium, he had them destroyed. He was dismissed from office the next year after the Opium War started. He earned a place among the group as the first official to take action against drug abuse in the country, a curse which contributed to the chaotic state and eventually led to the downfall of the country.

In modern Chinese history, the title "reformists" is generally given to a number of intellectuals who produced new political thoughts during the last years of the Qing period. It was into this distinguished company that Ho Kai and Hu Liyuan 胡禮垣 (more later) were admitted by virtue of their essays on reform. Some of the better-known members of this galaxy of thinkers will be briefly introduced.

Feng Guifen 馮桂芬 (1809–74) was a scholar who saw military service in the Taiping Rebellion, assisting Li Hongzhang. He established schools in Shanghai for the study of Western languages and sciences. In 1861, he edited fifty essays in which he examined the social and economic problems of the time. These were published as *Straight Talks from Jiao-bin-lu* (校邠廬抗議).

Wang Tao 王韜 (1827–97) was the founder of modern journalism in China. He was the Chinese editor of the *Mission Press* which was published by the London Missionary Society in Shanghai from 1849 to 1856. In 1860, he helped the militia to defend Shanghai against the Taiping rebels but, because of his dissatisfaction with the government administration, he became sympathetic with their cause. After the rebellion was over, he faced arrest but with the help of the British Consul in Shanghai he managed to escape to Hong Kong in 1862. He became Dr. James Legge's collaborator, and in 1867 the two went to the United Kingdom where they stayed for more than two years. Back in Hong Kong, with the help of Wong Shing, Wang founded the *Hsun Huan Jih Pao* 循環日報 in 1873, the first Chinese-language newspaper published by the Chinese in Hong Kong.

Yung Wing 容閎 (1828–1912) became the first Chinese student to obtain a degree from an American University when he graduated from Yale in 1854. He could also have been the first Chinese solicitor in Hong Kong. After studying in the States, he went back to Guangzhou where he served as secretary to Dr. Peter Parker. He then moved to Hong Kong and became an interpreter in the Supreme Court. With a view to become a solicitor, he entered the law firm of Ambrose Parsons as an articled clerk to serve a three-year apprenticeship. However, legislation to allow locally trained Chinese lawyers to practise was opposed by the Law Society. To add insult to injury, Yung's application for naturalization was also refused. He then left Hong Kong in 1856 and returned to Shanghai to become an interpreter in the Chinese Maritime Customs Office. In the latter part of his career, he was sent abroad by Zeng Guofan to buy military machinery for the Jiangnan Arsenal. He was given the task of forming and administering the Chinese Education Mission to sponsor young students to study abroad. It started functioning in 1870, but was abolished in 1881. Yung wrote an autobiography *My Life in China and America* (西學東漸記).

Xue Fucheng 薛福成 (1839–94) won fame for his response to an imperial edict inviting constructive suggestions for improvement of national welfare issued in 1875. He made six suggestions on efficiency in administration and another ten on coastal defence. He joined Li Hongzhang later and in 1899 he was appointed Minister to England, France, Italy and Belgium.

Ma Jianzhong 馬建忠 (1845–1900) was also in the diplomatic service and another of Li Hongzhang's protégés, noted for his work in Korea in 1882. A Western scholar who could read several languages, he had pleaded the government to build railways, develop industry, mining and education.

Yen Fu 嚴復 (1839–94) entered the School of Navigation where he learnt English. He was sent to England in 1877 and graduated from the Greenwich Naval College. Unhappy in the Chinese navy after returning to China, he turned to writing and journalism. He translated works of Darwin, Spencer, Mill and Adam Smith into Chinese.

Zhang Qian 張謇 (1853–1926) was in the service of Li Hongzhang and later Yuan Shikai 袁世凱 whom he assisted in administering Korea. An advocate of saving the country by industrial development and education, he set up cotton spinning mills and the Jiang-Huai River Conservancy Company. In 1908, he inaugurated a provincial assembly in Hunan province, the first of its kind.

Tan Sitong 譚嗣同 (1865–98) read the translations of Western books, and was an admirer of Kang Youwei and Liang Qichao (see later). At first he was active in Hunan, but he was summoned to Beijing in 1898 during the Hundred Days Reform to take up a post as imperial secretary. After the Wuxu Year Coup, others fled but he remained. He was then arrested and executed, thus becoming one of the first martyrs of the Reform Movement.

Zheng Guanying 鄭觀應 (1841–1923) came from an educated family but chose a business career. He was the author of a well-known treatise on reform, *Warnings to the Seemingly Prosperous Age* (盛世危言) dated 1880. He advocated the creation of a cotton industry to check the draining of wealth. He obtained the support of Li Hongzhang and, having been granted a monopoly for ten years, established the Shanghai Weaving Bureau in 1890 which he managed with great success.

These intellectuals published their writings individually and, following the dictate of their common ideas and proposals, formed factions and founded movements with which they became identified. Some of them belonged to the Foreign Enterprise Faction (洋務派), promoting the Self-Strengthening Movement (自強運動). The reformists inaugurated the Society for Strengthening through Studying (強學會), among them were undoubtedly the two most brilliant of the intellectuals, Kang Youwei and Liang Qichao, who were also associated with the Royalist Party (保皇黨).

Both Kang and Liang were Cantonese, Liang being the younger and Kang's disciple, though their thoughts differed somewhat. Kang regarded Confucius as a political reformer, whose concepts should be re-assessed, adopted and put into practice for the purpose of making changes in the government. He also had visions of a utopia and a league of nations to deal with international conflicts. With a long memorial, he managed to influence Emperor Guangxu to issue the first Imperial Reform Decrees in 1898. After the *coup d'etat* which ended the Hundred Days Reform Kang was condemned to death and had to flee to Hong Kong and then to Japan. However, Kang's loyalty towards the monarchy and his view that Confucian teachings should remain the guiding principles for reform were not acceptable to Sun Yat-sen. In 1917, when the Republic was in its sixth year, Kang actually supported the short-lived restoration of the Manchu dynasty master-minded by Zhang Xun 張勳. He was arrested, pardoned and subsequently retired.

Liang was more progressive, though, like Kang, he was a royalist and against a revolution. His thoughts represented a transition between the old idea of introducing reform within the bounds of Confucian tradition or sanctioned by Confucian principles, and the new ideas of the revolution. Unlike Kang he did not adhere strictly to the teachings of Confucius but moved towards socialism, as he realized that it was not practical to borrow Western technology and keep Chinese thoughts and institutions. He advocated a limited form of monarchy and supported Emperor Guangxu's new constitution. He too had to escape to Japan after the *coup d'etat* in 1898. In the early years of the Republic from 1913–17, Liang held the ministries of Justice and Finance under Yuan Shikai, who became president of China in 1913, proclaimed himself Emperor of China in 1915 and died ignominiously in 1916.

One more person who played an important role in the Hundred Days Reform was Weng Tonghe 翁同龢 (1830–1904). He too could be regarded as a reformist. He was appointed as tutor to the young Emperor Guangxu in 1876, thus starting a long and intimate relationship for twenty years as guardian, teacher and adviser. It was terminated in 1896 by the Empress Cixi but Weng still kept in touch with the Emperor. It was he who helped the Emperor to decide on introducing the reform policy. When it failed, he was forced to retire by the conservatives.

After the defeat of the reformists the reform movement was supplanted by the revolutionary cause. Both the reformists and the revolutionaries had one purpose in mind, to introduce political reform and new policies in order to save the country and the situation in which it now became involved. There was one major difference in approach between the two factions. The reformists were content with a constitutional monarchy but the revolutionaries wanted to abolish the monarchy altogether and establish a republic. Following the development of a relationship between them, Ho Kai rendered active assistance to Sun Yat-sen and his cause.

It has already been pointed out that Sun Yat-sen was Ho Kai's student at the Hong Kong College of Medicine for the Chinese. When the College was opened in 1887, Sun was twenty-two and Ho Kai thirty. In his memoirs, Sun said,

> From 1885, i.e. from the time of our defeat in the war with France, I set before myself the object of the overthrow of the Ch'ing [Qing] dynasty and the establishment of a Chinese Republic in its ruins. At the very beginning I selected for my propaganda the College at which I was studying, regarding medical science as the kindly aunt and who would bring me out onto the high road of politics. In the Canton [Guangzhou] Medical School, I made friends with Chêng Shih-liang

[Zheng Shiliang 鄭士良] who had a very large circle of acquaintances amongst widely travelled people who knew China well. When I began talking of the revolution advocating its ideas, he gladly agreed with me, and declared that he would immediately enter a revolutionary party if I would agree to lead it. After staying a year in the school at Canton, I learned that an English Medical School with a wider programme than that of the Canton School had been opened in Hong Kong. Thereupon, attracted by the thought that I should have a wider field for my revolutionary propaganda, I went to Hong Kong to continue my education. For four years I gave up all my free time to the cause of revolutionary propaganda, travelling backward and forward between Hong Kong and Amoy. At that time I had scarcely any supporters, Ch'ên Shao-pai [Chan Siu-pak] 陳少白, Yu Shao-wan [You Shaowan] 尤少紈 or Yu Lieh [You Lie] 尤烈 and Yang Ho-ling [Yang Heling] 楊鶴齡 and one man in Shanghai Lu Hao-tung [Lu Haodong] 陸皓東. The others avoided me, as a rebel, as they would one stricken with plague.

The four friends Sun, Chen, You and Yang were indeed known as the "Four Bandits" (四大寇) among their contemporaries. It was quite clear that Sun regarded the revolution as his primary concern and used medicine as his front. As his teacher, Ho Kai was not involved in Sun's activities during the latter's student days. It so happened that he began writing his essays on reform at this point in time.

Initially, Ho Kai was a reformist in favour of a constitutional monarchy rather than a republic. This was quite evident from his writings. According to Lo Hsiang-lin, it was Sun Yat-sen who influenced both Ho Kai and Zheng Guanying, to give their support to the revolutionary cause when they realized that the reform movement had failed. At that time, Ho Kai had already published some of his essays but must have been rather disappointed with the complete lack of response by the government. Ho Kai actually became associated with Sun Yat-sen after Sun graduated from the College. In 1894, two years after his graduation, Sun formed his Association for the Regeneration of China (Xing Zhong Hui 興中會) in Honolulu. A branch was also set up in Hong Kong, situated in No. 13 Stanton Street. Though he was not a member, Ho Kai helped in drafting a declaration of the aims of the Association. A year later, in 1895, an uprising, the first of its kind, was staged in Guangzhou. Ho Kai took part in the planning of this ill-fated coup, which was led by Zheng Shiliang and Lu Haodong, with the object of securing Guangzhou as a base. The coup ended in disaster and the execution of Lu who thus became the first martyr of the revolutionary movement. After the dust had settled, Sun had to leave Hong Kong and spent the next few years in exile.

The following passage appears in Norton-Kyshe's *The History of the Laws and Courts of Hong Kong*.

> Dr. Ho Kai, barrister-at-law and member of the Legislative Council, left Hong Kong with the Chinese Minister (Wu T'ing-fang), it was understood, with the intention of taking up an important appointment at Shanghai under the Chinese Government, and on his departure he was presented with an address and a valuable plate by the Chinese community. Not long afterwards, however, he returned to the Colony and resumed private practice and his seat in the Legislative Council.

The year was 1897, the month was March, because in a preceding passage it was revealed that "Friday the 5th March was a red-letter day in Hong Kong for the Chinese community, owing to a banquet given by them to His Excellency Wu T'ing-fang, the newly appointed Chinese Minister to the United States, Spain and Peru." In his thesis, Jung-fang Tsai wrote that "in March 1897, Ho Kai took a government position in Shanghai, handling matters in connection with railway and banking, only to quit in less than two months ...". In view of this episode, the possibility that Ho Kai was thinking of giving up his career in Hong Kong at this stage and throwing in his lot with the Chinese government should be examined. This is a very reasonable supposition because he had by then clearly defined his political philosophy in his writings and identified himself as a reformist as well as a royalist. He would be prepared to serve in the Chinese government although he had severely criticized it, provided he was able to put his reform ideas into action and so long as the Emperor's rule prevailed. According to the Legislative Council Report of 1897, the first meeting for that year took place on 25 February, at which Ho Kai was present. The Council was then adjourned sine die, and the next meeting was held on 3 May, which Ho Kai attended. Though he had been away from Hong Kong during the interval he obviously did not resign from the Council. Evidently, in spite of the lavish send-off he did not burn his boats before his departure. It can therefore be deduced that his intention was at best to explore the situation in Shanghai and not to leave Hong Kong for good. Some confusion has now arisen concerning this period of absence from Hong Kong since new evidence has been found. In Chapter II, it has been quoted from Wei Yuk's letter to Sir Francis May that Ho Kai was in such financial difficulties in 1896 that he went to Shanghai to serve under Sheng Xuanhuai 盛宣懷 on the recommendation of Wu Tingfang. Which of the two years, 1896 or 1897 was the right one? Presumably Ho Kai could not have left Hong Kong twice in two consecutive years? And what was his intention, to obtain a post in the Chinese government service or earn some money in the employ of big business? In one respect the two versions concurred: his sojourn in the North lasted for only two months.

The giant shadow of Li Hongzhang now cast itself on Ho Kai's path. In 1899, Li was acting Governor-General of the two provinces, Guangdong and Guangxi. Knowing that Li was receptive to reform ideas, Sun Yat-sen had written him a long memorial in 1893 or 1894. Sun probably thought that Li, as Patron of the Medical College, would be interested in what a graduate had to say about the political situation. In 1900 the Boxer Rebellion reached a climax in the North. Li was summoned to return to Beijing as Governor-General of Zhili, which appointment meant that he had to deal with the rebels as well as the foreign expeditionary force. It was not clear whether it was Ho Kai's own idea or the revolutionary group's, but they decided to make approaches to Li. They wanted Li to stay in the South, declare the two provinces independent, and be the head of an autonomous administration, with the group assisting him. They thought that their cause

would quickly succeed if Li would come over to their side. Ho Kai became actively engaged in this match-making, in which he involved the
Governor of Hong Kong, Sir Henry Blake, with whom he was on friendly
terms. Blake who was in sympathy with the revolutionary movement, was
prepared to arrange a meeting between Li and the group when the former
passed through Hong Kong. In the event, Li came but the Secretary of
State for the Colonies ordered Blake not to interfere with his movements.
Sun Yat-sen was away, banished from Hong Kong for taking part in activities against a friendly power, with a price on his head offered by the Qing
government. A meeting between Li and Sun therefore never took place,
but it was possible that their deputies had made contacts through intermediaries. In any case Li left Hong Kong for the North, and so ended the
hopes of the revolutionaries that he might be persuaded to stay in the
South. As a sequel to this episode, when Blake's term as governor was
about to expire in 1903, Ho Kai led a petition to the Secretary of State for
the Colonies to have it extended. The move was not met with universal
approval or enthusiasm. Members of the European community were especially against it. They accused Ho Kai of trying to keep Blake in office for
the purpose of helping Sun Yat-sen to return to direct the revolution.

In 1900, the revolutionaries staged a second uprising in Huizhou 惠
州. The leaders were Zheng Shiliang and Shi Jianru 史堅如. It also did not
succeed. It is not known whether Ho Kai had taken part in the planning of
this second coup. During the next ten years Sun and the revolutionaries
were extremely active in both China and abroad. But Ho Kai did not figure
any more in the events which led to their ultimate success in overthrowing
the Manchu dynasty and establishing a republic on "Three People's
Principles" (三民主義), namely, nationalism (民族), democracy (民權) and
livelihood (民生). For all that he had done for the revolutionary cause
directly or indirectly, he was named an adviser to the government of the
Republic of China when it was proclaimed in 1911.

Ho Kai wrote a number of articles on current events, in some of which
he expressed his views on reform in support of the movement. In the

section on his life in *Biographies of Famous Chinese in Hong Kong* (香港華人名人史略), a list of articles and letters written by him was given as follows:

1. A Critique on China (中國之評論)
2. Sleeping and Awakening (睡與醒)
3. China's Foundation and Reform (中國之基礎與改革)
4. On Commissioner of Customs of Guangzhou Dr. Hart's Plans for Land Tax and the Army and Naval Forces (談廣州稅務司喀博士之中國地稅與陸海軍計劃書後)
5. A Critique on Kang Youwei's Political Views (康有為政見之評論)
6. A Criticism of Zhang Zhidong (張之洞之批評)
7. On Encouraging People to Study (勵學論)
8. On Those Responsible for Reforming China (改良中國之負責人論)
9. On the Progress of Reform in China (中國改革之進步論)

Besides, Ho Kai, with Wei Yuk as co-author, wrote "A Memorial Addressed to Lord Beresford on the Open Door Policy" (與英國巴勳爵討論門戶開放書), and using his *nom de plume* "Sinensis", published "An Open Letter to Mr. John Bull on the Situation" (與約翰先生討論拳匪之公開信) in the *China Mail*.

To give some of these articles which were written in English a wider circulation, Ho Kai's friend Hu Liyuan translated the articles on reform into Chinese and published them in the local Chinese newspapers. Eventually, after further editing Hu produced a pamphlet consisting of seven essays under the heading of *The True Meaning of the New Government* (新政真詮). The seven essays were given the following titles:

1. A Review of Zeng Jize's Article (dated 1887) (曾論書後)
2. Discourse on the New Government (dated 1894) (新政論議)
3. Foundation of the New Government (dated 1897) (新政始基)
4. Administration of the New Government (dated 1897) (新政安行)
5. A Review of Kang Youwei's Speech (dated 1898) (康説書後)
6. A Review of *Exhortation to Study* (dated 1898) (〈勸學篇〉書後)
7. Flexibility in the New Government (dated 1901) (新政變通)

Born in Hong Kong Hu Liyuan studied at the Government Central
School from 1862 to 1872. As the school was opened in 1862, Hu's name
actually appeared on page one of the register. It will be recalled that Ho Kai
was there from 1870 to 1872, thus the two were schoolmates for a period of
two years. It would appear that when Hu was in Class 1 he was selected to
teach the lower classes. The intention behind this arrangement was to train
some of the best boys as teachers by having them spend alternate weeks in
study and in teaching for two years. He was well versed in Chinese classics
and literature. After he left school, he became a merchant in the shipping
business, but he was also actively engaged in literary work. He edited a
Chinese-language newspaper and compiled a book entitled *A Comprehensive Book on English Law*. Between 1878 and 1881 two successive Chinese
envoys to the United States, Chen Lanbin 陳蘭彬 and Zheng Zaoru 鄭藻
如, had requested his services as a counsellor in their missions but Hu
declined to join the Chinese diplomatic service. However in 1885 he accepted the offer by a group of British businessmen to assist them in developing what was then known as British North Borneo. While in the South
Seas he was invited by the Sultan of Sulu to visit his territory. It was said
that the Sultan liked Hu so much that he wanted to retire in the latter's
favour but Hu refused. When the Sino-Japanese War broke out in 1894 Hu
happened to be in Japan. He was held in such high esteem by members of
the Chinese Community in Kobe that they elected him as the honorary
consul. In that capacity he organized the repatriation of the legation staff.
After the war was over he returned to Hong Kong. For three years from
1895 to 1898 he was engaged as a translator by the Literary Society (文學
會). Besides the political essays for which he was best known, he wrote
many articles and poems, all of which have now been included in *The Complete Works of Hu Yinan* (胡翼南全集), which was Hu Liyuan's other name.

The seven essays on reform were essentially the combined efforts of Ho
and Hu, originating from articles and letters written by Ho and conversa-
tions between the two. They were not merely the Chinese version of Ho's
writings translated by Hu. Hu was very much a collaborator because in

these essays he had added his own ideas freely besides expanding on Ho's. As a matter of fact, the two shared common ideas on reform, and their names could not be separated in any discussion on their essays. Being a classic scholar who had taken the state examination, Hu used elegant phraseology and prose, and quoted profusely from Confucius and Mencius. To translate these essays back into English would be a formidable, long and tedious task. It is sufficient to provide a summary of the main ideas and proposals in each.

I. A Review of Zeng Jize's Article

Zeng Jize 曾紀澤 (1839–90), the son of Zeng Guofan, was Minister to France and Great Britain between 1878 and 1885. He successfully concluded the Treaty of St. Petersburg in 1881 with Russia, under which Russia restored the territory of Yili in Xinjiang to China. This was regarded as a rare diplomatic triumph for China at a time when she was under great pressure from foreign powers. After returning to China, he served in the Tsungli Yamen which was China's Foreign Office, the Board of Revenue, the Board of Admiralty and the Tong Wen Guan before he died at the early age of fifty-two.

Under the heading "Marquis Tsêng [Zeng] on China" an article appeared in the *China Mail* on 8 February 1887. The introduction to the article reads as follows:

> A most remarkable article on China "The Sleep and the Awakening" will appear in the forthcoming number of the *Asiatic Quarterly Review* (London, T. Fisher-Union). Any review would not be half so satisfactory to our readers as a republication in extenso, for the phraseology alone is extraordinary. The Marquis has previously let us read his journal, written shortly after his arrival in Europe but that entirely sinks into oblivion besides his present contribution.

In the article, Marquis Zeng said that China had been considered as among nations about "to vanish after a more or less prolonged existence of impaired and ever-lessening activity". He quoted a diplomat as saying, in 1849, that "with a fair seeming of immunity from invasion, sedition, or revolt, leave is taken to regard this vast empire as surely, though it may be so slowly, decaying". Zeng argued that China was asleep but she was not about to die. He traced the trouble to the Treaty of Nanjing of 1842 which opened four more doors, Amoy, Fuzhou, Ningbo and Shanghai besides Guangzhou to foreigners, and mentioned other events which took place subsequently. In a reference to Li Hongzhang, Zeng said that a series of preparations had begun which would make it difficult to repeat the history of that eventful year 1860 (when the Summer Palace in Beijing was burned down and the Russians gained concessions in Manchuria).

He assured the foreign powers that the awakening of 300 million people to a consciousness of their strength would not be dangerous to them for the Chinese had never been an aggressive race. "China has none of that land-hungering so characteristic of other nations", he wrote, "and she is under no necessity of finding in other lands an outlet for a surplus population." He explained that those Chinese who had emigrated to other countries left because of the "poverty and ruin in which they were involved by the Taiping and Mohammedan rebellions rather than to the difficulty of subsistence under ordinary conditions." "What China wants", he continued, "is not emigration, but a proper organization for the equable distribution of the population."

He advocated the colonization of those immense outlying territories such as Manchuria, Mongolia and Chinese Turkestan, for both economic and military reasons. Another way to absorb any overflow of population in certain provinces would be the establishment of factories, the opening of mines and the introduction of railways. "But even had these reasons not existed, the outrageous treatment which Chinese subjects have received, and in some countries continue to receive, would have made the Imperial Government chary of encouraging their people to resort to lands where legislation seems only to be made a scourge for their special benefit, and where justice and international comity exist for everybody except the men of Han," Zeng commented.

He then explained that in spite of the defeats and humiliations, China would maintain friendly relationship with the Treaty Powers. "Though China may not have attained a position of perfect security", he said, "she is rapidly approaching it. Great efforts are being made to fortify her coast and create a strong and really efficient navy." He did not further discuss reforms that would be advisable to make in the internal administration of China but returned to the subject of the foreign policy. "It will be directed to extending and improving her relations with the Treaty Powers, to the amelioration of the conditions of her subjects residing in foreign parts, to the placing on a less equivocal footing the position of her feudatories, as regards the Suzerain power, to the revision of the treaties, in a sense more in accordance with the place which China holds as a great Asiatic Power."

The Marquis referred to arrangements for the government of her vassal states and said that she would exercise a more effective supervision and accept larger responsibility. "Henceforth, any hostile movements against these countries, or any interference with their affairs, will be viewed by Peking as a declaration, on the part of the Power committing it, of a desire to discontinue its friendly relations with the Chinese Government." In conclusion, Zeng wrote:

> It behoves China, and all the Asiatic countries in the same position, to sink the
> petty jealousies which divide the East from the West, by even more than the East
> is separated from the West, and combine in an attempt to have their foreign
> relations based on treaties rather than on recapitulations. In her efforts to elimi-
> nate from the treaties such articles as impede her development, and wound her
> just susceptibilities, without conferring on the other contracting parties any real
> advantages, China will surely and leisurely proceed to diplomatic action. The
> world is not so near its end that she need hurry, nor the circles of the sun so
> nearly done that she will not have time to play the role assigned her in the world
> of nations.

On 16 February 1887, a letter, signed by "Sinensis" and dated 12 February was published in the *China Mail*. Introducing the letter the Editor wrote:

The ably written article which has appeared under the above title ["China, the Sleep and the Awakening"] and which is attributed to the pen of Marquis Tsêng has attracted a vast amount of attention here and in Europe, and we need offer no apology for publishing the communication below in which the views of the former Chinese Minister to London are freely discussed. As may be gathered from the "nom de plume" the writer "Sinensis" is a Chinese gentleman who takes a deep interest in the welfare of the Great Empire in the service of which the noble Marquis is so conspicuous an official; and if the discussion here entered upon should lead the more advanced and more highly enlightened of China's sons — her men of light and leading — to reconsider or to modify their views as to the time road to progress of the Chinese Empire, the object of the writer will undoubtedly be accomplished.

"Sinensis" was none other than Ho Kai. He first asked a question: "Is the sleeper really awake?" After repeating the list of the recommendations made by Marquis Zeng, he queried whether China would succeed without more. He then gave his views.

None will dispute the vast resources of the Chinese Empire, nor is there anyone who doubts the unceasing industry and latent strength of her teeming millions. All the materials essential to the building of a mighty nation are there and in abundance. At the commencement, however, she requires some wise architects and the laying of a firm and lasting foundation. What that foundation is or ought to be one has not to go far to seek. It has been, and is, and ever shall be the true foundation of every truly great nation. It may be summed up in a sentence, viz., equitable rule and right government. China can never be what her many well-wishers fondly desire her to be unless she will first cast aside all her unjust dealings with her own children and learn to dispense justice with an impartial hand — to discountenance official corruption in every form and to secure the happiness and unity of her people by a just and liberal policy. In short, before undertaking anything else, she should look after the all-necessary reforms in her administration. She must not wait for another more convenient session, but begin at once "to set her house in order", even before "she feels she can rely on the bolts and bars she is applying to her doors".... After such considerations, is it strange that I should refuse to accept the signs which the Marquis gives us as indicative of the awakening of China. Until I see China earnestly at work pushing on her internal reforms, and thus striking at the roots of these evils that have beset her for ages, evil which has made her what she is — so weak, so unmanly — and which were the frequent and sole causes of her numerous humiliations — I shall not believe she is awake in spite of the improvements in her coastal defence, her army and her navy.

He then offered his own prescriptions to the patient. Firstly, he recommended changing the three methods of selecting officials, by literary examinations, by purchase and through military service. The examinations he regarded as entirely worthless as a test of ability and talent, while "the longest purse will win the day and the purse will become longer at the expense of the people and their ruination". Military service would seem more rational and just "were it not for the enormous mass of corruption that surrounds it".

Secondly, he said that while China needed a really efficient navy and strong fortifications along her coast, she was in greater need of competent hands to man her forts and attend to and fight her ships. He was aware that there was the Naval College at Fuzhou but he wondered whether the students were properly paid and treated fairly after they had been commissioned. He quoted the encounter between the Chinese and the French fleet at Fuzhou (in the Sino-French War of 1884) in which the former was sunk in half an hour.

Thirdly, he said his remarks on the navy applied equally to the army. "The Chinese make fine soldiers if properly disciplined and armed, and placed under brave leaders." After pleading for better treatment for the soldiers, he stressed the point that the internal administration of the army must first be reformed. As an example of what a properly led and administered Chinese Army could achieve, he mentioned the "Ever Victorious Army" under General Charles Gordon in the Taiping Rebellion.

Fourthly, on China's foreign policy, he said "[China] is bound down by treaties to do much that is incompatible with her rights and dignity as an independent sovereign state. I deeply sympathise with China in every wrong she has suffered, and I long with every true-hearted Chinese for the time to come when China will take her place among the foremost nations and her people be welcomed and esteemed everywhere." On the Marquis' reference to China's vassal states, he warned that it was not the wisest plan to accept any increased responsibility before China was ready for it.

Fifthly, he turned to what he considered the real weakness of China, her loose morality and evil habits, both social and political.

> What makes the several Foreign Powers insist upon the violation of the sovereign right of China to bring every foreign resident within her territory, except the various Ambassadors and their suites, under their law, and to try such offenders in their own courts and mete out punishment in their own way? The Marquis Tsêng would say that is because China has not a formidable army and navy, but I would rather suggest that it was owing to the distrust with which Europeans universally regard the Chinese system of law and especially its administration.

Finally, he asked a question: "Where is China to find all the funds to pay her increased armament, to work her mines, to run her railways and to establish and maintain her factories?" He advocated raising a loan among her own people. He said that every nation had a national debt but he was afraid that China might not possess the confidence of her people regarding money matters. The alternative would be to let private enterprise undertake the development of the various projects, but the government must give the assurance that there would be no injustice, underhand dealings and undue interference.

He ended his letter by paying tribute to the Marquis.

> Marquis Tsêng did a good service to his country by the publication of his able and masterly-written article in question. The only drawback is that he mistook the effort for the cause, while the cause itself was entirely lost sight of because it was

not looked for. The Marquis should have directed the wanderers to the fountainhead instead of to its various ramifications.

In the letter, Ho Kai quoted from the Chinese classics four times, including a long passage at the end. Quite remarkably, the *China Mail* printed these quotations in the original Chinese.

With this letter, Ho Kai began his advocacy for reform. This exchange, in English, was read with interest by the European community. Hu Liyuan translated Ho Kai's letter into Chinese and published it in a Chinese newspaper, the *Chinese Mail* (華字日報) on 11 May 1887. It attracted even wider attention. In fairness to the Marquis, he did say in his article that "it is not the object of this paper to indicate or shadow forth the reforms which it may be advisable to make in the general administration of China." He maintained that "the changes which may have to be made when China comes to set her house in order can only profitably be discussed when she feels she has thoroughly overhauled, and can rely on the bolts and bars she is now applying to her doors." This was the point quoted and taken up by Ho Kai in putting forward his argument that reform in the government must come before other changes.

This letter was subsequently transformed by Hu Liyuan into an essay entitled "A Review on Marquis Zeng's Article", which was longer than the original as the result of much elaboration and embellishment. It became the first in the series of "Essays on Reform" attributed to Ho Kai and Hu Liyuan.

II. Discourse on the New Government

This essay was based on a letter written by Ho Kai in English to Hu Liyuan in 1894, the year the Sino-Japanese War broke out, when Hu was in Japan. Both Ho Kai and Hu wrote introductions to this essay. Its main theme was to propose the retention after revision of seven existing administrative measures and the introduction of nine new ones.

The seven existing administrative measures to be retained after revision were:

1. To appoint candidates who passed a revised state examination which would include law and other subjects, to the government administrative service and to select them on merit and ability.

2. To review the salaries of government officials, with the object of offering them adequate pay so that they would not have to augment their income by accepting bribery.

3. To abolish the payment of contributions as a condition for obtaining an appointment, a promotion, or an honour or award, and instead put the emphasis on achievements and services.

4. To establish schools for the training of scientists, lawyers, doctors, engineers, mineralogists, agriculturists, etc., all of which being essential for the future development of the country.

5. To promote literary studies not only with the view to preparing candidates for the state examinations but training teachers for schools and academies.

6. To constitute prefectural, county and provincial councils, each consisting of sixty members to be elected from among the three ranks of scholars, i.e. *xiucai* 秀才 to the prefectural council, *juren* 舉人 to the county council and *jinshi* 進士 to the provincial council; all members to serve for three years, and all males over twenty years of age except those infirm and incapacitated would be eligible to vote.

7. To constitute a national assembly consisting of the provincial councillors meeting once a year in the capital under the chairmanship of the Prime Minister, thus opening up the government to the people.

In making these proposals the authority of the Emperor to enact laws, approve appointments and make constitutional changes was emphasized. The views of Ho Kai and Hu Liyuan were quite clearly in favour of reform under the monarchy rule in this and the other essays.

The nine new administrative measures to be introduced were:

1. To build a railway system to link up various parts of the country, allowing the use of private capital for its construction and development, in order to facilitate communications and the transportation of local products.

2. To build steamships to facilitate the export of goods; the government-owned China Merchants Steam Navigation Company (招商局) not being a success, private shipping companies to be given government assistance.

3. To encourage the use of private capital for the development of the country's natural resources in the fields of forestry, mining, agriculture, fishery and metallurgy.

4. To keep a census in every prefecture and a record of the personal details and addresses of all inhabitants, to require hotels and inns to keep records of all guests and to re-organize the police force by appointing inspectors to be in charge of companies of policemen and improving their crime-detection and communication methods.

5. To re-organize the government by establishing eight ministries, viz. commerce, education, finance, defence, justice, industry, interior and foreign affairs, under a prime minister, all answerable to the Emperor; the appointments of all cabinet posts, including the Prime Minister's, to be recommended by the provincial councillors.

6. To maintain a land force for the protection of the country's territories, with a strength of 300,000 soldiers in each province in peacetime, to be increased to 1,000,000 in wartime, all regulars and reserves to be properly trained in military academies.

7. To maintain a navy consisting of three fleets, designated as the southern, northern and eastern fleets, each with its own battleships, cruisers, destroyers, and torpedo-boats, under a well-organized command structure and led and manned by properly trained personnel.

8. To develop a fair rate-evaluation system for the collection of revenue in order to finance all new projects and also for the provision of certain services such as night-watch, fire-fighting, street-lighting and water-supply etc. to the people.

9.   To publish newspapers in every province, county and prefecture so as
      to disseminate information and news to the general public and to
      gather the views of the people.

III. Foundation of the New Government

In his introduction to this essay, dated 1897, Ho Kai said that some of their
recommendations in "Discourse on the New Government" had been accepted but not carried out. He gave the example of the rejection of foreign
capital for the development of certain projects such as railways, banks, mines
and heavy industry. Ho Kai thought that without the backing of foreign
capital the Chinese investors would not be interested and foreign powers
would again make territorial claims if they were not allowed to have a
share in financing these projects. He wanted Hu to write another essay but
the latter said that if the defeat at the hands of the Japanese in the Sino-
Japanese War could not rouse the government officials there was nothing
more to say. But after Hu returned from his travels, they had another
discussion, as a result of which this essay was written. In Hu's introduction, it was mentioned that Ho Kai made a trip to the North where he
stayed for less than two months because he was not used to the climate
and fell ill.

This essay's main theme was national finance. It began with a description of the shameful defeat of the Chinese forces in the Sino-Japanese War
three years ago and the peace terms which included the annexation of
Formosa and the payment of indemnities. The armed forces were criticized
for their poor performance and government officials for the inept handling
of the situation. The difficulty of finding the right kind of people to occupy
important government posts was, as in the two previous essays, again
stressed. A list of loans which China had borrowed from foreign banks was
given. With a total of over $500 million in silver currency already incurred,
China was to find another $100 million to pay the Japanese. Furthermore,
China had to pay interest on the loans, and if the debts were not paid in

the years to come the amount of accumulated interest would exceed the principal sum. China would not be able to solve her financial difficulties unless national expenditure was cut and such main sources of revenue as the railway service, the banks, the mines and the heavy industries could be developed. The unsatisfactory manner in which these sources of revenues were being administered or exploited was then discussed in detail.

Regarding the railway service, it was pointed out that the existing arrangement of government supervised merchant managed enterprise was a failure because of distrust and lack of co-operation between the two sides. The rejection of foreign investment was unrealistic; more than one foreign power could be invited so as to avoid any one claiming territorial rights or special privileges as a result of monopoly. Also, the Chinese investors would probably feel safer if the enterprise was also supported by foreign investment. To borrow money from foreign sources instead of inviting foreign capital to invest was not a good idea because the revenue would then have to be used for paying interest and the railway system itself mortgaged as a guarantee for repayment. The payment of a fixed percentage of the revenue irrespective of profit or loss as a condition for allowing private investors to run the railways was regarded as unfair.

On fiscal policy the chaotic tariff system was criticized. So was the land policy or the lack of one. The harmful effect of the imposition of an export duty on such products as tea was discussed. There was a reference to opium-smoking in which it was estimated that one or two dollars per year on every smoker would provide a very large amount of revenue, even though only a percentage of the 300 million population were addicts. This measure was regarded as meaningful from the point of view of discouraging opium-smoking and it would also result in more revenue than imposing an import tax on Western medicines and drugs. The low wages or earnings of the Chinese compared with the Americans, Austrians, British, French and Germans were discussed. It was said that a Chinese residing in Hong Kong could enjoy better living because of more working opportunities and higher wages. The method by which China floated its national loan was compared unfavourably with Japan's. On account of poor pay, government officials accepted bribes but would not part with their personal wealth to help the country to tide over its difficulties. After comparing the defence budgets of various countries, it was suggested that the number of soldiers in the armed forces should be reduced but their pay should be increased. From an article written by the British Consul in Shanghai, it was found that there was no surplus in China's national budget. Apart from figures published by the customs service which was run by a foreign staff, the government did not reveal its income and expenditure, in any case, the figures returned by the provincial authorities could not be trusted. For the purpose of increasing the amount of total revenue, a land tax, a salt tax, a tax on opium, a tax on local products carried by Chinese vessels and a revaluation of tariffs were proposed. New sources of revenue such as licence fees on barges, inns, shops, sedan-chairs etc. and stamp duties on title deeds, drafts, wills, legal documents etc. were mentioned. It was suggested that some revenue should be used to provide social services such as free education, assistance to destitutes including orphans and widows, free medical care, and free burial service, and to finance public works such as building roads and bridges, and installing street-lights and drains. It was further suggested that local Councils at various levels should be set up under the chairmanship of a government official with local dignitaries serving as members to be responsible for the collection of taxes and the administration of social services. A scheme for the re-organization of the finance ministry was described in detail. The ministry was to set up departments in the twenty-one provinces, each department to have a head and a deputy and an accountant and a deputy, these four to be responsible for submitting detailed accounts every quarter which would be published in the capital. This organization was to be applied to the countries and prefectures throughout the provinces as well. A national bank with provincial branches would handle all monetary transactions. The employment of foreigners in this reorganization was said to be necessary because there would not be sufficient Chinese officials with experience to fill all the vacancies.

IV. Administration of the New Government

This essay was written in 1897. In the introduction, Ho Kai wrote that China was not unwilling to introduce a new government but did not know how to proceed. The purpose of writing the essay was thus to discuss practical ways of administering the new government. After repeating the proposals in "Discourse on the New Government" to retain seven old measures and introduce nine new ones, the authors stressed that the new government should be a benevolent one. The example of the Japanese Royal Family whose members personally looked after the wounded soldiers in the Sino-Japanese War was quoted. Four cardinal rules were laid down: (1) to facilitate the course of justice (平理), (2) to be concerned with public feeling (近情), (3) to follow the principles of the law (順道), and (4) to apply clemency (公量).

The example of the British government was also quoted. Its home government was able to control its far-flung territories overseas such as Canada, Australia and India, while China's was unable to exercise its authority over its provinces. Great Britain spent a large amount of money on social assistance for which there was still no provision in China. Recommendations made in the earlier essays such as to impose new taxes, encourage private and foreign investment on public works projects, revise the fiscal policy and reorganize the administration of the finance ministry were repeated.

To run the new government efficiently, the following proposals were made:

(1) To departmentalize the administration by setting up ministries of defence, internal affairs, foreign affairs, finance, justice, education, etc. It was said that Russia and Japan selected some forty officials every year and sent them abroad for training. As a result, all their consuls and ministers were able to learn a foreign language and Western ideas. They also had good promotion prospects. But in China, the officials in charge of ministries and departments were ignorant of Western methods nor could they understand new ideas. It was suggested that while making changes in the

administration, care must be taken to ensure that the new and the old staff would not become opposing factions, unwilling to co-operate with each other.

(2) To reduce redundant civil and military staff so as not to waste public money. The Emperor's relationship with his ministers was discussed, and it was concluded that their loyalty could be guaranteed only if they were properly remunerated, and given promotion according to merit. The lack of co-ordination between the forces during the Sino-Japanese War was attributed to the lack of leadership and the appointment of the wrong people to the commanding posts.

(3) To train specialists for the government service by revising the state examination system and the academic curriculum, both being unsuitable and inadequate. It was suggested that besides literature other subjects should be introduced, especially the natural sciences as hitherto no candidate had any scientific training at all. It was pointed out that other countries offered scholarships with generous allowances whereas China would only pay its scholars a small salary. In any case, the number of scholars selected was far too small, only one out of a hundred candidates being successful. The need of China for specialists trained in, for example, astronomy, physics, medicine and law was emphasized. The appointment of foreign and foreign-trained teachers and the award of diplomas and licences to specialists were also suggested.

Having made these proposals, the author commented that they could only be carried out if people did not oppose the introduction of reform for various personal reasons, such as being members of parties or factions, supporters of separatist rule, and opponents to the principle of democracy and the freedom of the press. A long dissertation on the evil of corruption followed a list of benefits brought to China by foreigners, such as the establishment of schools, translation of books, provision of free medical service, relief of flood victims, care of orphans and handicapped and infirm persons, suppression of opium-smoking and binding of feet, their sense of fair-play and justice and their charity and sympathy.

V. A Review of Kang Youwei's Speech

Kang Youwei made a speech at a meeting of the Society for the Protection of the Country (保國會) in April 1898. This essay was written with the purpose of challenging Kang on some of the views he expressed. Hu Liyuan acknowledged that he was persuaded by Ho Kai to write it. Although Ho Kai's ideas were incorporated, his name did not appear as co-author in the original version when it was first published. Hu explained that as Kang indirectly attacked Ho in his speech, he wanted to avoid involving Ho in confronting Kang. In his speech, Kang lamented the decline of China in recent years, as a result of foreign invasion with loss of territories. He did not agree with people who urged co-operation with foreign powers in order to strengthen the administration. He thought that this could only result in further demands by foreign powers for more territories and special privileges. He gave a list of twenty instances of foreign powers obtaining such concessions which greatly weakened the strength and authority of the country. His support was for the self-strengthening movement initiated by a group of scholars and also for limited reform of the government. Kang made a scathing attack on people who looked up to foreigners, specifically the Chinese in Hong Kong where he said poor Englishmen could become a taipan yet the Chinese, even though they might be wealthy or holders of an official rank, would regard it as an honour to serve as their comprador. He pleaded that the Chinese themselves should save their country without foreign help and cited the example of Japan who became a power by introducing reform, using foreign technology but not foreign nationals.

Hu admonished Kang for his excessive pride and caution in his analysis of the present situation. He said that some people had not learned lessons in geography, mathematics and astronomy introduced by Matteo Ricci and Adam Schall and therefore did not realize that China was not the centre of the earth nor the biggest country in the world. He considered the action taken by military commanders to attack foreign forces who were superior in arms though often outnumbered in strength as foolish, and the wrong way to deal with foreign powers. Hu believed that the present situation was the result of mishandling of the initial contacts with foreign powers by government officials who were ignorant of the outside world and the importance of foreign trade. As the Chinese did not have the military strength to oppose foreign forces, the government should institute reform and abandon all anti-foreign thoughts and measures. Hu particularly eulogized General Charles Gordon, known in history as Chinese Gordon, for helping China with his sword against the Taiping rebels. He said that had a Chinese accomplished what Gordon did he would be inundated with honours and rewards but Gordon remained a soldier without even a title, and, much to Hu's sorrow, was killed by rebels in the Sudan. Zuo Zongtang and Zeng Guofan were mentioned by Hu as having received excessive treatment, and after lavishing Li Hongzhang with praises, Hu regretted that he was unable to succeed in saving the situation. He defended the British administration in Hong Kong by pointing out that instead of preparing students for the State Examination, schools were established to give them training in modern science and technology. He estimated that of about two thousand students, some ninety per cent were Chinese. Chinese had acted in posts occupied by the British, also, they had been appointed to the Legislative Council and as justices of the peace and members of the jury. Their standing was considerably higher than Kang thought. As a legislative councillor, a Chinese had almost the same power as the governor, and as a justice of the peace, he would have the same authority as a magistrate. The compradors filled the majority of such appointments, furthermore, they rendered other public services, such as providing medical care for the sick and relief for the destitute and victims of disasters. Hu further explained that the servile attitude of the Chinese towards the foreigners was simply a display of courtesy and good manners, which the foreigners reciprocated. He expressed his admiration for foreign officials of high standing who would take up farming or other humble pursuits after they retired and refuted Kang for mistaking them as being poor people occupying high positions. In conclusion, Hu indicated that he did not disagree with the Confucian and

Mencian conceptions of protecting, supporting and educating the common people but he thought that posterity should not be burdened with the harmful effects of such outdated thoughts.

VI. A Review of *Exhortation to Study*

Exhortation to Study was a collection of twenty-four essays written by Zhang Zhidong who was a no less powerful or eminent figure than Li Hongzhang in the last years of the Qing dynasty. After passing the State Examination with flying colours he started his colourful career holding junior positions in the provinces. Some ten years later, he was appointed a tutor in the Imperial Academy. Having been posted to the capital he became interested in national policies. In 1880, he wrote a memorial calling for repudiation of the Treaty of Ili, by which Russia was paid a large indemnity and given a wide tract of the territory. It was because of such opposition that Marquis Zeng Jize was made an envoy to re-negotiate the terms of the treaty with the Russians, a mission he performed successfully. In 1882, Zhang was made Governor of Shanxi, and two years later he became Governor-General of Guangdong and Guangxi provinces where he stayed for six years. During his governorship he reformed the tax collection system, built an arsenal and some warships, and opened a mint and a printing press. During the Sino-French War which ended in the annexation of Annam to France, he sent troops from his provinces to take part in the campaign. In 1889 he was appointed Governor-General of Hubei and Hunan provinces, and was succeeded by Li Hongzhang in Guangdong and Guangxi. He remained in that post for eighteen years. During his term of office, he introduced new measures into the administration of his territory such as constructing railroads, subsidizing industrial projects, building more schools and sending students abroad for further study. After the outbreak of the Sino-Japanese War, he was at one time temporarily posted to Nanjing. Although he himself advocated reform, he turned against the reformist after the *coup d'etat* in 1898 which brought the Dowager Empress back in power. In 1900 he discovered a plot to depose the Dowager Empress and restore Emperor Guangxu, and ordered the capture and execution of the leaders. During the Boxer Rebellion, he displayed his political adroitness by playing up to the two sides, protecting the foreigners on the one hand and remaining loyal to the Dowager Empress on the other. He ended his career as Grand Secretary and Grand Councillor in 1907 and died two years later.

After its publication in 1898, the *Exhortation to Study* was immediately adopted by some reformists as their manifesto. Even Emperor Guangxu was much impressed, as he ordered its distribution to all government officials. Zhang was credited with initiating a new line in political thinking: Chinese learning for substance, Western learning for function (中學為體，西學為用). He advocated a gradual and moderate approach to reform the government by educating the people. Though he was in favour of adopting occidental methods, his thinking was essentially based on Confucian and Mencian principles, emphasizing on the relationship between Emperor and minister, father and son, husband and wife, and the qualities of benevolence, righteousness, propriety, wisdom and faithfulness.

The twenty-four essays were assigned to two sections: internal and external. There were nine in the former and fifteen in the latter. The nine essays in the internal section were:

1. On Achieving a Common Purpose (同心)
2. On Inspiring Loyalty (教忠)
3. On Understanding Principles (明綱)
4. On Differentiating Kinds (知類)
5. On Believing in the Classics (忠經)
6. On Defending People's Rights (正權)
7. On Observing Orders (循序)
8. On Keeping Promises (守約)
9. On Eradicating Evils (去毒)

The subjects covered by the fifteen essays in the external section included:

1.   On Gaining Knowledge (益智)

2.   On Studying Abroad (游學)

3.   On Establishing Schools (設學)

4.   On Curriculum (學制)

5.   On Propagating Translation (廣繹)

6.   On Reading Newspapers (閱報)

7.   On Changing Laws (變法)

8.   On Changing the State Examination (變科舉)

9.   On Agriculture, Industry and Trade (農工商學)

10. On Soldiering (兵學)

11. On Mining (礦學)

12. On Railways (鐵路)

13. On Blending of Thoughts (會通)

14. Against Disarmament (非弭兵)

15. Against Persecution of Religion (非攻敎)

In his introduction to the review, Hu Liyuan wrote that he agreed with Zhang Zhidong's views but not his solutions. He proceeded to present his arguments against various points raised in all the essays, leaving "On Defending People's Rights" to the last as the main target. No doubt he was also expressing Ho Kai's views. Hu was as much a supporter of Confucian and Mencian principles as Zhang, and he thought that under the existing government reform could be carried out, but he found that some of the solutions proposed by Zhang were unacceptable because they were either not practical for China or not used by European nations.

In discussing "On Defending People's Rights", Hu made a strong plea for a constitutional monarchy with parliamentary rule. He enumerated the advantages of a parliamentary system which Zhang did not support and criticized in his original essay. In fact, Zhang went so far as to say that "the doctrine of people's rights will bring not a single benefit but a thousand evils" to China. In his analysis of the state of affairs in China, Hu wrote that even while the country was being pressurized by foreign powers,

government officials tampered with justice, the military commanders were
incompetent, there were not enough schools and little progress was being
made to develop commerce and industry. He attributed all these failures to
the fact that the people had no rights. He defined people's rights as the
principles and rules by which a country was administered along a middle
and equitable course. The rights of people were given to them together
with their life, and not devised by them to suit their purposes. Hence the
policy of a country should follow the will of the people and be determined
by representatives elected by the people. Hu pointed out that during the
Yao and Shun dynasties in ancient times people's rights were respected
though not to the same extent as at present in the European countries
where people could participate in administering the government through
parliamentary representation. The duties and responsibilities of members
of a parliament or assembly were to help and serve the people, by enacting
laws that would benefit them and removing those that would harm them.
Some of Zhang's main objections to parliamentary rule were singled out for
comment. For instance, Zhang said that the responsibilities were so heavy
that it would be difficult to find suitable candidates. Hu argued that members of a parliament were not expected to be knowledgeable in all fields but
only in some, thus, the responsibilities would be shared by all and not borne
by just a few. Zhang also thought that as the lower house was usually responsible for raising funds and the upper house for enacting legislation,
members of the lower house would have to be people with means. Hu
retorted by saying that any one could become a member, regardless of his
means, as he would be taxed at the same rate as everybody else and not
more. As in a previous essay, Hu objected to the policy of government
control of enterprises financed by private capital. He said that Chinese
merchants were renowned for their creditability. A better policy would be
to entrust them with the management of the affairs of the enterprises and
make them accountable to parliament. A parliamentarian system would
not weaken the authority of the government, instead, it would strengthen
it because the government would have the backing of the people. Zhang

considered it more realistic to establish more schools to educate the people, while Hu went further to say that a universal education programme should prepare the people not only to fill official appointments but as representatives to take part in parliamentary rule. As members had no specific authority or assignments such as overseeing arsenals and shipyards or purchasing ammunitions and commodities, Zhang regarded them as a handful of people who could not even put up a fight. But Hu insisted that government would have to rely on their efforts to supervise the financial aspects of all important projects as the main source of revenue was collected from the people they represented. He admitted the existence of malpractice in the electoral system in other countries, but thought it had done no great harm and could be prevented. Zhang also wrote that if people insisted on exercising their own rights, there would be no central authority, and the weaker elements would be subjected to the will of the stronger. He was afraid that when people got elected, they would only work for the advancement of their own purpose and interest. After refuting these views Hu concluded that Zhang was basically ignorant of the principle of parliamentary rule and his essay on People's Rights was the most harmful among the collection.

VII. Flexibility in the New Government

This essay was written in 1901 by Hu Liyuan after he decided to publish the other six in a pamphlet under the title *The True Meaning of the New Government*. It was meant to round off the series. In the introduction Hu wrote that some people had made some statements, seemingly in support of the reform movement. However, having done so they did not elaborate, instead, they went on to present negative arguments which they thought were more compelling. He wanted to convince these people by showing them that their pronouncements could be positively defended. He quoted from both Confucius and Mencius that there should be flexibility in politics, hence, he chose "Flexibility in the New Government" as the subject for his last essay. In it, Hu applied this principle to discuss five statements, each of which describing a situation or a fact, which might or might not be conducive to the success of the reform movement.

1. "The powerful nations in the world are at present competing with one another in their struggle for supremacy." The implication was that China would not be strong enough to offer armed resistance against invading forces. Hu contended that to gain time for strengthening her defences and putting her house in order China would have to parley and negotiate with foreign power. Hu considered the offering of concessions and leases as better alternative to cession in meeting territorial demands because such arrangements could be revoked once the country became strong again.

2. "The reason why foreign nations are powerful is because they are rich." China should follow the examples of Portugal and Spain in the past, and Great Britain and the United States in recent times, Hu stated, these being countries which became rich and powerful by trading with all other countries in the world. With its resource of materials and supply of products, China could gain entry into the international market but in the first place, farmers, industrialists and merchants must be given strong backing and the transportation system improved.

3. "Reform proposals in China cannot be carried out while she is being surrounded by foreign powers." Hu considered it the more reason for reform, but progress was hampered by stubborn and senile government officials occupying high positions. They ignored the views of the people and considered the country as their private concern. By their corrupt practices, they not only deceived the Emperor but created a gulf between the government and the people. The entire government administrative structure would have to be completely overhauled, and a new breed of government officials who had studied natural sciences and foreign languages recruited.

4. "China would be partitioned by foreign powers if she does not rouse herself." This was conceded but the government should regain the confidence of the people in order to have their co-operation in re-habilitating the country. It was suggested that the government should abolish some of its unfair and unpopular policies, such as excessively severe punishment of criminals, imposition of heavy export duty instead of import duty, the practice of favouritism and bribery, and disregard for public opinion.

5. "China is so weak and demoralized that there is no hope for her recovery." The people, not the Emperor or the government officials, were held responsible for this because so many of them were illiter-ate. The best remedy would be to establish more schools and instil more knowledge into the students by using textbooks translated into Chinese from foreign languages. A modern nation with a new-style administration and a new social order could thus emerge from a universal education programme.

Hu went on to analyse the situation in China and discuss the benefits of reform, by repeating most of the views and proposals he had already men-tioned in the preceding essays. This last one was of considerable length, written in Hu's characteristic classic prose, and profusely illustrated with quotations from the classics.

It is clear that at that time the essays on reform by Ho Kai and Hu Liyuan probably did make some impact and were widely read. But compared with the contributions of the other intellectuals in China, who occupied commanding positions or enjoyed wider reputations, they were of less sig-nificant value. For all the ink and paper used, not to mention the time consumed and the mental energy spent on these literary efforts, the results achieved were minimal. No great influence was exerted on either those in power or others similarly engaged in advocating reform. Research scholars, Dr. Jung-fai Tsai foremost among them, rightly concluded that with their background, Ho Kai and Hu Liyuan could not possibly make any significant impact. It should be remembered that even Sun Yat-sen could not maintain his position as provisional President for long after the establishment of the Republic because he was also a western-educated intellectual and a southerner.

On "Open Door Policy" and "The Situation"

In the year 1899, Ho Kai wrote an address and in 1900 an open letter. The address was on the "Open Door Policy". It was signed by Ho Kai and his colleague on the Legislative Council, Wei Yuk, and presented to Rear-Admiral Lord Beresford who was leading a trade mission to China. The open letter was published in the *China Mail*. Ho Kai signed himself as "Sinensis", as in his review of Marquis Zeng's article on "China: The Sleep and the Awakening". It was known as "An open letter to John Bull to discuss the situation". The situation was that which China was now facing as the allied troops were soon to relieve the siege of Beijing, and put an end to the Boxer Rebellion. A few days before Ho Kai's letter was published two editorials appeared in the *China Mail*, also discussing "the situation". It was conceivable that these two editorials were written by Thomas H. Reid who was editor of the *China Mail* from 1894 to 1905, but inspired by Ho Kai, who apparently enjoyed a special relationship with the paper.

When China concluded the Treaty of Nanjing with Great Britain in 1842, it was agreed that all nations should enjoy access to any of the ports open to trade in the Empire. After the Sino-Japanese War of 1894–1895, Russia, France and Germany created "Spheres of Influence" in various parts of China. In these spheres, the foreign powers enjoyed other kinds of privileges besides trading, such as capital investment in Chinese enterprises, setting up business firms and factories, stationing of troops and extra-territorial rights for their nationals. Great Britain also claimed the Yangzi Valley, and established a number of trading centres along the river on which ships flying the British flag freely sailed. In 1899, the American Secretary of State, John Milton Hay, asked Great Britain, Russia, Japan, France and Germany to agree that within their respective spheres, the interests of other nations would not be interfered with, the same tariffs to all merchandise would be applied, and the same duties and charges would be levied. This call for equal trading rights for all nations in China became known as the "Open Door Policy" and Hay as its author. The obvious difference between "Open Door Policy" and "Spheres of Influence" was that the former was concerned with free trading for all while the latter might lead to the breaking up of China into economic segments each dominated by a single power or the division of the country into colonies.

Charles William de la Poer Beresford (1846–1919), later first Baron Beresford, attained the rank of Rear-Admiral in the Royal Navy, but while serving on half-pay, he also pursued a career in politics as a member of parliament, which he first entered in 1874. He led a trade mission to China in 1898, on behalf of the Associated Chambers of Commerce. He subsequently wrote a Report and a book entitled *The Break-Up of China*. He was an advocate of the "Open-Door Policy". In the introduction in his book, he stated that "every effort has been made on the part of [the] Mission to promote friendly feeling and to prove that the policy of Great Britain as expressed in the 'Open Door' is not a selfish policy for the British Empire but one which must equally benefit the trade of all nations."

Admiral Beresford's tour started with his arrival in Hong Kong on 30 September 1898 and ended when he left Shanghai on 9 January 1899. He visited "places in China where British Communities resided and wherever there was a Chamber of Commerce, convened meetings, obtained the opinions of the members, and received a number of resolutions." But he also inspected armies, visited forts and arsenals and ships of the Chinese navy. He was received by Prince Jing (靖親王) and Li Hongzhang at the Tsungli Yamen and by viceroys of the provinces which he visited. He explained that "although the Mission I undertook was essentially commercial, I found that it was absolutely impossible to ignore the political issues."

When the Admiral arrived in Hong Kong on his way to China, he found that Kang Youwei was there and had an interview with him. Kang came under police protection, Beresford recorded, as he had a price of $10,000 on his head. He told Beresford that the object of the Reform Party was to introduce Western ideas in order to modernize the country, but keep China as an Empire by supporting the dynasty. Beresford paid another visit to Hong Kong before he left China. On this occasion, he attended a meeting of the Chinese Chamber of Commerce and received a number of resolutions on China trade. After his return to England, he further received an address from the Chinese merchants in Hong Kong, which was signed by Ho Kai and Wei Yuk and dated 20 January 1899. In it, the views of the Chinese community in Hong Kong, as represented by Ho and Wei, on the Open Door Policy and the political situation in China were expressed.

The address began with a discussion on some problems concerning British-born or naturalized Chinese. "It is nothing less than the dread of the Chinese Mandarins, and the total absence of protection from the British Government, that has hitherto kept the British-born or naturalized Chinese from taking openly any intelligent interest or active part in the political and commercial relationship between these two great nations. For some reasons or other the Consular Authorities representing the British Government in China have persistently refused recognition and protection to British subjects descended from the Chinese race who happened to be in Chinese territory, or travelling for commercial or social purposes, and they are left to the tender mercies of the Chinese officials who have thus golden opportunities for filling their pockets or paying off old scores." It went on to say that "there were some irksome and impracticable regulations which effectually block the claim of protection by the great majority, if not all, Chinese subjects. As an example we may mention the rule of distinctive dress, where it is provided that a British Chinese subject claiming British protection must cut off his queue and change his long-accustomed mode of dress". Ho Kai himself, it will be recalled, had long discarded his queue and turned to wearing European-styled attire.

The Open Door Policy was warmly acclaimed. "The policy of the 'Open Door', so ably enunciated and advocated by you, met with their [the Chinese in Hong Kong] cordial approval and support, as being the only means whereby Great Britain's commerce in China can be preserved and extended, the Chinese Empire kept intact and her trading and political relationships with foreign nations improved." However doubt was expressed if China could support or adhere to the policy. "She has no army or navy worth recognising as such. She is nearly rent asunder by internal dissensions and rival factions. Her officials are the most corrupt and notoriously incompetent; her revenue is ridiculously insufficient and already overcharged with payment of interest on foreign loans; her land is infested with rebellious bands and lawless mobs; her people are ignorant and full of prejudice and pride."

What then was the solution to the problem? "It is quite apparent that immediate reformation must be inaugurated. It is also clear that without external aid or pressure China is unable to effect her own regeneration. In this predicament we venture to think that England, having the predominant interest in China and being the country most looked up to and trusted by the Chinese, should come forward and furnish the assistance and apply the requisite pressure." Ho Kai's views in the essays on reform were repeated, namely that the two most urgent reforms were firstly, a system of adequate salaries to the officials, and secondly, a thorough overhaul of her system of collecting revenue, taxes and crown rents. "We recommend further that if China be unable or unwilling to undertake these absolutely necessary reforms, Great Britain, either single-handedly or in conjunction with some other Power, should render China substantial assistance, and, if need be, apply firm pressure on the central authorities in Beijing." The authors of the address then went on to describe in detail the defects in the two existing systems.

The concluding passages are worth quoting in full:

We think that there is a mighty force available for the British Government, a force which has been hitherto lying dormant and undeveloped — either willingly neglected or perhaps never dreamed of. That force is the unchallenged commercial acumen of the Chinese. By a proper system of organisation and greater encouragement to British subjects of Chinese parentage, they can be made an arm of strength to Great Britain commercially, and that proud position which she has held in China can yet be maintained despite the rivalry and underhand schemes of her enemies. We humbly suggest that Britain's Chinese subjects be sent to the interior to occupy every possible source of trade and to act as commercial scouts or living channels of communication to the different Chambers of Commerce. Well organised and instructed to make inquiries within their trade spheres or to penetrate further, if need be, into the interior or any special region, these intelligent merchants may perform wonders and help to maintain the commercial supremacy of Great Britain. It may be stated as an irrefutable fact that, wherever the goods may come from, whether Britain, Germany, France, America, or Japan, they ultimately reach the Chinese market through those Chinese merchants who know exactly what is needed and the best mode of supplying the people's wants. They act the necessary part of middle-men between the foreign merchants and the large mass of native consumers. They can visit places where Europeans would only arouse suspicion; they can extract information where foreigners would only close the natives' mouths. Where Chinese of the interior would willingly interchange views with British subjects of Chinese parentage and Chinese dress, foreigners would have to be content with vague and evasive answers given grudgingly and with circumspection.

With the support and good-will of these British subjects of Chinese parentage, with the removal of the likin (釐金) [transportation tax] barrier and other obnoxious Customs' regulations, British goods, assisted by superior carrying powers, can supply the Chinese market, and there would be such a ramification of British commercial interests in the whole Chinese Empire that China, in its entirety, would become a complete sphere of British influence, which, as Great Britain is a nation of free-traders, may be considered as synonymous with the "Open Door". We are hopeful of seeing the day when Great Britain will emerge from this commercial and political conflict with untarnished lustre and unsullied glory.

In conclusion, we beg to offer your Lordship our most sincere thanks and the thanks of all the enlightened Chinese for the personal interest and trouble you have taken in the Chinese question; for your lucid enunciation of the policy of the "Open Door", and for your strong support of the same, which, if maintained, would not only be beneficial to Great Britain and other nations, but would confer lasting benefit upon China herself; and, lastly, for your kind reception of this address, imperfect as it is. On your Lordship we place our implicit reliance, knowing as we do that you will champion the cause of commercial and political freedom and liberty with the most distinguished ability and success.

At that time, the Boxer Rebellion had burst upon the already chaotic scene. The slogan of the Boxers was "Protect the Qing dynasty, exterminate the foreigners" (扶清滅洋). With it they won not only popular support but tacit approval of the Imperial Court. In Chinese, they called themselves "Yi He Quan" (義和拳) or "Righteous and Harmonious Fists", signifying that they would unite to uphold the cause of righteousness by the use of force if necessary. They were called "Boxers" by foreign missionaries whose extermination was the target of their uprising. Fanned by patriotism, the Boxers resented the impact of foreign influence on China's economy and regarded the foreign missionaries as tools planted by the foreign powers in China to dominate her people. They were essentially members of a secret society, being mostly peasants. Unlike the Taiping rebels they had no united leadership. Though they considered themselves as militia men and were dressed in a uniform which distinguished them from regular soldiers, they had no military training. Loosely organized, they operated as units, in some instances attached to the regular army. Having convinced themselves that they possessed supernatural powers to resist bullets and cannon balls, the Boxers staged their uprising in Shandong province in 1898. At first they confined their activities to attacking Chinese converts and burning down churches. It was not until the last day of 1899 that they killed their first foreign missionary. The uprising soon spread across the northern provinces. The Imperial Court issued

ambiguously-worded edicts which in effect instructed the provincial officials not to oppose them but to stand aside. The climax of the uprising was
the siege of the Legation Quarter in Beijing which the Boxers reached by
the end of May 1900. The Allies assembled a force to relieve it. By August
it was clear that once again the capital would be occupied by foreign troops.
On the eleventh the Dowager Empress fled with the Emperor, and on the
fourteenth the Allied troops entered Beijing. Li Hongzhang was left
behind to negotiate with the Allied occupation powers. It was widely feared
that the foreign powers might even include the partition of China in their
terms. In the two editorials in the *China Mail* and Ho Kai's open letter the
overall situation was discussed. The physician now offered to prescribe
for the ailing patient. He did not advise surgery but advocated various
remedies under strict supervision and control.

On 1 August 1900, an editorial appeared in the *China Mail*. It read
strangely like one of the essays on reform. After recommending that the
Emperor should be reinstated or if he was dead an official of high rank
should be appointed as administrator of the government, the editorial continued as follows:

An Advisory Board formed of the foreign ministers or some other representatives
from each of the powers should sit at the capital to control the government.
Some system of local government could be relegated to the provinces in which
the viceroys would have control of the domestic legislation. The provinces should
be governed separately or in groups such as Kwangtung [Guangdong] and Kwangsi
[Guangxi] and Hunan and Hupei [Hubei], where for centuries the government
has been administered by one viceroy from each of the provinces. At the seats of
the different viceroyalties the senior councils of the foreign powers should form
a provincial or local board for supervision of the local government. At present
the local communities are governed by village elders and gentry to whom the
officials delegate a certain authority to deal with minor crimes. Under the proposed scheme the influence of these village councils would be enlarged and representatives would be nominated from the leading villages and centres to form

provincial assemblies under each viceroy to assist in the administration of the government The viceroy with his provincial assembly would have the control of the policing of the territory and the granting of mining and railway rights, the promotion of educational and other domestic legislation. But the collection of the taxes must not on any account be entrusted to the Chinese officials. Owing to the inherent custom of squeezing which is a recognised source of revenue among Chinese officials it would be difficult to formulate a Chinese collectorate entirely above suspicion.... Another collectorate similar to the imperial maritime customs should be formed to collect the taxes and the books of the collectorate would be open for inspection and other terms printed as is done in the case of the imperial maritime customs. Revenue from the taxes would be handed over to the different viceroys who would transmit a certain proportion to the capital for the expenses of the imperial government and retain so much for the expenses of the provincial government.... We propose that the provinces should also have a say in the imperial affairs of the Empire and this is to be achieved by direct representation. Besides the board of foreign advisers to sit at the capital, there should also be an assembly of people's representatives. The Chinese are not yet ripe for elective principles but ten to twenty members could be sent from each of the provinces to form what might be called a national assembly. This would be quite in consonance with former Chinese practice.... At first this would simply be an advisory board. It would not be wise to invest it with too much power at first but as the country advanced, to increase its control, otherwise they might come into loggerheads with the foreign advisory board. The supreme power would be vested in the central governor with his foreign dictators and their control would be somewhat similar to that held by the central authority of the United States at Washington. On the institution of this scheme of government many radical reforms would have to be instituted with regard to the salaries of the officials and other matters.

Only three days later, on 4 August another editorial appeared in the *China Mail*, giving support to the reform movement instead of the idea of dismemberment of the country. The editor advised that:

To strike at the very roots of the corrupt Chinese customs the whole system of the education must be thoroughly revolutionised.... The Government system of examination of candidates for civil appointments is from a practical point of view even worse than this system of education.... Another urgent reform that will have to be accomplished in establishing a strong government in China affects the salaries of the officials.

A few facts concerning the wretched pay of the Chinese officials mentioned in the memorial address by Ho Kai and Wei Yuk to Rear-Admiral Lord Charles Beresford were quoted. The editorial concluded with the following passage: "... The only chance for emancipation of the common hordes of China is by the reform of the system of government under the direction of the foreign powers and two of the principal measures that should occupy their attention is the payment of adequate salaries to the officials and the education and enlightenment of the people." Again this editorial could have been inspired by Ho Kai because it read like one of the essays on reform.

On 22 August 1900 "An Open Letter on the Situation" dated 21 August and signed by "Sinensis" appeared in China Mail. It was addressed to Mr. John Bull.

You have been duped and imposed upon by interested persons who have selfish needs to serve. You have been led to believe that the weak and generous policy on your part would result in a better understanding and relationship between Great Britain and China, and that international commerce and inter-course would be improved thereby. On the one hand you have been lured with promises and prospects of extensive increase of trade and on the other threatened with disturbance and ultimate destruction of existing business on celestial soil. You did not know that your meekness has been regarded by the Chinese government as weakness and that your generosity and forbearance as signs of timidity and cowardice. Hence of late years you have had a succession of mishaps culminating in the present crisis. You failed also to recognise that your trade with China could only be materially developed by increasing the prosperity and welfare of

the Chinese people which in turn depend upon the establishment of an enlightened government in the place of the present ignorant, corrupt and tyrannical
regime.

Do not, Mr. Bull, be misled again as to the cause of the present trouble. You
have been told I know, both officially and privately, that the whole affair was
directly or indirectly caused by foreign missionaries and their converts. This is
absolutely false and don't you believe it. Your missionaries, with very few ex-
ceptions, are good and worthy men, and, if left to themselves, will make many
more friends than enemies in China. But they have always been hated by the
Mandarins and their underlings, by the literati and expectant officials, for bringing to the people of China not only religion but also enlightenment and
civilisation, thus rendering them less amenable to the arbitrary and oppressive
policies of their superiors, and more difficult to be squeezed and fleeced by their
corrupt rulers. You must know that your missionaries do not simply preach the
gospel, but they do a great deal of educational work among the natives, many of
whom have doubtless derived from their foreign missionaries their first notion
of the principles underlying good government, the necessity for reform, the right
of personal liberty and of resisting unjust demands and impositions. All these
must be detestable to the official and literary classes. They saw that your missionaries, though innocently enough, had been undermining their influences, and
indirectly taught the masses to rebel against their authority.... Thus, for a long
time past, the mighty mandarins and literati have regarded the foreign missionaries as their deadly enemies, and have either covertly or openly stirred up the
ignorant populace against them. Sometimes by false reports and infernal lies,
other times by obscene and malicious writings, they worked upon the fear and
superstitions of the people, and incited them to exterminate or drive out the
missionaries. Frequently they aggravated the situation by publishing official proclamations which are couched in such ambiguous terms as to encourage instead of
deter the rioters or by sending soldiers with such secret instructions as to cause
them to assist in, rather than prevent the riotous proceedings. The present rising
of the so-called Boxers against missionaries and native Christians has been got
up and supported by the high mandarins to drive out the missionaries.... Read,

John, the numerous Imperial edicts which have been translated and published in the newspapers and see how some of them extol and encourage the Boxers …

It is alleged that they have from time to time interfered in the litigations and with the dispensation of justice between native Christians and their co-nationals. This is a serious charge, if true. But first of all show me a single yamen in the whole of China whose justice is dispensed equitably between the litigants without fear or favour. Is it not notorious and bribery? The biggest purse will always win the suit, The suitors are not allowed to get legal experts to represent them in their cases, and the mandarins can deal with the matters coming before them in any way they chose. Under these circumstances it is quite possible and even probable that some of the native converts who have suffered injustice did lay their cases and their complaints before their respective foreign spiritual advisers and request them to make representations directly or indirectly to the proper authorities for redress and justice. It is also quite conceivable that some good-natured and zealous missionaries, sympathising with them regarding their grievances, did make the appeals on their behalf, and perchance obtain justice too. This is not interfering with the dispensation of justice, but assisting in procuring it.…

How to deal with the present crisis will doubtless exercise your mind not a little. Of course you must capture not only Peking, but also the lawless band of mandarins and their confederates the leading Boxers. You must also have enough military forces in China to see that the various provincial authorities do keep the peace in their respective localities. After this you might think of the all-important and absorbing question; what to do with China and its 400,000,000 inhabitants? I take it that you are well agreed upon the principles so fearlessly propounded by your Under-Secretary for Foreign Affairs that China shall be for the Chinese, and there will be no partition of the Middle Kingdom by the Foreign Powers. The Indianising of China you will not have, but then you must not go to the other extreme to leave China severely alone and permit her to get along as before. Otherwise you will have a repetition of the present trouble at no distant date and may be something worse into the bargain. The present rotten and corrupt system of government must go and radical reforms should be introduced. It will not do after having vindicated your honour to make a hollow peace with the Chinese Government, exact an indemnity, sign a new treaty, have some more ports opened to trade, get more concessions, and then let the Manchu Government do as they like thereafter. Pray remember that Manchus are not Chinese, and it will only be fair to leave China for the Chinese and Manchuria for the Manchus. All the enlightened sons of China are earnestly looking to and praying Great Britain and United States of America for deliverance from the yoke of an oppressive and corrupt Government. If emancipated their gratitude to their deliverers will be lasting and boundless, but if they be left to the tender mercies of an unreformed and corrupt government as before, they will rise up to a man and do their utmost in gaining their just rights and liberty.

Some again may suggest to you that it would be better for you to leave the regeneration of the Chinese alone otherwise they may get to be so enlightened and powerful as to become a menace and a positive danger to the whole world. Don't you be frightened by this pure alarmist's suggestion for these reasons. Firstly, it will take centuries to make China a very powerful nation. Secondly, the Chinese are not a war-like and aggressive race, they are mostly composed of peaceful scholars, traders, agriculturists and they are generally contented with what they do. Thirdly, as the Chinese advance in wealth and strength other nations are not stationary and the relative position will be maintained centuries hence. Fourthly, Chinese of different provinces have their several distinctive characteristics and in the distant future they are more likely to separate into distinct states than to unite into an immense nation. Once more, Sir, it may be represented to you that the task of reforming China is tremendous and that it would be opposed by other foreign nations. To save trouble and possible complications with the European powers you will be urged to allow matters in China to drift on as before. Let me assure you most sincerely that the task of reforming China is not so great as you may imagine. China is about ripe for reformation and many of her intelligent and gifted sons are most enthusiastic over it. Their co-operation may be counted on and with it the labour will become easy and profitable. I very much doubt whether any foreign power would actively and openly oppose the much desired reformation seeing that the benefits resulting therefrom will be shared by all alike. But whatever may be the opposition I feel sure that if Great Britain and America led the way, Japan will fall in readily enough, and after all the Far Eastern Question will have to be settled mainly by these three powers conjointly as they are the most interested parties.

Lastly, as regards the sort of reform you should introduce into China and the form of Government you might establish, I regret that I have neither the time nor space here to touch upon them but I may refer you to the two leading articles published in the *China Mail* on the 1st and 4th of August 1900, respectively. In them you will find many suggestions for your consideration and adoption.

Some views expressed by Ho Kai in these two literary efforts were strangely naive and simplistic and some arguments were seriously flawed. Did he really think that by using this method of communication he could draw the attention of the parties to whom he addressed? Did he really expect "John Bull" and Li Hongzhang, both busily engaged in peace negotiations in Beijing in the aftermath of the Boxer Rebellion, would have time to read his letter? Let us consider a few points he raised. He suggested that Hong Kong Chinese should be posted to the Chinese government because of their knowledge of English. However, China had already started training young Chinese as diplomats by teaching them foreign languages at the Tong Wen Guan which was established in Beijing in 1862. The granting of consular protection to Chinese holders of British passports had never been considered by both the Chinese and the British governments because neither would set aside the issue of dual nationality. He pleaded that the foreign powers should bring their economic strength and military power to keep the "Open Door Policy". To save the "situation" his solution was that China should be governed by foreign powers after saying that China should not be carved up by them. He said, with probably in mind the work done by missionaries, that since China had benefited by contact with the West, therefore the survival of China could only be achieved by the direct participation of foreign powers in the government of China in ruling the country. All these suggestions could well be regarded as tantamount to high treason. It might as well that he published these two letters in a British colony. Had he done so in China he would have been arrested and executed. Even if he could manage to escape back to Hong Kong, he would have a price on his head like Sun Yat-sen. In any case, for making such suggestions Ho Kai earned the contempt of modern scholars who regarded him as an imperial capitalist or comprador ideologist and politician, thinking that the salvation of China could only be brought about by subjecting the country to not only western cultural influence but political and economic dominance as well.

Final Assessments

I n his lifetime and after his death, Sir Kai Ho Kai was lionized and eulogized as a leading spirit, a shining light and an excellent example of a native son who had succeeded in every way. For all that he had done for Hong Kong, he well deserved all the honours and tributes which he had received. Besides working for his own advancement he had laboured for others to improve their quality of life, spending more of his time and energy on public affairs than on his own practice as a barrister during his active life. There was the other part of him. Although his roots were deeply planted in a British colony, and he himself was thoroughly anglicized, he never forgot his Chinese origin. Undoubtedly motivated by patriotism, he considered it his duty, while watching the life-and-death struggle which was going on in China, to try to enlighten his compatriots with modern ideas of political reform and give the revolutionaries his active support. To pass judgment on him, it will be necessary to consider what impact his contributions and achievements had made on the local affairs in Hong Kong, and the reform movement and revolutionary cause in China.

In Chapter IX, it was pointed out that members of the Legislative Council were nominated by the Governor and not elected by the people and yet they were regarded as representatives of the community. In any case the people expected them to speak up, either in debates at the Council meetings or on other occasions when topical issues were discussed. In the process of enacting or amending legislation, unofficial members would have opportunities to speak on a wide range of topics whether supporting or opposing a motion before the Council. Because of the single official majority in the Council in Ho Kai's time, the defeat by only one vote of a motion could still be regarded as a protest or objection registered by all the unofficials. Another important function of the Legislative Council was to exercise control of the public purse through its finance committee. In the annual debate on the budget presented by the Financial Secretary as the appropriations bill, far-reaching as well as short-term proposals could be made. It would indeed be the duty of the unofficial members to present the views of the community on the effects of such proposals. The contacts of unofficial members with the official members, including the Governor himself, outside the Council chamber were just as important as matters could often be discussed and settled by this approach. It was well known to the Chinese community that when Sir John Pope Hennessy appointed the first Chinese, Ng Choy, to the Legislative Council, he met with opposition from the European community. Hennessy was the first Governor of Hong Kong who was distinctly in favour of having the Chinese to take part in both public life and the public service. If he had had his way, there would have been more Chinese in the forefront, advising on or administering the affairs of the Colony. Ng Choy, as has been recorded, served for only two years. After this precedence, other Governors obviously felt that it should be followed. Thus, Wong Shing was appointed by Sir George Bowen to succeed Ng Choy, and six years later, Ho Kai was appointed by Sir William Des Voeux to succeed Wong Shing. To these men's credit, they were no "yes-men" who would only put a rubber-stamp on all business transacted in the Council. As no other language but English was spoken, Chinese members would of course have to be Western-educated. But it was not essential that they should be in the legal profession in order to be able to read legislation and follow the proceedings of the Council. It so happened that both Ng Choy and Ho Kai were barristers, but Wong Shing who served in between the two was a businessman. They were all excellent choices.

Perhaps the first indication that Ho Kai was no "yes-man" was his opposition to the increase in the defence contributions which Hong Kong had to make towards maintaining the garrison. He sided with some other unofficials in a debate on this issue shortly after he joined the Council. One would have thought that the acquiescence by a new unofficial member would surely put him in a favourable light in the eyes of the Governor and the General, the two most influential men in the Colony. He was also soon involved in another sensitive issue, the clamour for a representative assembly in the Colony. However, the petition for elected representatives to sit on the Legislative Council and Executive Council presented by Ho Kai and three of his European colleagues to the Home Government was not allowed. Hong Kong was not to have even a municipal council but only a sanitary board on which a few elected representatives sat. Ho Kai could have kept away and taken no part if he had wanted to avoid controversy. A further example that he could be outspoken to the point of being courageous was his reference to police corruption in connection with the gambling bill which must have ruffled the feelings of some government officials.

As a representative of the Chinese community, it fell on Ho Kai's lot to look after their interests and protect them from any discrimination. His attitude towards the so-called four vices — prostitution, gambling, drinking and opium-smoking — could be easily understood from the speeches he made on bills concerning these issues. As a Chinese, he was apparently not opposed to concubinage because he agreed that the clause protecting girls under sixteen would interfere with the custom of the Chinese in choosing a concubine who might be under that age. But apart from this, he supported all measures to stamp out prostitution, and he was responsible to a very large extent for putting the business of the Po Leung Kuk in order, including finding it new premises. He stated that he was against gambling but he would not wish the government to use gambling laws to prevent the Chinese from enjoying their leisure hours in their private clubs. As a medical man, he was aware of the consequences of opium addiction but he was unable to do much as the opium trade was still a substantial source of revenue which the government would not like to have seen reduced, and opium-smoking was yet another Chinese custom. Ho Kai did not object to the imposition of a tax on liquor, his only worry was that the law could not be effectively enforced. In all these issues, Ho Kai's thinking was that of a member of the conservative Chinese society.

In others, Ho Kai had done his best to see that his fellow Chinese were treated fairly. His remarks on solitary confinement might at first give the impression that he was being harsh to deny prisoners more privacy and some comfort. But on reading his arguments carefully it was clear that he was speaking with deep knowledge of the psychology of his people. He considered that solitary confinement might turn out to be a luxury that would induce criminals to seek imprisonment, rather than a deterrent against crime. It must have been difficult for the local courts to administer justice sometimes in view of the proximity of Hong Kong with the mainland where criminals could easily find refuge, and the lack of co-operation from the mandarins on the magistrate courts in Guangzhou. On the other hand injustice was being done to the Chinese in Hong Kong as they could be summoned before local magistrates for questioning without regard to proper procedures. As a legal man, Ho Kai was able to give his expert advice in solving these problems. He was also aware of the difficulties experienced by the Chinese in settling legal matters, usually those concerning properties and land, particularly following the lease of the New Territories. He managed to persuade the government to make things easier for them.

The biggest test in Ho Kai's long years in public life was admittedly the Public Health Ordinance. As a member of the Sanitary Board, he raised his objections to the provisions of the draft bill. However, not yet being a member, he did not take part in the debate on its second reading in the Legislative Council. It might seem inconceivable that as a medical man he would not support the bill which aimed at improving the living conditions in the Chinese quarters by the introduction of certain health standards and sanitary measures. The provisions of the bill have been discussed in detail in Chapter VII. From the technical point of view, the objection to the incorporation of certain building standards in a public health ordinance instead of specifying them in a separate building ordinance was reasonable and valid. But why should there be any objections to the provisions for better ventilation, more living space, latrines, drains and sewers, which aimed at preventing overcrowding, ensuring proper disposal of night-soil and protecting the water supply? In his arguments, Ho Kai mentioned the difference between the European and Chinese constitutions. There were indeed differences in living and dietary habits between the two races. The Chinese were living in crowded and insanitary conditions, but even if they were not ignorant, they had no choice. They might not appreciate the nutritional value of milk and steak but even if they did they probably could not afford them. Under such circumstances, "the difference between the European and the Chinese constitutions" should be that the Chinese were the weaker of the two. Because of their poor resistance, they would be more susceptible to diseases such as tuberculosis. Coming from one who had received a Western education and who was a medical doctor, the statement: "hence arise the several provisions in this ordinance and bye-laws in question which I have no hesitation in characterising as wholly unnecessary" would seem to be very strange indeed. It was not logical for Ho Kai to argue that since the Chinese were quite content with the kind of houses they lived in and the surroundings around which these houses were built, they should be left alone. It would be far better from the point of view of public health to bring about improvements by building the Chinese-style houses with more living space, front- and backyards, separate kitchens and toilets, unless it was not an economically viable proposition to both the landlords and the tenants. It will be recalled that in his report, Chadwick already commented on the vested interests of the landlord, and so did the Colonial Surgeon in his annual report. In this respect, Ho Kai was more explicit and candid. He did not see why so much land should be sacrificed in order to improve the health and welfare of the Chinese. He thought that public confidence would be shaken if investors were unable to get the fullest benefit from the land they bought. Though he said he was not siding with the landlords and he was not defending vested interest, he argued that "the poor tenant would be forced to pay enormous rent for less space than before, plus all sorts of sanitary improvements which, however good in themselves from a European standpoint, they did not care for, and which they thought at least their constitutions did not require". Ho Kai would have done better if he did not insist that the Chinese did not care for improvements and that they did not require them because their constitution was different. Since there were economic reasons against using a piece of land to build a restricted number of houses according to the standards laid down in the draft bill, he could protect the interest of the landlords by making alternative proposals to the government to assist them. For instance, he could persuade the government to regulate land prices so that bidders could still make a reasonable profit even though the number of houses to be built was restricted. Or he could propose to the government to subsidize the landlords by bearing the cost of such additional works as stabilizing the hillside, forming the front- and back-yards and laying drains and sewers for the standardized houses. Even more generously, the government could give the landlords such encouragement as reduction or exemption of rates or property tax for a limited period of a few years. Or, the government could subsidize the tenants by assisting those who could not pay a reasonable rent to live in the standardized houses. But Ho Kai did not make any such proposals. In spite of what he said, the impression one gained after reading his arguments against the Public Health Ordinance was that he had been more concerned with protecting the interests of the landlords rather than, as expected of him as a medical man, promoting better health for the tenants.

It is entirely justifiable to link the filthy insanitary conditions in Hong Kong with the outbreak of the bubonic plague epidemic, but would it also be justifiable to say that the so-called drastic provisions in the original draft public health bill might have prevented its occurrence? This must be regarded as an imponderable for the case could never be proved. It is not really fair to lay the blame for the epidemic at the door of those who had opposed the bill. In any case, the Colonial Surgeon wrote that the bye-laws and regulations of the bill were not carried out properly. Bubonic plague was such a virulent disease that it would not be preventable once the epidemic reached Hong Kong. But it was nevertheless a great pity that it took the full force of the epidemic to make people realize that after all some sacrifices would have to be made. By then the economic loss suffered by the community was far worse, not to mention the heavy loss of lives.

The greatest debt which Hong Kong owes Ho Kai is undoubtedly his contribution to the provision of medical care and medical education at a time when both were lacking. In introducing Western medicine to the Chinese he proved himself to be a man of foresight and vision and an indefatigable worker. We had ample evidence that he followed and respected Chinese customs and habits, so we would not expect him to oppose traditional medicine especially as the alternative, medical care with Western medicine, was not available. But as a Western trained doctor he realized that an alternative must be provided for the people. Unfortunately there were no other Western doctors besides himself, and he was unable to build up a practice. The idea of building a hospital started by others soon obtained his full support. It was an entirely unselfish act as he had turned to practise law instead. After the hospital was completed, not being concerned with patient care, he continued to be responsible for the administration of its affairs. It was built by him as a monument to his wife but it was also a monument to himself. As soon as the idea of establishing a medical school was proposed, and it could only be possible because a hospital was available as its teaching hospital, Ho Kai became its most enthusiastic supporter. With characteristic energy, he helped in raising funds, drafting its constitution and forming its administration. After the school was opened, he joined its staff as a part-time teacher to give the students lectures on the relationship between medicine and law. He lived to see the next step in the development of medical education for the Chinese in Hong Kong, which was the establishment of a university with a faculty of medicine for the award of a degree. Again he was a prime-mover and much of the speedy and successful work in planning and organization was done by him. In the field of medical education, Ho Kai was thus an invaluable link in the chain of events which extended for more than two decades. The medical profession in Hong Kong should forever be indebted to Ho Kai for initiating medical education in Hong Kong and ultimately making it part of a university education.

Another contribution to medicine in Hong Kong for which he should also receive credit was the introduction of Western medicine into the Tung Wah Hospital. The appointment of a Western-trained doctor as its superintendent was a historic move of the greatest importance because it marked the first step towards making changes in that stronghold of traditional medicine. Ho Kai was a member of a committee which made the recommendation. With his concurrence and authority behind it, there could be no question of its acceptance by the Board of Directors who naturally looked up to him for advice and guidance.

Apart from the place he earned for himself in the history of Hong Kong, Ho Kai won another in the history of China together with his friend and collaborator, Hu Liyuan, on account of their essays on reform. It would seem rather presumptuous for the pair of them, residents in a British colony, one a lawyer and a physician, the other a merchant and a man of letters, neither having had any experience in government administration or training in political science and economics, to urge the Chinese government to reform, challenge the views of some of China's most prominent administrators and intellectuals, and make proposals based on their own thinking. There was no doubt that they were driven by their patriotism and sense of duty, but being no expert authorities on the subject matter, and in spite of the elegance of the prose-style and the profusion of quotations, did their essays on reform make any real impact at all? If the answer to the question was to be based on the number of proposals and ideas accepted or adopted by the Chinese government then it must be a resounding "No".

Ho Kai's first essay, after his review of Marquis Zeng's letter, was commented on in an editorial which appeared in the *China Mail* on 18 October 1895. The first half read as follows:

China is entering more and more definitely into the era of experimental reform movements, the inevitable outcome of her persistent degeneration crying aloud for amendment. Her condition of helpless misery of chronic disorder defying control, of Manchu despotism and legalised anarchy, of hopeless heartrending poverty among the masses and irredeemable rottenness among the classes, has been glossed over the centuries by the educated section of the Chinese, who found it conducive to their interest; but it has steadily grown worse, while at the same time there has been steadily growing a class of Chinese who have acquired more or less enlightenment through residence among foreigners, and have had their ideas of justice and right stifled by the pernicious influence of Chinese official life and the lying classical literature which supports it. Thus whereas formerly the only class that might have had education enough to see what was wrong and how to remedy it, was the class that lived on the miseries of the land, there are now more and more who know and have no advantage in suppressing their knowledge. Hence arises a healthy feeling in favour of the reforms, the need of which is so manifest to any intelligent and independent observer. This feeling, feeble and hesitating in its infancy cannot but grow until it attains some day strength enough to sweep away the colossal iniquities of the Chinese social and political fabric. Whether that day is near or still remote, the most experienced student of China would be puzzled to say; and it would equally baffle the ability of the cleverest to predict exactly by what means the reform will be effected. There are now several very different movements in progress tending to the same end. Early this year there was a great stir made over the publication of Dr. Ho Kai's reform pamphlet, the foundation stone of Chinese regeneration; and there were rumours of a violent upheaval to overthrow the Dynasty and establish a new constitution on Ho Kai's lines. That was one method of reform that seemed to promise well, but the promise shows no sign of fulfillment yet.

The personal friendship between Ho Kai and the editor of the *China Mail* was probably responsible for the gross exaggeration in the second last sentence and the seeming despair in the last. Nevertheless, in Hong Kong the essays did receive some attention from the editors of the local press, both Chinese and English.

But it would appear that no comments on Ho Kai's writings had been made by any of the reformists in China, apart from the contemptuous reference to Hong Kong Chinese by Kang Youwei. In the foreword, Ying Lianzhi 英斂之 (1867–1926), the editor of the Shanghai edition of *The True Meaning of the New Government*, wrote: "… if the [Chinese] government had accepted his suggestions, would China still be the same China to-day? This shows that he [Ho Kai] had not been properly treated. Should we say this is his misfortune or China's misfortune?" Ying founded the *Ta Kung Pao* 大公報 in Tianjin in 1916. Being a Catholic, he had worked to establish a Catholic university in China, but the Fu Jen University in Beijing did not come into being until 1925, a year before his death. His comments on the essays of reform might also be regarded as biased, for an editor entrusted with the task of editing some author's works could not but be complimentary, or in this case, flattering.

Historians and scholars, however, have not neglected the essays. In works on the history of political philosophy in modern China, the Reform Movement and the Revolution, the names of Ho Kai and Hu Liyuan have often been mentioned and their writings discussed. A number of papers have been published, and at least two doctor of philosophy theses have been written, on the subject. The ideas for reform put forward in the essays have been examined critically. Whether the comments are favourable or not, it has been emphasized that the background of the authors is the most important single determining factor. To some, the fact that they had both received a Western education and lived among foreigners in a capitalist society is the reason why their ideas were not acceptable and therefore of no value. For precisely the same reason, praise is given to them by others for their democratic and enlightened proposals which regrettably were not adopted. Some of these contradictory views expressed by various authorities will now be presented.

1.   Xiao Gongquan 蕭公權 in *History of Chinese Political Philosophy* (中國
     政治思想史) (1954):

> In their essays, although Ho and Hu often quoted from the Chinese
> classics, they aimed at applying Western democratic principles to intro-
> duce radical reform in the political system in China. Their views were
> basically different from those of Kang Youwei and Liang Qichao, both of
> whom were still adhering to absolute rule and classical concepts. Deeply
> impressed by the success of Western politics, education and culture, Ho
> and Hu braved criticism to proclaim that there was nothing to be learnt
> from the classics in their attempt to eradicate Confucian thoughts which
> Kang and Liang still harboured. They also refuted Zhang Zhidong's prin-
> ciple of "Chinese learning for substance, Western learning for function",
> pointing out that both substance and function were embodied in Western
> learning. Ho and Hu considered people's rights or democracy as the true
> foundation of a government but they also supported the monarchy. They
> proposed that China's political system should be changed to a system of
> representation with a constitutional monarch. They described in detail
> how members of a national assembly should be elected and how cabinet
> ministers and the prime minister should be chosen from among them, and
> suggested that members of the national assembly should have the auth-
> ority to dismiss cabinet ministers and the prime minister. These proposals
> were not practical and would be difficult to carry out. Two other proposals
> by them were worth mentioning, one was to divide the country into sep-
> arate administrative areas, and the other to give support to the keeping of
> international peace.

2.   Shi Jun 石俊 in *Lecture Notes on the History of Thoughts in Modern
     China* (中國近代思想史講授提綱) (1955):

> The reformists began to realize that the feudalistic rulers of the Manchu
> dynasty were collaborating with foreign capitalist aggressors, with the
> result that China was gradually losing its independence. Ho Kai, who had

received an education of the English capitalist class, wrote a review on
Zeng Jize's article. In it he disclosed that the reactionary groups of feudalistic warlords, land-owners and compradors were selling the rights of
China by raising foreign loans to build railways and open up mines. He
and Hu Liyuan considered the policy of "officially supervised and merchant managed enterprise" was a pretext made by the pro-Western faction
using the government's name to squeeze the merchants and common people
in order to profit themselves.

3.   Ren Jiyu 任繼愈 in "The Reform Thoughts of Ho Kai and Hu Liyuan"
       (何啟與胡禮垣的改良思想) (1958):

Same as other reformists, Ho Kai and Hu Liyuan were not thinking of
taking over the government but were hoping that the rulers would open
up the government to satisfy the demands of the people. They were one
step ahead of other reformists by bringing up the concept of "people's
rights" or democracy which was not even mentioned by the others. They
hoped that a more powerful government would then be able to protect the
financial interests of the capitalist class both within and without the country. They expressed their economic ideas on reform which were largely to
protect the interest of merchants and businessmen both in China and
overseas. Although democratic rule was exposed by the labour class in
Europe as reactionary, in the Orient, people like Ho and Hu who used the
slogan could be regarded as progressives. They were right in protesting
against feudalistic culture, such as the old classics and class distinction,
but they were still unable to discard imperialism altogether.

The final assessment by this author was as follows:

The thoughts of Ho Kai and Hu Liyuan reflected the interest of the overseas bourgeois at that time in making proposals on the political economy.
These were the same demands by the national bourgeois. They had
definite anti-imperialism sentiments, but they were afraid of imperialism,
hence they adopted a comprising attitude towards imperialism. They were

against feudalism, but because of the weakness of their class, they were unable to develop radical thoughts against feudalism. On account of the prejudice of the oppressing class, they could not see the strength of the peasants, instead, they adopted a contemptuous attitude towards the peasants. They were not demanding to take over from the ruling government, they only hoped for a partial opening up of the government to satisfy the demands of the national bourgeois.

They publicized the political system of Western capitalism, disclosed the rotten state of feudalism, exposed the reactionary faces of the pro-Western faction, protested against conservative feudalistic thoughts, and supported learning from the West. These thoughts, from the objective point of view, were in harmony with the "Hundred Days Reform" movement when they saw their hopes for reform vanished, they showed definite sympathy with the subsequent revolutionary movement.

4.   Onogawa Hidemi 小野川秀美 in "Ho Kai and Hu Liyuan's Discourse on the New Government" (何啟・胡禮垣の新政論議) (1958):

After summarizing the main proposals for reform in the essay, the author wrote that Ho Kai and Hu Liyuan appeared to have the inclination to speak and argue on behalf of the Hong Kong government. This was about the only remark the author made on the two. To substantiate it, he pointed out that the English version of the declaration of policy by the Xing Zhong Hui was written by the two of them in collaboration with two English news editors, Chesney Duncan and Thomas H. Reid. Also, when Chen Shaobai was sent to Hong Kong by Sun Yat-sen to start a newspaper for the Xing Zhong Hui, he first asked his old friends Ho Kai and Au Fung-chi 區鳳墀 to find out what was the attitude of the Hong Kong government officials towards the Chinese revolutionaries. The author explained that Ho Kai was not a member of the Xing Zhong Hui but he gave it support behind the scene. In their first essay, Ho and Hu showed that they were in agreement with Sun Yat-sen. They further expounded

their proposals in later essays, in which they criticized the ideas of
Kang Youwei and Zhang Zhidong.

5.   Watanabe Tetsuhiro 渡邊哲弘 in "Ho Qi and Hu Liyuan's Discourse
        on the New Government" (何啟‧胡禮垣の新政論議) (1961):

In this article, the author concluded that he did not agree with the
philosophy of Ho Kai and Hu Liyuan on reform. He wrote that Ho
and Hu gave the fundamental reason for China's weakness as the isolation of the emperor from the people and the opposing stands taken
by government officials and the people; they offered as a salvation
the promotion of trade and industry to eliminate foreign influence.
The author explained that this would lead to further difficulties. In
the capitalist state which governed China, the power of the officials
would have to be broken fast. One of the gravest harms done by the
government was to have negotiated foreign loans, which policy was
regarded as providing foreign powers with the motive for reducing
China to a half-colony status. Ho and Hu proposed to change this
into increasing the national debt and said that the key to the problem of strengthening the country was to adopt the policy of "officially
supervised and merchant managed enterprise". However, this policy
change still involved the co-operation and investment of foreign
capital. Under the circumstances, the foreign powers would achieve
the dual purpose of first the modernization of China and second the
suppression of Chinese capital. The end result would thus be the over-
taking and annexation of the basically weak Chinese commercial
capitalist class by all-powerful foreign capital. The author quoted that
in attacking foreign aggression, Kang Youwei expressed his patriotic
thoughts in his famous speech in which he said that the mistaken
views of the overseas Chinese Ho and Hu could not be given silent
consent. The proposal of merchant managed enterprise under government supervision still involved too much official participation to be
considered as free commercial enterprise. As to discussions on parliamentary constitution, Kang Youwei's aim was to reorganize the lower

echelon of government officials and using their departments as the nuclei for a new government structure, while Ho and Hu's attempt was to use the commercial capitalists to strengthen it and Zhang Zhidong advocated supporting its establishment on traditional lines. Ho and Hu not only attacked the formation of factions by government officials, they also criticized the trend of people of different philosophies to form parties. They therefore also turned their criticism towards the political-party system advocated by supporters of Sun Yat-sen but as their most horrifying thought was the possibility of an uprising staged by the peasants or anti-foreigners, they would nevertheless prefer to co-operate with the heavily capitalist-tinged Sun Yat-sen party.

6. Hu Bin 胡濱 in *Reform Philosophy in Modern China* (中國近代改良主義思想) (1964):

> Ho Kai and Hu Liyuan, from the standpoint of the overseas Chinese capitalist class, severely criticized the "self-strengthening" proposals for the government by Qing officials who were pro-Western. Based on their personal experience as permanent residents in Hong Kong, they earnestly expressed the hope that their mother country would become prosperous, but they were deeply disappointed that under Manchu rule, China was losing territories and becoming weakened. They pointed out with regret that though they lived elsewhere they would not like to see their mother country in such a sorry state. Stimulated by their patriotism, they expressed their dissatisfaction with the proposed measures for reform by the pro-Western Chinese officials. They maintained that the strength of a country could not be determined by its military power but by the support of its people, the loss of which was attributed by them as the cause of China's weakness. They opposed the government's policy of raising foreign loans to build railways and open up mines, the result, they said, would be infringement of the rights of the country. They also opposed the policy of "officially supervised and merchant managed enterprise" which they

regarded as a form of suppression imposed on private enterprise, there being always mutual distrust between government officials and private businessmen.

Disseminating Western capitalist class political theories, Ho and Hu said that the key to a democratic government was a system of representation. They severely criticized the absolute rule of the Qing dynasty, whose feudalistic system of government was responsible for China's weakness and poverty. Their thinking was therefore more advanced than that of Zheng Quanying and Chen Chi 陳熾. However, in aiming at overthrowing feudalism, they praised capitalism and exaggerated its strength. Their proposal to allow foreign powers to make investments instead of borrowing money from them would only encourage foreign powers to extend their influence in China, and result in putting China's economy under the protection of foreigners.

Though they deserved credit for refuting Zhang Zhidong's "three principles" and other outmoded ideas, still Ho and Hu declared their support for the monarchy. Their compromising attitude towards feudalism showed that they were incapable of radically eradicating ideas that were based on feudalistic culture.

7.   Li Ao 李敖 in *Sun Yat-sen and the Westernization of Medicine in China* (孫逸仙和中國西化醫學) (1968):

In a chapter on the Hong Kong College of Medicine, this author discussed Ho Kai whom he regarded as a frustrated Westernized essayist. In his assessment, Ho Kai's political essays contained some very advanced thinking at the time, but unfortunately it did not gain wide support or exert much influence. He pointed out that Ho Kai had influenced Kang Youwei by quoting the following passage which appeared in a footnote in an article by Lo Hsiang-lin entitled "The Influence of Sun Yat-sen's Revolutionary Views on Ho Kai and Zheng Guanying and Others" (國父革命主張對於何啟與鄭觀應等之影響).

> Ho Kai published "China the Sleep and the Awakening" in 1887.... Both
> Kang Youwei and Ho Kai were born in Xiqiao in Nanhai. Kang did not
> know English. His knowledge of Western learning was obtained from
> reading one or two recently published papers in Hong Kong and Shang-
> hai. His earliest essay, the "Ten-Thousand Word Proposal" (萬言策), in
> which he advocated reform, was written in 1888, after Ho Kai's essay.
> Undoubtedly, Kang had been influenced by Zheng Quanying, Ho Kai and
> others.

The author then wrote that:

> Unfortunately, circumstances did not grant Ho Kai the opportunity
> which Kang Youwei had of gaining access to the throne and advising the
> Emperor on policy matters. Ho Kai's principal area of activities was con-
> fined to Hong Kong, where at any rate he wrote his essays, taught medical
> jurisprudence and physiology, practised law and founded a hospital.

8. Chiu Ling-yeong 趙令揚 in *The Life and Thought of Sir Kai Ho Kai*
    (1968):

    In his thesis, after quoting the remarks made by Ying Lianzhi in his
    foreword to *The True Meaning of the New Government*, the author
    wrote: "If one accepts the implication of Ying Lien-chih's [Ying Lianzhi]
    foreword, one cannot deny that in the history of modern China, Ho
    Kai was a great but ultimately unsuccessful figure." He went on to say:

> There is no doubt that Ho Kai's reform proposals were timely and far-
> sighted. The achievement of Ho Kai lies not in his association with Dr.
> Sun Yat-sen or other contemporary reformers and revolutionaries, but in
> the new concepts he expressed in his writings.... No one would deny that
> the ideas of K'ang Yu-wei [Kang Youwei], Liang Ch'i-ch'ao [Liang Qichao]
> and Ho Kai had never been in complete accord, however, it must be pointed
> out that they were aiming at the same target, to build a new China.... If
> China had had more men like Ho Kai, his appearance would certainly
> have seemed less remarkable and his influence would not have been so

notable. It was indeed a great loss to China that Ho Kai was never able to give his services to his own country. But because of his background China was quite unwilling to accept those services.

9.   Jung-fang Tsai in "Comprador Ideologists in Modern China" (1975):
     In this thesis, the author called Ho Kai and Hu Liyuian "comprador ideologists". It has already been explained that a comprador was a Chinese manager of a foreign business concern in the treaty ports of China. He served as the middleman in the firms dealing with Chinese customers. But the word was used by the author to mean someone who collaborated with foreign imperialists in one way or another to serve his own interest and the imperialistic interest at the same time. It was also used as an adjective, hence, comprador politicians, comprador intellectuals and comprador reformists. According to the author, Ho and Hu thought in Confucian terms and their ideas were a synthesis of indigenous and alien elements. It was pointed out that they were not interested in forming a political party, but they were champions of private enterprise and their economic philosophy was related to class interests. The proposals they made concerning commercial and industrial development, tax and tariff reform, patent rights and a system of representation were not original as they had been put forward by others. In conclusion, the author considered Ho and Hu as spokesmen for the emerging capitalist class in China, expressing bourgeois demands and seeking political rights to safeguard the economic interests of their own class. Their reform thoughts were linked with comprador commercialism, the ultimate goal being the reorganization of the bureaucratic system with the commercial capitalist class as its cover, hence to protect their own interests.

10. Yü Weixiong 余偉雄 in *The Causes and Effect of the Wuxu Reform* (戊戌變法之原因及其影響) (1977):
     In a chapter on Ho Kai and his efforts, it was suggested that his idea of a constitutional monarchy for China, following the lead by

Wang Tao, had greatly influenced the political philosophy of the Hundred Days Reform. His writings were much admired by Ying Hua or Ying Lianzhi, who reviewed his *The True Meaning of the New Government* favourably. The comments by Yan Huiqing 顏惠慶 (1877–1950) in his biography were also quoted. Yan was a career diplomat, known as W. W. Yen, who had held ministerial and ambassadorial posts in both the Qing and the Republican governments. He considered Ho Kai's writings were important but had not attracted much attention. The conclusion of the author was that the ideas which generated in Hong Kong had had great effect on political philosophy in China and greatly influenced events in modern China, especially the adoption of foreign ways and the Coup of the Wuxu year.

11. Paul A. Cohen and John E. Schrecker in *Reform in Nineteenth Century China* (1977):

Ho Kai was among what the authors called "the new coastal reformers". "Although the new coastal reformers differed from each other in many ways", they wrote, "their biographies and careers reveal common patterns, including attendance at missionary schools, study and travel abroad, knowledge of foreign languages, conversion to Christianity, employment with foreigners, and involvement in new kinds of careers such as law, journalism and modern business." They continued:

> The new coastal reformers shared a common world outlook, one aspect of which was their cosmopolitanism. Although some were much more Westernised than others, all of them were on close familiar terms with Westerners and saw the West as having important contributions to make to China in both the institutional and technical realms. At the same time, they all retained commitments to Chinese culture or to the Chinese nation, the nature and depth of the commitment varying from individual to individual. A second feature of the outlook of the coastal reformers was their nationalism. The social gulf between Chinese and Westerners in the

littoral was great, and Chinese, even the most influential, seldom achieved full respectability in the eyes of the Westerners. The Westerners' sense of superiority was also reflected in their continual disparagement of Chinese culture and government. In the face of this assault, feelings of inferiority, shame and anger were easily aroused in Chinese living in the littoral, and nationalism for many of them provided new access to dignity and self-respect. Finally, the new coastal reformers shared a strong commitment to the development of Sino-Western commerce, partly for reasons of self-interest, partly because of the positive benefits that would accrue to Chinese society, and partly out of a spirit of economic nationalism.

The authors' final assessment was as follows:

> In terms of the overall process of change in nineteenth century China, the most important contribution of the coastal reformers lay in the realm of innovation. This is seen both in the activities they engaged in and in the reforms they advocated in their writings. The cultural environment of the littoral was ideally suited to encourage innovation. It furnished a whole range of positive stimuli, in the form of new ideas, new institutions, new practices, and new technologies. Equally important, the littoral was relatively free of the taboos and constraints which, in the hinterland, often served to discourage or inhibit production of the new.

They also explained that in the context of China as a whole, the coastal reformers worked under very real limitations; which were divided into two basic types: lack of political power and lack of social and cultural standing or legitimacy. Though some of the coastal reformers gained some status by working for people like Li Hongzhang and Zhang Zhidong, they had no power, and, frustrated in their efforts to introduce comprehensive reform, the best they could hope for was to serve as instruments of limited defensive modernization. As regards the lack of social standing and cultural legitimacy, there were two facets which seriously undermined whatever leverage the coastal reformers might have had for promoting change in the hinterland culture: collaboration and acculturation. Collaboration with Westerners could be regarded as a "sell-out", while the advantage of a greater exposure to Western-derived influences turned into a liability.

12. Jung-fang Tsai in "The Predicaments of the Comprador Ideologists" (1981):

In this other paper the author expounded on his concept of comprador ideologists (see 9). He compared Ho Kai with Kang Youwei. The reformists were willing to accept foreign help and Kang wished to collaborate with the British or the Japanese in the hope that after the suppression of the Boxer rising he himself could resume power and introduce reform. But the author contended that Kang could hardly approve Ho Kai's scheme for re-organizing the Chinese army under the British or the establishment of a government under the control of a foreign "advisory board". "The difference between Kang and the Hong Kong reformists lay in their social background", the author commented, "Kang and Liang were gentry who had received traditional Confucian education and passed civil service examinations. In contrast, Ho Kai and Hu Liyuan belonged to the western-orientated bourgeoisie which was economically tied to foreign capitalism. With such ties to Britain it was not surprising that they actually sought to collaborate with foreign powers, especially the British to regenerate China, even at the price of compromising the nation's sovereign rights".

13. Xu Zhengxiong 許政雄 in *The Variation and Development of the Civil Right Thinking in the Late Qing Period* (清末民權思想的發展與岐異) (1992):

The author's assessment was along the same line as Tsai's. He compared Ho Kai with Yan Fu 嚴復, after agreeing that Ho Kai was a comprador ideologist. He wrote that Yan was an intellectual among the government officials, a patriot who held the traditional belief that the "ordinary individual bears a responsibility for the rise and fall of his country" (天下興亡，匹夫有責). With this as the starting point, whether out of loyalty to the Emperor or nationalism, Yan regarded liberty and people's right as essential in saving the country. He was therefore sympathetic with the reformists' proposal to change the constitution but maintaining the monarchy. On the other hand, because of differences in conditions and circumstances, Ho Kai was neither an intellectual nor a Qing official. Having received a colonial education and under the influence of a foreign culture, he lacked the traditional value of a national Chinese. What he called people's right was viewed from a personal standpoint with emphasis on the profit to be gained by the individual in obtaining better competition and prospects. The author concluded that when the comprador ideologists realized that their ideas were unacceptable by the authorities and they were unable to exert any influence they then turned to others whose thoughts were somewhat similar and hence to Sun Yat-sen.

Not surprisingly, Ho Kai's ideas and proposals were not favourably reviewed by modern writers. The main themes of the reform movement were still concerned with support for neo-classical concepts, constitutional monarchy, private enterprise with the injection of foreign investments and parliamentary rule, all of which were unacceptable according to present-day ideology. In the Hundred Days Reform, measures such as pursuing Western studies, adopting Western military skill, abolition of the traditional way of conducting the state examination, establishment of schools, promulgation of a published budget of annual receipts and expenditures, abolition of sinecure posts, removing of ineffective officials, etc., could hardly have originated from Ho Kai's proposals as others had made the same. He should be content that he had joined a distinguished company, and been given the credit of having contributed to the reform movement and later the revolutionary cause. He and Hu made in fact a curious literary combination. He wrote in English, which would not have been understood by the Chinese, while Hu's Chinese prose-style was such that it was difficult and dull reading for posterity.

There is also another question to be considered. Apart from his essays on reform, did Ho Kai's other activities contribute in any way towards either the reform movement or the revolutionary cause? It was evident that Ho Kai's personal contacts with the well-known reformists of the day were minimal. Kang Youwei, for instance, had fled to Hong Kong after the Hundred Days Reform in 1898. The two could have got together, but by that time, Ho Kai was already helping the revolutionaries. In any case, it was said that Ho never had any faith in Kang's concepts and even predicted that Kang would fail. Ho Kai won an admirer in Ying Lianzhi, who, however, arrived rather late on the scene. Although he was a reformist to begin with, Ho Kai was actually much more active in helping the revolutionaries and their cause in general, and Sun Yat-sen in particular.

It would appear that Sun was sufficiently influenced by Ho Kai to entertain the idea of joining the reformist group at first. As an "outsider", meaning someone who was not holding any position in China and had received a Western rather than a traditional education, Sun realized that it would be difficult for him to get into the reformist movement. The same could of course be said about Ho Kai. Sun changed his tactics after he had made some unsuccessful approaches to the reformists with his letter to Li Hongzhang, and started fighting for his own cause. Ho Kai went over to his side. In his writings, Sun had acknowledged his intellectual debt to Ho Kai. This relationship between Sun and Ho and the part Ho played in the revolutionary cause had been critically reviewed by H. Z. Schiffrin in his work: *Sun Yat-sen and the Origins of the Chinese Revolution:*

> Without formally enrolling in the organisation, (Ho Kai) attended meetings of
> the high command and pledged his secret support. Ho's support, however surrep-
> titious, opened new vistas for the conspirators. Here was a man of wealth and
> standing in the British Colony, eminently qualified to provide the movement

with respectable standing when it shook off its conspiratorial cloak and emerged into public view. Once a foothold was secured in Hong Kong, the plotters would need a spokesman to present their case to the foreign powers, of which Great Britain was the most important. Who was better suited than Ho? Yet there was no reason to assume that Ho Kai would have been contented to remain behind the scene had a revolutionary plot succeeded in attaining its initial objectives and taken on larger dimensions. He was more than an influential sympathiser. Of all those connected with the Hsing Chung Hui [Xing Zhong Hui] at this time his was the only name linked to the political programme and it is hard to believe that he did not anticipate a hand in its realisation. For obvious reasons, he could not expose himself and at this stage he only took on the responsibility of drafting proclamations, etc.

In the event nothing seemed to have happened, in fact, Sun's relationship with Ho came to an end. Wrote Schiffrin:

> In retrospect, the Hong Kong based intrigues appeared to have been a watershed in Sun's career. This was the last occasion when Ho Kai would act as his spokesman. Sun had outgrown him. Ho for all his patriotism and interest in constitutional government, still bore the burden of a dual allegiance. Though many of his specific proposals soon found their way into Sun's political vocabulary, his active participation was limited to present a revolutionary case to foreigners whenever the occasion arose. He was essentially a conditional revolutionary who could not conceive an activism, except when supported by British gunboats.

Sun Yat-sen had apparently wanted to make use of such people as Ho Kai and Yung Wing as envoys to foreign countries after the republic was established. Sun, however, was never in command of the republican government after it was inaugurated in 1911. He did make an attempt to keep Ho Kai in touch with the new government. He told Hu Hanmin 胡漢民, Governor of Guangdong, to consult Ho Kai on foreign policy. Ho Kai however proposed that the provincial revenue should be deposited into the Hong Kong and Shanghai Bank for the purpose of safekeeping. Hu was unwilling to accept this arrangement and on the whole was unimpressed by Ho Kai's advice. Ho Kai made no further contribution and withdrew from the political scene thereafter because of ill-health.

What then was the reason why Ho Kai could not succeed if he had wanted a role in the new government? "By background and training", wrote Schiffrin, "these men were eminently fitted for leadership roles in this difficult transitional period in Chinese history, yet their influence was limited by their conflicted loyalties. A Western-educated non-literatus like Sun could respect Ho Kai but modern intellectuals of literati antecedents demanded a more definite enunciation of national aim. Nor could Ho find it easy to work for the Mandarins in China." History could therefore only regard Ho Kai as having at one time been Sun Yat-sen's eminence gris.

Postscript: Hong Kong and China, 1914

By the time Ho Kai retired and died in 1914, a lot of changes had taken place in Hong Kong and many of his good deeds had borne fruit. To identify these changes, we could make a survey of the scene by studying the Administrative Report of that year which was written by the Colonial Secretary, Sir Claude Severn, while recalling to our minds the past events described in the preceding chapters for comparison.

The estimated total population at the middle of the year 1914 was 501,304. Apparently some 60,000 Chinese hastily returned to China in August and September that year owing to fears of a bombardment of Hong Kong following the outbreak of the European War. This exodus produced a beneficial effect on the overcrowded conditions in the Chinese quarters but in spite of the relief, there was no sharp fall in the number of plague cases. There were 2,146 cases with 2,020 deaths, a mortality rate of 94.1 per cent. Vital statistics figures were now available. The birth-rate was 9.3 per 1,000 among the Chinese community and 16.8 per 1,000 among the non-Chinese community. It is difficult to account for the significant difference between the two birth-rates, unless the Chinese were slack in registering their births. The general death-rate was 23.8 per 1,000 among the Chinese community and 12.9 among the non-Chinese community. The difference here might well be expected. The number of deaths from malaria was 241, including a large number of workmen employed in the construction of the extension to the Tytam Reservoir. Smallpox deaths numbered 91, all Chinese, with the exception of a Portuguese infant and a

British shipwright. Pulmonary tuberculosis and phthisis claimed 724 Chinese victims, while other forms of tuberculosis represented an additional 312 deaths, making a total of 1,034 or 11.3 per cent of the total deaths among the Chinese community. Beri-beri was responsible for 399 deaths. Some efforts were being made to prevent this deficiency state:

> During the past few years circulars have been distributed to all large employers of coolie labour calling their attention to the fact that beri-beri is produced by the consumption of white rice as the staple article of diet without a sufficiency of other foods, and advising that beans should be supplied with the rice, when fresh meat or fresh fish cannot be afforded.

In 1914, government hospitals consisted of the Civil Hospital, to which was attached an isolated Maternity Hospital, the Victoria Hospital for Women and Children, and the Kennedy Town Infectious Diseases Hospital.

The Civil Hospital contained 150 beds in 19 wards, the number of in-patients treated was 2,742, and out-patients 13,828. The Maternity Hospital contained 12 beds for Europeans and 4 for Asians. The number of confinements was recorded as 261. The Victoria Hospital at the Peak contained 41 beds, and 158 patients were treated there during the year. At Kennedy Town Infectious Diseases Hospital, which contained 26 beds, cases admitted were mainly of smallpox. There was a lunatic asylum, under the direction of the superintendent of the Civil Hospital. European and Chinese patients were separated, the European portion containing 8 beds in separate wards and the Chinese portion 16 beds. During the year, 187 patients of all races were treated with 15 deaths.

The Tung Wah Hospital was supported by voluntary subscriptions from the Chinese community, but received an annual government grant of $8,000. Various other services not appertaining to a hospital were performed by the institution, such as the free burial of the poor, the repatriation of destitutes, and the organization of charitable relief in emergencies. Chinese as well as European methods of treatment were employed in accordance with the wishes expressed by the patients or their relatives. About half the number of patients were treated by Western medicine. The hospital was under the supervision of a visiting physician, who was a member of the Medical Department, whilst a Chinese house-surgeon trained in Western medicine was appointed to the hospital staff. There were 323 beds in the buildings and 4,683 patients were accommodated during 1914. In the branch hospital for Chinese smallpox cases at Kennedy Town, there were 58 beds and 17 cases were treated there. The new Kwong Wah Hospital for Chinese in the new Kowloon Peninsula, which was opened in October 1911, provided accommodation for 210 patients. The existing buildings contained 70 beds and 1,787 patients were admitted in 1914. The hospital received a grant of $8,500 per annum from the government.

In the continuous campaign against plague, to avoid the complete seclusion from friends and relatives which removal of Chinese plague patients to the Kennedy Town Infectious Diseases Hospital would entail, four district plague hospitals had been established, under the management of the Chinese Public Dispensaries Committee. These hospitals were maintained by the Chinese but the government provided an annual grant of $2,000.

The Alice Memorial and Affiliated Hospital, managed and controlled by the London Missionary Society, now consisted of four hospitals, the Alice Memorial Hospital opened in 1897, the Nethersole Hospital opened in 1893, the Alice Memorial Maternity Hospital opened in 1904 and the Ho Miu Ling Hospital opened in 1906. The number of in-patients treated by the group was 1,330, in addition, the number of labours in the Maternity Hospital was 250. With the expenditure amounting to $17,938.85, the group received an annual grant of $300 from the government.

Not supported by the government were the Chinese Public Dispensaries the management of which was in the hands of a Committee under the chairmanship of the Secretary for Chinese Affairs. These public dispensaries were described as institutions maintained in order to provide the Chinese with the services of doctors, whose certificates would be accepted by the Registrar of Deaths, and with the services of interpreters who could assist the inmates of houses, where a case of infectious diseases had oc-curred. Coolies were engaged and ambulances and dead vans provided in order to remove cases of infectious diseases to the Infectious Diseases Hos-pital and dead bodies to the mortuary. The Dispensaries also received sick infants and sent them to one or other of the Convents and arranged for the burial of dead infants. Free advice and medicine were given and patients were attended at their houses. There were eight dispensaries in existence including one for the boat population on a hulk in Causeway Bay. The total cost of maintenance, which was $39,664.60 for 1914 was defrayed by voluntary subscription.

Another institution not supported by the government was the Po Leung Kuk defined as a Society founded in 1878 for the suppression of kidnapping and trafficking of human beings. The Society's buildings had been declared a Refuge under the Women and Girls Protection Ordinance, and almost all women and girls detained by the Secretary for Chinese Affairs under the Ordinance were sent to the Po Leung Kuk. During 1914 the number of persons admitted was 435 and at the close of the year 41 remained under the care of the Society. The inmates were under the immediate charge of a Chinese matron, and instructions were given them by the matron and a Chinese teacher in elementary subjects and needlework.

At the Hong Kong University, at the end of the year 1914 the number of students was 147: 79 of whom were taking Engineering, 36 Medicine and 32 Arts. While most of the students had studied in Hong Kong schools, a number came from Guangzhou, the coastal ports of China and the Straits Settlements. The idea of the University was stated as "to pro-vide, close to China, education for Chinese similar to that given in the British Universities, but at a much cheaper cost, for if a Chinese goes abroad to be educated, he has to pay, besides travelling expenses, some $2,000 per annum, whereas at Hong Kong the expenses of the University are $540 per annum for board and tuition, or, including extras, from $600 to $650". All students were required to become boarders and thus their whole lives were under supervision whilst they were there. Of the three faculties, Medical, Arts and Engineering, the Medical has already been described in Chapter VI. The establishment of the Arts Faculty was largely due to the munificence of a Chinese gentleman in the Straits Settlement, Mr. Cheung Pat-sze 張弼仕. Its special object was to provide training suitable to those who desired to enter the public service or the higher branches of mercantile life. The Engineering Faculty, the largest with nearly two-thirds of the students belonging to it, was divided into three branches: Civil, Electrical and Mechanical. With an exceptionally large equipment of machinery and apparatus, and fourteen laboratories and workshops, it was stated that "there is practically no place in China where students have such an opportunity of seeing all kinds of machinery in actual working and of learning their practical management". Instructions at the University were carried on in English, but all students were required to have a proper knowledge of their own language. The first Vice-Chancellor of the University was Sir Charles Eliot, who later became the British Ambassador to Japan.

What happened to the opium trade and opium-smoking? In the Administration Report for the year 1910, Sir Frederick Lugard reported that "in pursuance of the policy of His Majesty's Government all opium divans in the Colony and the New Territories were closed on the 1st March, 1910". On that date, all the provisions of the Ordinance to amend and consolidate the laws relating to opium and its compounds, No. 23 of 1909, came into force. In 1913, with a view to obtaining a better control over the sale of prepared opium the government decided to institute a Government Monopoly of the sale of the prepared drug in the Colony on the expiration of the lease of the existing Opium Farm. The Opium Farmer was allowed to renew his lease for a further period of one year from the 1 March 1913, but a special clause was inserted in the agreement reducing the amount of opium to be prepared in the farm during the year from 900 chests to 540 chests for local consumption and 120 chests for export. The Opium Ordinance was also amended during the year in several important respects, the most noteworthy in this connection being the provision rendering it illegal for any person other than the Farmer or his licencees, to be in possession of a quantity exceeding five taels of opium. The results achieved were considered as having been satisfactory. In 1914, it was reported that the Opium Farm was taken over by the government in March and the restrictive measures adopted had already had a good effect.

Meanwhile even more significant and dramatic changes had taken place in China, which became a republic. The first few years of the infant Republic turned out to be a bitter disappointment to the revolutionaries and democrats. The Republic was established in eighty-three days, from the Wuchang uprising on 10 October 1911, to the proclamation of Dr. Sun Yat-sen as Provisional President on 1 January 1912, a speedy success rare for revolutions. Success, however, was largely due to Yuan Shikai's betrayal of the boy Emperor Xuantung, and Sun soon stepped down in favour of Yuan in February 1912, in order to bring about peace and unification. By September, Sun was appointed Director of Railways and started touring overseas again; and by December, the Kuomintang led by Song Jiaoren 宋 教仁 won an overwhelming majority in the first Parliamentary election.

President Yuan soon revealed his ambitions. In March 1913, Song was assassinated, in all probability by Yuan's order. In April, Yuan negotiated the "reorganization loan" of £25 million from a Five-Power Consortium without Parliament's approval. What Sun called the "Second Revolution" against Yuan started in July, but was easily suppressed. Sir John Jordan, the British minister, was especially helpful to Yuan in arranging the loan, supplying munitions, and barring Sun from Hong Kong. The Kuomintang Parliament was dissolved in November and Yuan became virtual dictator. He sanctioned the extension of his own presidency to ten years in May 1914, and later to "President for Life". The stage was set for the monarchical attempts in 1915 and the downfall of Yuan, only to usher in the decade of the warlords.

As expected, the overthrow of the Qing dynasty in China made considerable impact on Hong Kong. The following observations were made by Sayer:

Whereas in the spring of 1911 a Chinese discarded his queue at the risk of losing his head, in the spring of 1912 he risked his head who left his queue. With this abrupt change of fashion, Western clothes and effects were now in much demand and even though pins and walking sticks made no greater appeal than in the past, cigarettes were widely smoked and pipes occasionally. Small fortunes were made in foreign caps, paid for by the forsaken queue, thanks to a steady demand among the countries of the West for human hair. The old order had gone, giving place thus far only to disorder, and while young China in its foreign cap saw no inconsistency in vociferously denouncing the foreign treaties, old China, in the person of the scholar and official, crept silently away and the immemorial pirate and brigand ventured from his hiding-place again. When the overthrow of the Chinese empire began, and Tartar General and bannerman had been driven from Canton, Hong Kong's rust reaction was to await the return of more normal times. But as the months passed and lengthened into years the sad truth dawned: that happy state of peace, progress and prosperity which Englishmen in China had begun to regard almost as their birthright had been swept away. When the neighbouring continent, besides the familiar scourges of plague, pestilence and famine, had now to face simultaneously all those other evils — sedition, privy conspiracy, rebellion, battle, murder and sudden death — from which a Christian litany so quaintly asked deliverance, one had to expect a certain repercussion in Hong Kong.

With this wind of change other new fashions and ways of living were adopted by the Chinese. Though they began to enjoy certain novelties they remained conservative in many aspects, and there had been few signs that the old society or social order was rapidly changing. The tramway service was inaugurated in 1904, sixteen years after the funicular service for the European residents on the Peak came into operation. For going uphill the Chinese used sedan-chairs but to commute in the city they would ride in rickshaws. By 1912, motor cars began to appear on the roads, though reserved for the very rich. The streets, which had been lit by gaslight since 1865, were illuminated by electric light for the first time on 1 December

1890. Gradually, most houses in the urban area were supplied with electricity. Besides lighting, another innovation was the moving fan which brought gentle breezes to cool off the summer heat. Water, of which Hong Kong is always short, was as much a problem then as now but at last it started to flow from service reservoirs to the taps in some houses instead of being drawn from wells. There was still not much mixing of the two communities. Their clubs were exclusive to their members. They occupied different stands at the race-course. The Chinese had not yet taken up any kind of sport or games enjoyed by the Europeans, not even swimming. "The elders take their caged birds for an airing on the cricket ground; the youngsters kick a shuttlecock in a back-street or furtively fly a kite", wrote Sayer. The homes and business firms of the Chinese were still located in the eastern and western districts, though the wealthier members were beginning to take up residence in the mid-level. In the field of education, there was no longer a school for English teaching that was open to all regardless of race. However, in the new University, students of all nationalities were admitted. Having received an education, a new Chinese élite had emerged. They were divided into the following classes: interpreters including other civil servants, compradors, professionals, and advisers to the government, or members of councils and committees, with some of the compradors and professionals among them. One must say this about the new Chinese élite, a large number of early charitable institutions such as schools and hospitals were started and financed by them, for the promotion of the welfare of their compatriots.

In the year 1914 in which Ho Kai died the First World War began. It is generally agreed that this event marks the end of an era in European history because of the political, economic and social changes which occurred in most European countries as a result. It could also be considered that an era in the history of Hong Kong ended with this great war. During the war years, the volume of trade which passed through Hong Kong was much reduced owing to diversion of shipping, which also resulted in shortage of supply of commodities. For instance, the government had to take over the purchase and distribution of rice, the staple food of the Chinese population, to ensure an adequate supply and prevent the steady rise in price, and thereby to forestall labour unrest and increase in crime rate. After the War, with her share of world trade and industrial production decreased, Great Britain had to abandon free trade. In the face of tariff barriers and protectionism Hong Kong remained a free port but only under increasing difficulty. The economy of Hong Kong was therefore much affected, in fact, depression was experienced during the period of adaptation which followed. On the other hand, Hong Kong was not affected by the increasing spread of socialism in Great Britain, which aimed at the creation of a welfare state for her own people, and greater freedom or trusteeship for her colonies. The people of Hong Kong had no desire to break away from *laissez-faire* or to demand self-government or independence. If the emergence of a new China close by did not affect Hong Kong's status quo or the thinking of its people, it was not likely that changes in far-away Great Britain would have any consequence in her very special colony in the Far East.

In the preface which he wrote for Lam Yau Lan's 林友蘭 *Hong Kong Historical Notes* (香港史話) Lo Hsiang-lin divided the history of Hong Kong into four periods. The first was from 1842–1912, during which Hong Kong was developed into a port; the second from 1912–1941 was devoted to cultural and educational development; the third from 1941–1945 was when the place was under Japanese Occupation; and the fourth, from 1945 up to the present time, has seen the emergence of Hong Kong as a commercial and industrial centre. He apparently chose 1912 as the beginning of a period of cultural and educational development in Hong Kong because the University was opened in that year. From another point of view, we can also consider that an era in the history of Hong Kong came to an end when Lord Lugard departed in 1912. It so happened that with the appointment of Sir Henry May as Lugard's successor, a new breed of governors became occupants of Government House in Hong Kong. They would be former cadets who, having been trained in Hong Kong or elsewhere and served for some years in various territories in the colonial service, eventually reached the zenith of their careers with the coveted post. The departments too would be headed by such cadet officers from then on so that the quality of the administration was much strengthened and improved although its structure remained the same. If Sayer thought that Hong Kong had already reached adolescence as early as 1862, then unquestionably she should have become an adult by 1912. In any case, at this point in time, be it 1912 when the May regime began, or 1914 when the guns of August brought on the Great War, we have come to the end of our story.

—ɔ Epilogue ɔ—

Ho Kai died suddenly at noon, on 21 July 1914, at his residence, No. 45B Robinson Road. Although he was known to be in poor health, the sudden death came as a shock and profound regret was felt throughout the Colony. Only the evening before, he was one of a party of bathers at Junk Bay, as reported by the *China Mail*. The funeral took place on 22 July at 4:45 p.m. It was attended by a large number of his friends and colleagues, besides his large family. Three fellow members of the Order of St. Michael and St. George, the Governor Sir Henry May, and Legislative Councillors E. A. Hewett and Wei Yuk, followed the cortege to the Protestant Cemetery in Happy Valley. "The interment took place in one of the prettiest spots in this pretty ground", the *China Mail* correspondent wrote, "the grave, shaded by a wealth of tropical foliage, being next to the one in which his first lady was laid to rest."

Members of the Hong Kong Bar Association gathered in the Supreme Court the day after he died to pay him tribute. Addressing the gathering, the Attorney-General said: "Though his life was not a long one he succeeded in crowding into it many and varied activities. He took a prominent part in almost every department of public life and his influence has been felt more than twenty years directly or indirectly in the statute laws which your Lordships have to administer in the Imperial Courts of the Colony."

In response, Mr. H. E. Pollock, Q.C. made the following remarks:

When I first arrived in the Colony he was still actively engaged in the profession of barristers, and I can well remember the keenness and ability which he displayed in the conduct of the various cases in which he was engaged. Of late years he seldom appeared in the Courts but confirmed his energies almost entirely to matters of public interest, and as a colleague who has been for several years on the Legislative Council I can bear witness to the patience and diligence which he brought to bear upon the study of various measures put forward by the Government from time to time with a view to their amendment or improvement. His record of service rendered in the Colony, covering so many fields of varied public interest, is one of which any man might well be proud.

The Acting Chief Justice, Mr. H. H. J. Gompertz also spoke. "He worked for many years", he said, "for the regeneration of his native land and those responsible for the destinies of China have freely availed themselves of his sagacious and broad-minded counsel and his eminent moderation and common sense."

In the Legislative Council on 23 July, the Chairman delivered the following speech:

It was only on the 6th February last that this Council recorded its great appreciation of the eminent services rendered to it and to the Colony by Sir Kai Ho Kai during the long period of 24 years during which he had been a member of the Council, his seat upon which he was obliged to resign owing to ill health. Today I have to ask you to record our deep sorrow at his untimely death and our heartfelt sympathy with his widow and his family in their bereavement The Council has so recently expressed its sense of the devoted and valuable services of Sir Kai Ho Kai, and the Chinese community in the address which they presented to him, and the public press in numerous appreciative articles at the time of his resignation and again on his death have recorded so fully the splendid work done for the Chinese community and for the whole Colony of our deceased colleague and friend, that it is unnecessary for me to dilate further upon his memory. With respect, we treasure with admiration the example he has set us all of devotion to public duty. It is with a heavy heart that I move the resolution which in terms too inadequate records our feelings at this hour.

The resolution, seconded by Wei Yuk, was in the following terms: "This Council desires to record its deep sorrow at the death of Sir Kai Ho Kai, for 24 years one of its most brilliant and devoted members, and to tender to his widow and family its heartfelt sympathy with them in their bereavement." Having passed the resolution in silence the Council adjourned out of respect for his memory.

Ho Kai's grave in the Colonial Cemetery can still be seen today. It is situated in Section 8, bearing the serial numbers $\frac{4712}{8043}$ 10250. Its description by the correspondent of the *China Mail* no longer applies. There is no wealth of tropical foliage shading it, only a young tree stands nearby. According to the inscriptions on the tombstone, Ho Kai, his first wife Alice Walkden and his second wife Lai Yuk-hing, were buried underneath it. On the four sides of the tombstone are the following inscriptions:

North side:	In loving memory of
	Sir Kai Ho Kai, Kt. C.M.G.
	M.B.C.M. Aberdeen, M.R.C.S. England,
	Barrister-at-law, Member of Lincoln's Inn,
	Unofficial Member of Legislative Council,
	Hong Kong, 1890–1914
	4th son of the late Rev. Ho Tsun-sin
	Born 21st March 1859, Died 21st July 1914.
West side:	In loving memory of
	Alice
	The dearly loved wife of Ho Kai
	Eldest daughter of the late John Walkden Esqre.
	of Lawrence Lane and Blackheath
	Born in London February 3rd 1852
	Died in Hong Kong, China, June 8th 1884
East side:	"And God shall wipe away all tears from
	their eyes and there shall be no more death,

neither sorrow, nor crying, neither shall
there be any more pain, for the former days
are passed away." Rev. XXI, 4
She though dead yet speaketh

South side: The grave of Lady Ho Lai Yuk Hing
born the Tenth Year of Tongzhi
died the thirty-fourth year of the Republic
(in Chinese Characters)

In the Colonial Cemetery, there are many more tombstones on which famous names associated with the history of Hong Kong had been carved. They were expatriates who came here as administrators, educators, lawyers, doctors, merchants and soldiers, and native sons who had served their birthplace in similar capacities. Some of them and their wives and children had been victims of disasters and typhoons, cholera and plague epidemics, malaria and typhoid fevers, riots and disturbances. In the well-kept and peaceful grounds of the Cemetery, they had come to eternal rest, forever belonging to the place where they once lived. Let us remember that the miracle which is Hong Kong today began with people like Ho Kai who could truthfully be regarded as pioneers. They had long departed after making their many and varied contributions, but there still remain their indelible footprints on the sands of time.

∼⊱ Appendices ⊰∼

APPENDIX I

Governors of Hong Kong, 1843–1919

June 1843–May 1844	Sir Henry Pottinger
May 1844–March 1848	Sir John Davis
March 1848–April 1854	Sir George Bonham
April 1854–May 1859	Sir John Bowring
September 1859–March 1865	Sir Hercules Robinson
March 1866–April 1872	Sir Richard Macdonnell
April 1872–March 1877	Sir Arthur Kennedy
April 1877–March 1882	Sir John Pope Hennessy
March 1883–December 1885	Sir George Bowen
October 1887–May 1891	Sir William Des Voeux
December 1891–January 1898	Sir William Robinson
November 1898–November 1903	Sir Henry Blake
July 1904–April 1907	Sir Matthew Nathan
July 1907–March 1912	Sir Frederick (later Lord) Lugard
July 1912–February 1919	Sir Henry May

APPENDIX II

Colonial Secretaries of Hong Kong, 1843–1912

1843	G. A. Malcolm
1844	Sir Frederick Bruce
1846	W. Caine
1854	W T Mercer
1868	J. G. Austin
1879	Sir William Marsh
1887	Frederick Stewart
1890	Sir Francis Fleming
1892	Sir George O'Brien
1895	Sir James Stewart Lockhart
1902	Sir Francis May
1911	W. D. Barnes
1912–1926	Sir Claude Severn

APPENDIX III

Registrar-Generals, 1845–1913

1845	S. T. Fearon
1846	A. L. Inglis
1849	W. T. Mercer
1850	Charles May
1856	D. R. Caldwell
1862	T. Turner
1864	C. Clementi Smith
1881	James Russell
1883	Frederick Stewart
1887	J. H. Stewart Lockhart
1901	A. W. Brewin
1912–1913	E. R. Halifax

APPENDIX IV

Colonial Surgeons and Principal Civil Medical Officers, 1843–1912

Colonial Surgeons:	1843	Alexander Anderson
	1844	F. Dill
	1846	Peter Young
	1847	William Morrison
	1854	James Carroll Dempster
	1858	William Aurelius Hasland
	1859	John Ivory Murray
	1872	Robert W. McCoy
	1873	Phillip Bernard Chenery Ayres
Principal Civil Medical Officer:	1897	John Mitford Atkinson
	1912–24	John Taylor Connell Johnson

APPENDIX V

Chinese Members of the Legislative Council, 1880–1922

1. Ng Choy 伍才   1880–1882   (2 years)
2. Wong Shing 黃勝   1884–1890   (6 years)
3. Ho Kai 何啟   1890–1914   (24 years)
4. Wei Yuk 韋玉   1896–1914   (18 years)
5. Lau Chu Pak 劉鑄伯   1913–1922   (9 years)

APPENDIX VI

Morbidity and Mortality of Plague Cases, 1894–1923

Year	No. of Cases	No. of Deaths	Mortality Rate
1894	2679	2552	95.3%
1895	44	43	97.7%
1896	1204	1078	89.5%
1897	21	21	100.0%
1898	1320	1175	89.0%
1899	1486	1428	96.0%
1900	1057	1034	97.8%
1901	1651	1561	94.6%
1902	572	572	100.0%
1903	1415	1251	88.4%
1904	510	495	97.1%
1905	304	287	94.4%
1906	893	842	94.3%
1907	240	198	82.5%
1908	1073	986	91.9%
1909	135	108	80.0%
1910	25	23	92.0%
1911	269	253	94.1%
1912	1847	1768	95.7%
1913	408	386	94.6%
1914	2146	2020	94.1%
1915	144	144	100.0%
1916	39	38	97.4%
1917	38	38	100.0%
1918	266	266	100.0%
1919	464	464	100.0%
1920	138	120	87.0%
1921	150	130	86.7%
1922	1181	1071	90.7%
1923	148	136	91.9%
Total	21867	20489	93.7%

Sources: Compiled from Colonial Surgeon's Reports and *Historical and Statistical Abstract of the Colony of Hong Kong* 1841-1930.

APPENDIX VII

Distribution of Plague Cases in 1894 According to Nationalities

Nationality	No. of Cases	No. of Deaths	Mortality Rate
Chinese	2619	2447	93.40%
European	11	2	18.18%
Japanese	10	6	60.00%
Philippino	1	1	100.00%
Eurasian	3	3	100.00%
Indian	13	10	76.92%
Portuguese	18	12	66.67%
Malay	3	3	100.00%
West Indies	1	1	100.00%
	2679	2485	92.76%

APPENDIX VIII

Age and Sex Distribution of Plague Cases in 1894

Age	Male	Female	Total
Under 5 years	18	27	45
5–10 years	65	73	138
10–20 years	281	190	471
20–30 years	244	84	328
30–40 years	323	75	398
40–50 years	233	74	307
50–60 years	127	86	213
60–70 years	56	49	105
Over 70 years	21	24	45
	1368	682	2050

APPENDIX IX

Population of Hong Kong, 1894–1923

Year	No. of Non-Chinese	No. of Chinese	Total Population
1894	10782	235224	246006
1895	10828	237670	248498
1896	12709	226710	239419
1897	13700	235010	248710
1898	15190	239210	254400
1899	15522	243490	259312
1900	14778	247900	262678
1901	20096	280564	300660 (Census)
1902	18524	293300	311824
1903	18581	307050	325631
1904	18900	342304	361206
1905	17977	359873	377850
1906	21560	307388	329038 (Census)
1907	18550	395818	414368
1908	19786	401713	421499
1909	20479	408409	428888
1910	20826	415180	435986
1911	18893	445384	464277
1912	21163	446614	467777
1913	21470	467644	489114
1914	20710	480594	501304
1915	13390	495840	509160
1916	13390	514620	528010
1917	13500	521600	535100
1918	13500	548000	561500
1919	13600	584500	598100
1920	14682	615625	630307
1921	14798	610368	625166
1922	16000	622300	638300
1923	17000	650900	667900

Source: *Historical and Statistical Abstract of the Colony of Hong Kong 1841–1930.*

APPENDIX X

Chronology of Events in China, 1839–1911

1839 — Opium War between China and Britain

1842 — Treaty of Nanjing

1843 — Hong Kong ceded to Britain

1850 — Taiping Rebellion

1856 — "Arrow" War

1857 — Canton occupied by British and French Troops

1858 — Treaties signed with Britain, France, Russia and U. S. A.

1860 — Peace terms reneged, Beijing occupied

1864 — Nanjing retaken and Taiping crushed

1871 — Ili region in Xinjiang occupied by Russia

1884 — Sino-French War

1894 — Sino-Japanese War

1896 — Sino-Russia Treaty, construction of Manchurian Railway

1898 — Hundred Days Reform

1899 — Boxer Rebellion

1900 — Occupation of Beijing by Allied Troops

1911 — Manchu Dynasty overthrown, Republic founded

APPENDIX XI

Chronology of Events in Ho Kai's Life, 1859–1914

1859 — Born

1870 — Entered Government Central School

1872 — Went to England

— Tung Wah Hospital opened

1879 — M.D.C.M. Aberdeen, M.R.C.S. England

1881 — Called to Bar

1882 — Returned to Hong Kong

— Chadwick Report published

1886 — Appointed to Sanitary Board

1887 — Alice Memorial Hospital opened

— Hong Kong College of Medicine for the Chinese opened

— The Marquis Zeng – Ho Kai correspondence on "China: The Sleep and the Awakening"

1888 — Public Health Ordinance passed

1890 — Appointed to Legislative Council

1892 — First Graduation Ceremony of Hong Kong College of Medicine

1894 — Plague Epidemic broke out

1896 — Po Leung Kuk Building opened

1898 — New Territories leased

1912 — Hong Kong University opened

1914 — Died

⟶ Bibliography ⟵

A. Government Publications

Administrative Report. 1912, 1913, 1914.
Annual Report, Medical and Health Department, Hong Kong. 1880–1914.
Blue Book 1894–1904, Regarding the Bubonic Plague in Hong Kong.
Blue Book Reports on Bubonic Plague 1894–1907.
Historical and Statistical Abstract of the Colony of Hong Kong. 1841–1930.
Hong Kong Government Gazette. May 7, 14 May and 22 July 1887.
Hong Kong Sessional Papers. 1886–1914.
Laws Relating to Public Health and Sanitation. Hong Kong, December 1895.
Legislative Council Report. 1890–1914.

B. References in English

Airlie, S. *Thistle and Bamboo.* Hong Kong: Oxford University Press, 1989.
Alice Ho Miu Ling Nethersole Hospital 1887–1967. Hong Kong, 1967.
Beresford, C. *The Break-up of China.* London, 1899.
Boorman, H. L. (ed.). *Biographical Dictionary of Republican China.* New York: Columbia University Press, 1967–1979.
Cameron, M. E. *Reform Movements in China 1898–1912.* New York, 1974.
Cameron, N. *Barbarians and Mandarins.* New York: Walker/Weatherhill, 1970.

————. *Hong Kong: The Cultured Pearl*. Hong Kong: Oxford University Press, 1978.

Cantlie, N. and G. Seaver. *Sir James Cantlie*. London: Murray, 1939.

Chadwick, O. *Report on the Sanitary Conditions of Hong Kong, with Appendages and Plans*. 1882.

Cheng, T. C. "Chinese Unofficial Members of the Legislative and Executive Councils in Hong Kong up to 1941." *Journal of the Hong Kong Branch of the Royal Asiatic Society*, Vol. 9, 1969.

China Mail. 8 February, 16 February, 12 May 1887; 15 August 1888; 24 July 1892; 14 October 1895; 30 April 1896; 1 August, 4 August, 21 August 1900; 26 February, 27 February, 21 July, 22 July, 23 July, 30 July 1914.

Chiu, Ling-yeong. "The Debate on National Salvation: Ho Kai versus Tseng Chi-tse." *Journal of the Hong Kong Branch of the Royal Asiatic Society*, Vol. 11, 1971.

————. "The Life and Thoughts of Sir Kai Ho Kai," Ph.D. Thesis, University of Sydney, 1968.

Choa, G. H. "Chinese Traditional Medicine and Contemporary Hong Kong," in *Some Traditional Chinese Ideas and Conceptions in Hong Kong Social Life To-day*. Hong Kong Branch of the Royal Asiatic Society, 1967.

————. "A History of Medicine in Hong Kong." *Medical Directory of Hong Kong*, 1970.

————. *Heal the Sick Was Their Motto: The Protestant Medical Missionaries in China*. Hong Kong: The Chinese University Press, 1990.

————. "Hong Kong, Medicine and Sun Yet-sen," *Journal of the Hong Kong College of General Practitioners*, Vol. 14, No. 5, May 1992.

————. "The Lowson Diaries," *Journal of Hong Kong Branch of the Royal Asiatic Society*, Vol. 33, 1993.

————. "A Hisotry of Medical Education in Hong Kong." *Synapse, Hong Kong College of Physicians, Supplement 2*, 1994.

Chu, S. C. *Reformer in Modern China: Chang Chien 1853–1926*. New York: Columbia University Press, 1965.

Coates, A. *Prelude to Hong Kong*. London: Routledge & K. Paul, 1966.

Cohen, P. A. and J. E. Schrecker. *Reform in Nineteenth Century China*. Cambridge, MA: Harvard University Press, 1976.

Collis, M. *Foreign Mud*. London: Faber and Faber, 1964.

————. *Wayfoong*. London: Faber and Faber, 1965. 22

Development of the Tung Wah Hospital (1870–1960). Hong Kong, 1961.

Discovery Magazine. Cathay Pacific, Vol. 27, No. 9, September 1996.

Eitel, E. J. *Europe in China*. Hong Kong: Luzac, 1895.

Endacott, G. B. *Government and People in Hong Kong*. Hong Kong: Hong Kong University Press, 1964.

————. *A History of Hong Kong*. Revised edition. London: Oxford University Press, 1973.

Gittins, J. *Eastern Windows, Western Skies*. Hong Kong: South China Morning Post, 1969.

Haffner, C. *The Craft of the East*. District Grand Lodge of Hong Kong and the Far East, 1977.

Harrison, B. (ed.), *University of Hong Kong: The First Fifty Years, 1911–1961*. Hong Kong: Hong Kong University Press, 1962.

Hsu, I. C. Y. *The Rise of Modern China*. Hong Kong: Oxford University Press, 1975.

Hummel, A. W. *Eminent Chinese of the Ch'ing Period*. Washington: U.S. Government Printing Office, 1943.

Li Chien-nung. *The Political History of China, 1840–1928*. Stanford, CA: Stanford University Press, 1956.

Manson-Balir, P. and A. Mcock. *The Life and Work of Sir Patrick Manson*. London, 1927.

Norton-Kyshe, J. W. *The History of the Laws and Courts of Hong Kong*. Hong Kong: Vetch and Lee, 1971.

One Hundred Years of the Tung Wah Group of Hospitals 1870–1970. Hong Kong, 1971.

Paterson, E. H. *A Hospital for Hong Kong*. Hong Kong, 1987.

Perham, M. *Lugard, the Years of Authority, 1898–1945*. London, 1960.

Perleberg, M. *Who's Who in Modern China*. Hong Kong, 1954.

Pope-Hennessy, J. *Verendah*. London, 1964.

Ride, L. T. *Robert Morrison: the Scholar and the Man*. Hong Kong: Hong Kong University Press, 1957.

Rudolph, R. C. "Early China and the West: Fertilization and Fetalization," in *China and the West, Culture and Commerce*. University of California, 1977.

Rydings, H. A. "Transactions of the China Medico-Chirurgical Society 1845–46." *Journal of the Hong Kong Branch of the Royal Asiatic Society*, Vol. 13, 1973.

Sayer, G. R. *Hong Kong: Birth, Adolescence, and Coming of Age*. London: Oxford University Press, 1937.

———. *Hong Kong, 1862–1919*. Hong Kong: Hong Kong University Press, 1975.

Schiffrin, H. Z. *Sun Yat-sen and the Origins of the Chinese Revolution*. Berkeley: University of California Press, 1968.

Schurmann, F. and O. Schell. *Chinese Readings 1, Imperial China*. Pelican, 1967.

———. *Chinese Readings 2, Republican China*. Pelican, 1967.

Sinn, E. *Power and Charity*. Hong Kong: Oxford University Press, 1989.

Smith, C. T. "The Emergence of a Chinese Elite in Hong Kong." in *Hong Kong, the Interaction of Traditions and Life in the Towns*. Hong Kong Branch of the Royal Asiatic Society, Vol. 11, 1971.

———. "English-educated Elites in Nineteenth Century Hong Kong," in *Hong Kong, the Interaction of Traditions and Life in the Towns*. Hong Kong Branch of the Royal Asiatic Society, 1975.

———. "Sun Yat-sen's Middle School Days in Hong Kong: The Establishment of Alice Memorial Hospital." *Ching Feng*, Vol. 21, No. 2, 1978.

Smith, C. T. *Chinese Christians: Elites, Middlemen and the Church in Hong Kong*. Hong Kong Oxford University Press, 1985.

Smith, C. T. and J. Hayes. "Visit to Tung Wah Group of Hospitals' Museum, 2nd October 1976." *Journal of the Hong Kong Branch of the*

Royal Asiatic Society, Vol. 16, 1976.

Stewart, J. C. *The Quality of Mercy*. London: George Allen and Unwin, 1983.

Stokes, G. G. *Queen's College 1862–1962*. Hong Kong, 1962.

Tsai, Jung-fang. "Comprador Ideologists in Modern China: Ho Kai (Ho Ch'i) (1859–1914) and Hu Li-Yüan (1847–1916)." Ph.D. Thesis, University of California, Los Angeles, 1975.

———. "Syncretism in the Reformist Thought of Ho Kai and Hu Liyuan." *Asian Profile*, Vol. 6, No. 1, 1978.

———. "The Predicaments of the Comprador Ideologists." *Modern China*, Vol. 7, No. 2, April 1981.

Des Voeux, G. W. *My Colonial Service*. London, 1903.

Warner, J. *Fragrant Harbour*. Hong Kong: John Warner Publications, 1976.

Wong, K. C. and L. T. Wu. *History of Chinese Medicine*. Tianjin. 1932.

Wright, A. (ed.). *20th Century Impressions of Hong Kong*. Singapore: Graham Brash Ltd., 1990.

C. References in Chinese

方　豪：〈清末維新政論家何啟與胡禮垣〉，《新時代雜誌》，第3卷，第12期，1963年12月。

王爾敏：《中國近代思想史論》。初版。台北：華世出版社，1977年。

石　峻：《中國近代思想史講授提綱》。第一版。北京：人民出版社，1965年。

《名牧遺徽》。

任繼愈：〈何啟與胡禮垣的改良思想〉，收入《中國近代思想史論文集》。第一版。上海：上海人民出版社，1958年。

李　敖：《孫逸仙和中國西化醫學》。初版。香港：文藝書屋，1968年。

李東海(編)：《東華醫院一百二十五年史略》。北京：中國文史出版社，1998年。

余啟興：〈伍廷芳與香港之關係〉，收入《壽羅香林教授論文集》。初版。香港：萬有圖書公司，1970年。

余偉維：《戊戌變法之原因及其影響》。初版。香港：珠海書院中國文學歷史
　　研究所，1977年。

林友蘭：《香港史話》。增訂版。香港：上海印書館，1978年。

吳醒濂：《香港華人名人史略》。初版。香港：五洲書局，1937年。

胡禮垣：《胡翼南先生全集》。初版。香港：胡氏書齋，1920年。

胡　濱：《中國近代改良主義》。第一版。北京：中華書局，1964年。

《星島晚報》。香港。1981年5月12日。

陳邦賢：《中國醫學史》。修訂重版。上海：商務印書館，1954年。

許政權：《清末民權思想的發展與歧異》。台灣：文哲出版社，1992年。

湯志鈞：《戊戌變法人物傳稿》。第一版。北京：中華書局，1961年。

劉禺生：《世載堂雜憶》。第一版。北京：中華書局，1960年。

劉粵聲：《香港基督教會史》。初版。香港：香港基督教聯會，1941年。

黎晉偉：《香港百年史》。初版。香港：南中編譯出版社，1948年。

蕭公權：《中國政治思想史》。第四版。台北：中華文化出版事業委員會，
　　1965年。

薩孟武：《中國政治思想史》。增補再版。台北：三民書局，1972年。

顏路裔：《教會掌故》。初版。香港：道聲出版社，1970年。

羅香林：《國父之大學時代》。增訂台一版。台北：台灣商務印書館，1954
　　年。

羅香林：〈國父革命主張對於何啟與鄭觀應等之影響〉，收入《國父九十誕辰紀
　　念論文集 (一)》。初版。台北：中華文化出版事業委員會，1965年。

羅香林：《國父的高明光大》。初版。台北：文星書店，1965年。

關肇碩，容應萸：《香港開埠與關家》。香港：廣角鏡出版公司，1997年。

D. Major Works by Reformists
(Available at the Library of
The Chinese University of Hong Kong)

王　韜：《弢園文錄外編》。第一版。北京：中華書局，1959年。

左宗棠：《左文襄公全集》。影版。台北：文海出版社，1964年。

李鴻章：《李文忠公全集》。影版。台北：文海出版社，1962年。

林則徐：《林文忠公全集》。影版。台北：德志出版社，1963年。

─────：《林文忠公政書》。初版。上海：商務印書館，1935年。

馬建忠：《適可齋記言》。第一版。北京：中華書局，1960年。

翁同龢：《翁文恭公遺集》。影版。台北：維新書局，1970年。

─────：《翁文恭公日記》。影版。台北：嗣風出版社，1964年。

容　閎：《西學東漸記》。初版。上海：商務印書館，1916年。

張之洞：《張文襄公全集》。影版。台北：文海出版社，1970年。

康有為：《康南海先生遺著彙刊》。台北：宏業書局，1976年。

─────：《康南海文集》。影版。台北：文海出版社，1972年。

馮桂芬：《校邠廬抗儀》。影版。台北：文海出版社，1971年。

梁啟超：《飲冰室全集》。初版。上海：中華書局，1936年。

─────：《梁任公選集》。香港：崑崙出版公司，1972年。

張　謇：《張季子九錄》。影版。台北：文海出版社，1965年。

曾國藩：《曾文正公全集》。影版。台北：文海出版社，1974年。

─────：《曾文正公家書》。再版。台北：世界書局，1967年。

鄭觀應：《盛世危言》。台北：學術出版社，1966年。

薛福成：《薛福成全集》。台北：廣文書局，1963年。

魏　源：《魏源集》。第一版。北京：中華書局，1976年。

─────：《古微堂內外集》。影版。台北：文海出版社，1978年。

譚嗣同：《譚瀏陽全集》。影版。台北：文海出版社，1968年。

嚴　復：《侯官嚴氏叢刻》。影版。台北：成文出版社，1968年。

龔自珍：《龔定盦全集》。上海：國學整理社，1935年。

∽ Index ∾